KEEP THE FAI

KEEP THE FAITH

The Story of Celtic's
Historic Treble Winning Season
2000–2001

Ron Mackenna and Carlos Alba

MAINSTREAM
PUBLISHING

EDINBURGH AND LONDON

THANKS TO Jonathan Russell of the *Scottish Mirror* and Kevin McKenna of the *Herald* for the use of match reports.

ACKNOWLEDGEMENTS: Thomas Jordan, Kevin McCarra, Jonathan Northcroft, Ian Campbell, Neil Cameron, Jim Traynor, Andrew Smith, Rob Robertson, Glenn Gibbons, Charlie Nicholas, Billy McNeill, Bobby Lennox, Jimmy Johnstone, Ronnie Simpson, Bob Crampsey, Chris and Eugene Cairns, Damian Rogers, Jim Smith, Joe Cook, David Norrie, Eddie Toner, Joe O'Rourke, Gerry Madden, Brendan Sweeney, Jim Divers, Jason Henderson, Stilian Petrov, Neil Lennon, Ramon Vega, Tom Boyd, Austin Barrett, Steve Clarke and www.e-tims.net, www.celticfc.co.uk, Tony Hamilton, Keith Sinclair, Frank Murphy, Phil Miller, Davey Paton, Adrian Cocozza, Brian Wilson, James Allcock, Chris Starrs, Willie Hughes, Alan Storer, David Welsh.Tony Murray, Graham Lynn, Kevin Cawley, Gerry Madden, Eddie Toner, Joe O'Rourke, Brendan Sweeney, Jimmy Divers and www.celticsupportersassoc.co.uk, John Paton, the North American Federation of Celtic Supporters Clubs, the Singapore Celtic Supporters Club, the Australian Celtic Supporters Clubs, www.thehuddle.co.uk and Tom Carruthers (President Western Australia Celtic Supporters Club).

First published in Great Britain in 2001 by
MAINSTREAM PUBLISHING COMPANY (EDINBURGH) LTD
7 Albany Street
Edinburgh EH1 3UG

ISBN 1 84018 547 3

A catalogue record for this book is available from the British Library

Typeset in Van Dijck and Univers
Printed and bound in Great Britain by Mackays Ltd

CONTENTS

1.

FIELD OF DREAMS

With a four-leafed clover on my breast
And the green and white upon my chest
It's such a joy for us to see
For to play football the Celtic way . . .
(*Four Leaf Clover.* The Peatdiggers & Peter Barry)

IT IS 10.40 P.M. Saturday, 26 May 2001. Bars can sometimes have a joyous feeling, a wall of warmth that hits you when you walk through the door. Tonight, Pier 17 on Glasgow's Clydeside is like that. In the semi-gloom of the spotlights people are sitting, talking, shouting, some of them are even singing. The babble of voices has got louder and happier with every round of drinks. This is more than a Saturday-night-out crowd. The men seem fitter, healthier, more handsome, even. And they are glowing with something more than alcohol: it is pride. Their wives and girlfriends are with them. Some of them have brought their parents too. The mood has swept everybody along with it. It is a celebration, a joyous celebration that is taking place, tonight, for the first time in 32 years.

Look closely and there are football players at every table. In their jackets and suits they look different than they did five hours ago. Over there, sitting together are Henrik Larsson, Ramon Vega and Chris Sutton. Amid the noise they have been laughing and telling stories. But Vega has stopped and, listening intently, he is turning his head towards the small stage. He looks at the others, laughing, and says, 'Tom Boyd is singing.'

It is a song they have all heard the club captain sing before. He sang it at his testimonial a few weeks ago. And he has hummed it almost every day since as he wandered around the training field or dressed in the changing-rooms. Usually he has a smile on his face and normally nobody pays much attention. But now everybody is listening. People seated with their backs to him have craned their heads around to see. The conversation has died down.

There is something different about his voice this time.

He stands with his head slightly tipped back and the microphone near his face: 'With a four-leafed clover on my breast . . . And the green and white upon my chest . . .' But the words are not coming out right. His voice is thick with emotion and breaking . . . 'It's such a joy for us to see . . .' Those are tears coming from his eyes.

The car horns are still sounding in different parts of Glasgow. The city centre is awash with celebrating fans in green and white. All around the country the same song Tom Boyd is singing and many more are being belted out by groups of euphoric people. On the other side of the world supporters are dancing. In Singapore, Sweden, Canada and the States the Celts are swinging. There are parties everywhere.

Tony Murray is at one of them in Clydebank's Duntocher Hotel, a pint in his hand, his wife and friends around him. A lifelong Celtic supporter, he too has cried at today's victory. He was sitting in the North Stand of Hampden. His eight-year-old son Anthony was on one side of him, on the other his best friend James McKenna, over from Australia for three days to see history in the making. Maybe it was the green-and-white bedlam that erupted around him at the final whistle. Maybe it was the sight of the team reappearing on the park in the traditional green-and-white hoops. Maybe it was the fact that he was the same age as his son is now when Celtic last won the Treble. It doesn't really matter.

And who knows what was going through Tom Boyd's mind when the tears came? The thought of all those hard, lean years being finally over? Flashing images of the night Celtic beat St Johnstone, or finally won the league, or the cups? Perhaps the closeness of the players in the first-team dressing-room?

Every player in the room, everybody associated with the football club had their own memories of the year at that moment. Put together like a flickering movie reel, they would reveal much more than just what happened on the park. Of course there would be the crushing defeats inflicted on Rangers, the moment in Perth when Stan Petrov broke his leg and the league was sewn up, the games when it all looked lost but the team fought back.

But there were the funny moments too. Martin O'Neill standing naked before Billy Connolly. Chris Sutton and the other players talking about,

Henrik Larsson meeting the *Chewin' the Fat* boys, or the team singing together in the dressing-room.

The people outside in the streets celebrating had their memories too; thoughts of crazy trips to Finland and France; of watching matches on the other side of the world at four in the morning; of dining with the team under the sun-kissed Florida sky.

And many people would have thought back to the beginning.

It is the morning of 29 July 2000. Outside a towering stadium which dominates Glasgow's East End a crowd of supporters, journalists, a few gawpers is growing; milling around, laughing, their shouts rising up into the summer air:. There is an air of expectation. The sun is shining. Deep inside, underneath the stands, a slim man in his late forties, at first glance unremarkable apart from his steel-rimmed spectacles, is turning to face a group of fit, healthy young men: athletes, football players, Celtic players.

'Gentlemen,' he begins. 'I will always be 100 per cent honest with you and the press. But in the coming weeks you will hear me tell a lie.' The man, the new manager, continues: 'When asked by the media if we can win the league I will say no, that we are too young and still developing as team and manager. Disregard it.

'We will win the league. Some of you believe it already and all of you will believe it shortly.' (31 August 2000, *Daily Mail*)

The game has begun.

The man is Martin O'Neill. The words are only extraordinary if you know what went before. And everybody in Glasgow, in Scotland, everybody who knew anything about football, knew what went before. What nobody expected was what was to come after.

Twenty-one points is a large gap between two teams in any sport. In football it is a gulf. In football, in the league championship in Scotland, when it is the gap between Rangers and Celtic, it is worse. It is humiliating.

Yet 21 points were not all that had separated the two sides at the end of the 1999–2000 season. As the month of May ended there was also the small matter of Celtic having lost their eleventh championship in twelve seasons; their fourth manager in four seasons and on the way having suffered the worst defeat in the club's history when they were ejected from the Scottish Cup, at home, by a team which five seasons previously had been playing in the lowly Highland League. And there is a painful footnote somewhere recording that one of the club's greatest idols, Kenny Dalglish, had been found, on returning to Celtic, to have feet of clay.

Across the city Rangers, deadly serious rivals for more than a century, had picked up every championship Celtic had lost in the last 12 years. They were rampant. They had coasted to their latest league victory. They were strong, confident, accepted across the UK and Europe as the real masters of Scottish football, and still building for the future.

For an ordinary club such a predicament would have been painful. But Celtic is no ordinary club. The heavy hand of history bears down on every season. The ghost of Jock Stein lingers in the dressing-room. His team, the Lisbon Lions, propelled Celtic to immortality in 1967 by becoming the first British club to win the European Cup. It was an extraordinary feat that has ensured that Celtic's name is known and spoken of with respect throughout Europe. Yet it has also brought with it a burden of expectation. A fear that with every passing season's slip the lustre dulls . . .

The club Martin O'Neill walked into in the summer of 2000 should, then, by any standards have been damaged, broken and spiralling downwards. In other cities in the UK, where the fortunes of two clubs are so tightly intertwined, the unbearable disappointments almost inevitably lead to one beginning the slow depressing march to the lower leagues. Celtic had had more than a decade of uninterrupted underachievement, broken briefly by Wim Jansen's glorious league win in 1998. A victory which was cruelly followed by the Dutchman's immediate departure and defeat in the next season, confirming the sceptics' claims it was just a one-off handed to Celtic on a plate by a temporarily exhausted Rangers. And the season that had just ended was a howler, the mother of all bad seasons.

Yet anyone studying the statistics and visiting Glasgow's East End for the first time to take the club's temperature was in for a shock. The patient was far from sick and wasting away. In fact the opposite was true. Celtic as an institution, as a football club, was in gloriously rude health, miraculously showing no signs of lasting damage.

The explanation lies in the emotions of more than 250,000 supporters. Sport is emotion. In Kevin Costner's movie *Field Of Dreams* Idaho farmer Ray Kinsella hears a voice telling him: 'Build it and they will come.' In the face of bankruptcy, divorce and the mounting suspicions of his neighbours he constructs a baseball diamond in his cornfield. People are drawn to the empty field from all over the country. Ghosts of the Chicago Black Sox walk out of the corn and start playing ball. Kinsella's father and the long-dead relatives of others join them. It is Hollywood nonsense but it is a film few men can watch without feeling a tear well up in their eyes.

There are no voices at Celtic Park but, like Kinsella's cornfield, the setting has been created for a return to the glory of days long past. Emotion has seen the building of a world-class football stadium that was until very recently the largest in Britain. It waits for the emergence of a team to rival the Lisbon Lions.

The supporters, who made it possible, wait too. Thousands of them became ordinary shareholders and bought and bought at a point when the business world said it was not possible. The share issue came at the end of a five-year trophyless spell and was derided as doomed to failure. It was not a rational purchase as *The Herald* (January 1995) ominously warned supporters, pointing out that the funding for the new stadium was not in place.

It was a fact the club, under Fergus McCann, had already pointed out themselves in the prospectus. They warned that only the money to rebuild the North Stand was in place and anything else would depend on 'the achievements of the first team, future availability of cash resources and bank and other facilities and the level of ticket revenue in future seasons'. It was, therefore, a leap in the dark. A leap of faith.

The share issue was oversubscribed to the tune of £5.4 million. More than 10,000 supporters paid a minimum of £620. It was the biggest share issue of its type in Britain.

It was also a new beginning.

The stadium rose from the rubble in the East End and the faithful rose to the occasion with it. Despite the lean years on the park the clamour to become part of what was going on became deafening. There are now 50,000 season ticket-holders and all signed up on no more than the dim expectation that things could only get better. They linger, like the people who came to sit around Kinsella's corn field. They are not alone. In the extremely unlikely event that they should change their minds there are 10,000 more sitting on the waiting list.

In Australia, Singapore, the United States, anywhere that Scots and Irish have gone to find work or a new life, people still cling on to Celtic. Distance does not dilute the extraordinary gravity-defying support for the club.

It's a sentiment embodied in the phrase 'Keep the faith'. A phrase that passes across the lips of Celtic supporters whenever they part company. A phrase that sums up the optimism of tens of thousands of ordinary people who have passed the Celtic torch down over generations.

The story of the Treble-winning season is their story as much as it is the story of the team on the park or the manager. It is a tale of a club in waiting and of faith repaid.

2.

MESSIAH?

Hail Hail, The Celts are here,
what the hell do we care,
what the hell do we care,
Hail Hail, The Celts are here,
what the hell do we care now . . .
For it's a Grand Old Team to play for,
for it's a Grand Old team to see,
and if you know the history,
It's enough to make your heart go,
nine-in-a-row.
We don't care if we win, lose or draw
what the hell do we care,
for all we know,
that there's going to be a show,
and the Glasgow Celtic will be there.

'IF HE CAN BEAT RANGERS to the title, he'll be a Messiah, the new Jock Stein.' So said Brian Clough, the legendary former Nottingham Forest manager who had taken more than a passing interest in Martin O'Neill's career (4 July, *The Herald*). Messiah or not, doubts still remained in the minds of a number of Celtic supporters over the former Leicester City manager's appointment. A few fans had made it known that they had wanted a foreign coach and the Celtic shortlist had included a glittering array. There was Guus Hiddink, the former Holland coach, Luis Fernandez, the former Paris Saint-Germain coach, Nils Arne Eggen of Rosenborg Trondheim, and Sven Goran Eriksson of Lazio.

Of them all Hiddink had come closest to being signed up for the job but when, eventually, O'Neill had let his interest be known, he was the clear choice. There followed a brief tug-of-love with Leicester, where he had had such recent success, as the club promised to make him the best paid manager in the Premiership if he would only stay. The negotiations ran on for so long that O'Neill's brother felt the need to intervene as O'Neill later admitted to *The Times*: 'He called me and said "Are you going to take this job or what?"'

John Barnes had been sacked in February, shortly after Celtic's defeat by Inverness Caley. A moment immortalised in the *Sun* headline: 'supercaleygoballisticcelticareatrocious'. Although Kenny Dalglish then took over the day-to-day running of the club until the season's end, for months there had been speculation over who was going to be the new manager. Despite the public pressure to get things sorted out, such was the club's desire to get it right and the difficulties over contract negotiations that O'Neill was not signed up until 1 June.

Celtic's major shareholder Dermot Desmond later revealed that throughout the arduous talks on Celtic's new manager O'Neill's name was the one that fired up most board members. 'We drew up a shortlist of managers right away and Martin O'Neill was on it,' he recalls. 'Our initial soundings regarding whether Martin would be interested in the job claimed he wasn't available. We learned this was misinformation and shortly after the Premiership reached its conclusion we contacted him again.'

O'Neill impressed right away. 'Within minutes of the interview it was obvious to everyone that Martin was the man for the job. We realised that the most important thing for the club was to ensure we got the person we wanted and that was Martin. There was no way we were ever going to give up the chase for him.' (6 June, *Celtic View*)

Even though there were protracted negotiations there has also never been any doubt that Martin O'Neill is a Celtic man through and through. He made the fact plain to journalists in a series of interviews on the day he signed for the club.

'I am not being patronising, nor am I being trite, when I talk about the lure of Celtic Football Club and what it means to me,' he told them. 'That is the way I feel about this club.

'I have felt that way ever since that day in 1967 when they won the European Cup, and then from a night in 1974, when I came up here to see a match and climbed all the way up to the top of one of these giant terracings. There was something special about that.

'And, of course, Jock Stein's achievements were fantastic. He is immortal, and you would have to be mad to think you could do what he did. I remember being at Nottingham Forest when Tommy Gemmell came down and I said to him – and you know I was in awe of him – "That was some goal in Lisbon." He said to me: "Which one, son?" and, you know, he was right.'

The new manager had a contract with the BBC to commentate on the European Championship finals and no sooner had he jetted in to address the players than he was off to Brussels to complete his obligations. It left pundits with a field day as Celtic seemed to be slipping further and further behind Rangers. In fact, when O'Neill arrived Rangers had already signed seven new players while Celtic had signed no one and had just parted company with their star striker Mark Viduka.

But softly, softly was the O'Neill approach, as he had indicated to his players in the dressing-room, and in repeated interviews he stressed that Rangers were the 'benchmark'. It was in some ways an obvious but dangerous tack to take, as the other side of the Old Firm had discovered more than 30 years before. In 1967, just before Celtic and Rangers both played in their European finals, Rangers chairman John Lawrence had admitted Celtic were their yardstick and despite being absolutely correct he was pilloried by members of his own support, furious at any suggestion, however logical, that Celtic could be in any way superior.

The passion might still be there but times had changed. The climate O'Neill walked into in Glasgow among Celtic fans was sober and reflective. Nobody in their right minds could have expected Celtic to win the league after the recent turmoil on the park and the talk, encouraged by the new manager, was of a season of rebuilding.

'Oh no, we didn't expect anything,' says Jim Smith, a 40-year-old drug counsellor and lifelong Celtic supporter who works in Motherwell. 'It had been such a grim season. Just depressing. Worse than anything I can remember. Worse even than the season when Mo Johnston signed for Rangers and they came here and hammered us. They were about 3–0 up after a few minutes, as far as I can remember, and the fans took it bad. They began showering the old board with Mars bars, scarves, season tickets and pies, and shouting abuse. But in those days you knew they were never going to spend any money on new players. You knew that Rangers were just going to bankroll their way to the top so your expectations were already low.

'The thing about the 21-point season was that we had expectations. I mean, I have been coming to Celtic Park all my life. I remember my first Celtic game, the League Cup semi-final at Hampden against Dundee. I was just a kid and I went with my dad, my uncle Jim and my Auntie Maureen. And I can remember getting my first season ticket in the '80s. In those days there were no season books or standing orders. You went up to the offices of Desmond White in Bath Street; he was one of the directors and was an accountant or a lawyer, and you handed over your cash, all of it in one go, and they gave you back this wee bit of paper, a sort of card. That was it. That was your season ticket.

'So I have been going for a few years and I have got to tell you, in terms of sheer disappointment about what was going on, it was the worst. You can understand when Martin O'Neill arrived we were just looking at a season of rebuilding.

'I wanted O'Neill to come, although others thought Hiddink was more glamorous. But Hiddink hadn't been having a great run and O'Neill definitely has something. He's got that sort of Irish toughness, self-belief. And he's got integrity too. You know it's the truth when he says he's a Celtic man. We all laughed in the old days every time we signed a new player and, no matter where they were from or their nationality, the first thing they'd say was "I have supported Celtic since I was a boy." You don't get that feeling with O'Neill. He likes to complete things too. When he was starting out as a manager at Wycombe Wanderers, Nottingham Forest came after him, but he stayed because he had a job to do. I admired that. But all the same nobody expected miracles when he came here. I reckoned at least ten weeks just to sort out the squad, see who he fancies and who was for the off. Then a few weeks of gelling together before we could start seeing decent results. Under these circumstances a league win was really out of the question.'

O'Neill himself was well aware of the turmoil that the club had gone through recently and with a passing wink at the rapid turnover of managers, three in as many years, he said, 'By deduction, I should have at least seven and a half months.'

O'Neill's immediate departure to take up his duties with the Beeb at the European Championships may have set hearts all a-flutter in Glasgow as the clock ticked by without any signings but it was there he spotted the player who was to be one of his key buys and play a pivotal role in strengthening the team's spine.

Joos Valgaeren had had a good European Championship playing for his national side Belgium. So good that 12 clubs were said to be chasing his signature from JC Roda, his home club, as the end of July came around. He was a big, tough defender with a no-nonsense style and a massive heart. Martin O'Neill had publicly stated that he was unlikely to buy any player on the basis of a two- or three-week showing at the championships. He had changed his mind.

'Wanting to win and having the deep desire to see that through are two different things,' he told the *Observer*'s Glenn Gibbons on 30 July. 'I've seen enough of Joos to know he has that deep desire. I think if you have a good, strong mentality, you're well on the way. I think it's inbred in top-quality sportsmen and I think Valgaeren is one of them. I like the way he talks when he's asked about himself and his qualities.

'You hear him say frequently, "I'm a sportsman, I want to win," and that is how a top-quality player should talk. There are parallels to be drawn between him and Matty Elliott, who developed into a marvellous player in the Premiership with Leicester after being around smaller clubs for a few years.'

It was to take weeks of wrangling before Valgaeren would arrive and he was one of only three big signatures the former Leicester manager was chasing. The others, Chris Sutton, a striker who had had a miserable time at Chelsea, and Neil Lennon, O'Neill's inspirational midfield battler from Leicester, would also take a while to arrive.

Before any of them were in place the new manager had to see what he already had. O'Neill had studied videos of Celtic's games during the previous season but video footage is no substitute for seeing players in the flesh. The biggest problem is the way cameras understandably follow the action, limiting the viewing of any particular player to a few fleeting moments unless he is having an outstanding game.

So, to Ireland and O'Neill's first chance to see his squad in action as he took them on a pre-season tour which dotted all over Europe from Dublin to Denmark and then into Germany.

Jonathan Northcroft, chief football writer at the *Sunday Times* Scotland, who was on much of the trip, calls the arrangement 'bizarre': 'They were left with a weird pre-season schedule which was an amalgam of a Kenny Dalglish arrangement, and an Allan MacDonald arrangement. They went to Dublin and then they went to Denmark and then they went on a bizarre mission to Leipzig in the old East Germany. O'Neill was saying, "Oh, my God. Who arranged this? Why are we doing this?" And Celtic were absolutely awful in much of it.'

O'Neill inherited a team low in confidence and a squad short of quality.

Outside Dublin, in the quaint Carlisle Grounds, home to Bray Wanderers AFC, Irish First Division champions in 2000, he was about to discover it. The game was billed in Ireland as the biggest Bray had ever seen. The club were on the brink of rebuilding themselves, a new league structure was being created and years of wrangling over the lease for the Carlisle Grounds lent an air of insecurity to their march up the league rankings.

In brilliant sunshine Martin O'Neill's side took to the park wearing Celtic's change strip in gold. Bray were wearing vertical green-and-white stripes, a variation on the Celtic hoops. The 6,000 capacity crowd was packed into the small ground and two cameras on giant hydraulic lifts hung over the top of the tin-roofed enclosure.

Neil Cameron, then a sports reporter with the Glasgow *Evening Times*, remembers the occasion: 'Because of the way the ground was laid out Martin O'Neill had to virtually walk around it from the corner flag to get to the dug-out. The reception was unbelievable. The Celtic fans, and there was a huge contingent, went absolutely wild. O'Neill seemed a bit bemused by the whole thing.'

Celtic supporter James Allcock remembers the mood was buoyant: 'Part way through the game we were pelted by a hail storm. A lot of people fled to the covered area (the area we were in behind the goal was just a grass bank) but quite a few braved the weather. Between us and the goal there was a dreadlocked guy with no shirt on. He spent the whole game cheering on Bobby Petta (the Dutch winger who, at the time, was getting torrid treatment from the fans), even during the storm.

'There was also the streaker. The team were shocking but got a good reception. The reception for Martin O'Neill was fantastic. As I remember, everyone was in good spirits but the feeling was that we didn't expect to win the league that year, just improve on the awful year before. No one was expecting a miracle!'

But the match was to be imprinted in the minds of the Celtic players for what happened at half-time after a particularly woeful performance. With Celtic 2–1 down O'Neill walked into the dressing-room, took off his glasses – a sure sign of an explosion to come, as the Leicester boys will testify – and let fly.

Celtic and Scotland star Paul Lambert, a European Cup-winner with Borussia Dortmund, admitted: 'That's when we knew that this guy had it, that he was for real.' (*Daily Mail*) After the Bray game, O'Neill displayed his ruthless streak by singling out Brazilian defender Rafael to tell him: 'We are the same, you and me.' The smile on the South American's face disappeared when the manager, in front of the team, added: 'I'm 48 and I can do everything you can do.' Rafael, a source of much disappointment to the Celtic fans following his £5 million signing the season before, did not figure much in the season to come.

9 JULY: CELTIC 3 BRAY WANDERERS AFC 2
(Report by Darryl Broadfoot: *The Herald*)

Tommy Johnson ensured his sixth manager in three years got off to a winning start, scoring a hat trick in a match more memorable for a virtuoso streaking performance than the entertainment provided by the fully-clothed men who hogged the field for 90 minutes.

His ovation as he was marched off wearing only handcuffs and a satisfied smile after an impromptu lap of dishonour, was greater than the one afforded to Martin O'Neill as he took to the bench for the first time.

While for Celtic the match was, in the words of the new manager, 'a training exercise', it was a rare opportunity for the boys from Bray to take on Parkhead's finest . . . and they came ever so close to making it a day to remember.

O'Neill, quite rightly, will pay little attention to the result, or the performances, but on yesterday's evidence, some are further along the road to full fitness than others.

Brazilian defender, Rafael, made a surprise appearance after a horrendous start to his Celtic career and looked desperately out of sorts in a back four that also included last year's other major injury victims, Tom Boyd and Alan Stubbs.

The man who signed from Gremio has been plagued by injury and illness since his £5m move from South America, succumbing to appendicitis within days of signing, and damaging a knee after recuperating from the operation. He looked ill at ease and bereft of pace against a nimble front line and, indeed, was caught cold for the opening goal.

Those Celtic fans present among the 6,000 who turned up will expect a marked improvement from Rafael by the time the real stuff gets under way but they will have been heartened by a typically solid performance from their captain, who at 34 is reaping the benefits of a disciplined career.

With Chris Sutton's imminent arrival, countryman Johnson sent out a timely reminder that he is determined to make up for lost time. Cruciate ligament damage and banishment to the reserves under Wim Jansen has blighted his stay in Glasgow, but his form towards the end of last season and the early signs this summer suggest the blow of losing Mark Viduka can be cushioned somewhat.

Bulgarian Stilian Petrov looks as though he is in for a punishing pre-season. Never the slightest of men, the midfielder looks as though he has piled on a few pounds during the hiatus and will have to make the most of the training camp in Denmark and the forthcoming matches against FC Copenhagen on Wednesday, and Sachen Leipzig in Germany on Friday.

The cobwebs were understandably apparent during a languid first-half performance from the visitors and Jason Byrne sounded an early warning when he shot just wide after a long ball breached the Celtic rearguard.

Worse was to follow when Rafael's lack of match practice enabled O'Brien to embarrass Jonathan Gould with a perfectly executed chip from the edge of the penalty box that sailed over the goalkeeper's head.

Celtic upped the tempo and within a minute drew level courtesy of Johnson. Berkovic picked out the Geordie's diagonal run from the left, and although his first effort was blocked by goalkeeper Trevor Wood, he equalised with a simple tap-in from the rebound.

Following a 15-minute lull, entertainment arrived in the form of the streaker. The male in question galloped past a disapproving Berkovic, but by the time he had completed his mazy run, followed, Benny Hill-style, by a half-dozen of the Garda's finest, the Israeli and Johnston were doubled up as the offender was rugby-tackled to the ground and huckled.

Johnston, regarded as the joker in the Parkhead pack, dedicated his second goal – a thudding 25-yard strike – to the man marshalled out of the stadium with a policeman's bib covering his modesty.

Reluctantly, we settled for the more conventional method of entertainment, but before long the Bray boys were buoyant when the busy Byrne shook off the attentions of Stubbs and drilled the ball into the net through Gould's legs.

The keeper's involvement ended on the hour mark when O'Neill introduced Stewart Kerr. Bray's manager, Pat Devlin, brought off his own No.1 in place of Alan Young.

O'Neill then made a triple substitution, pitching in the young guns, John Kennedy, Mark Fotheringham, and Stephen Crainey, in place of Stéphane Mahé, Tom Boyd, and Petrov.

Their eagerness to impress gave the match a much-needed injection of life and, in 73 minutes, Johnson completed a deserved hat trick, stroking the ball past the substitute goalkeeper after Jackie McNamara's cross had been laid into his path by Fotheringham.

'Hail! Hail!' sang the relieved Celtic faithful, but they wished they hadn't tempted fate as the heavens opened, unleashing the kind of torrential rain usually reserved for the Glasgow Fair.

While the fans scurried for shelter, the players darted off knowing there is much work to be done in Copenhagen.

Celtic's next stop was indeed Copenhagen, to play the Danish team of the same name, who had amongst their side one Harald Brattbakk. Brattbakk had been the striker whose name was on everybody's lips during his short spell playing for Celtic. Unfortunately it was for all the wrong reasons. The Norwegian had a stunning track record of goals when he was with Rosenberg so expectations were high. Yet, when he arrived at Celtic he seemed to wilt under the pressure. Even the feat of scoring the goal that won Celtic the league under Wim Jansen's reign was not enough to wipe away the wry smiles that spread across the faces of supporters from all camps when his name was mentioned.

But before facing Harald and Copenhagen, Celtic had to welcome O'Neill's first signing, Chris Sutton. Sutton arrived the day before the Copenhagen game dragging the baggage of a big name and a bad season at Chelsea behind him. He had been one of the rising stars in English football with a career only sullied by the miserable time he had had at the London club. But inevitably questions were being asked about the wisdom of forking out £6 million for him and whether he could cope with the incredibly intrusive pressure-cooker atmosphere in Scottish football. Sutton hadn't sampled an Old Firm clash in the flesh but he had watched one on TV in Glasgow – at probably the most famous Celtic bar in the world, Baird's in the Calton. It wasn't his only stop for a beer on the trip, as regulars at the Hoops Bar in the Calton, another great Celtic pub, remember. Sutton and Billy McKinley, his Scots pal at Blackburn Rovers, both arrived in a white stretch limousine to watch the game. They joined in with the fans in mucking about and having a great time. At one point the Blackburn striker was behind the bar taking orders from the bemused fans. Until very recently photographs of Sutton pulling pints at the Hoops adorned its walls.

With impeccable timing he arrived as a Celtic player virtually straight from a court case in England where he had been fined £300 for his role in a restaurant row. The experience had left him extremely wary of the press: 'The whole situation was farcical,' he said (13 July, *Daily Record*). 'If a situation where three people collaborate to stitch me up is repeated, then the same thing could happen. If I had not been a footballer with a profile, it would not have come to that. But that's now behind me and I just want to talk about Celtic.'

But if his confidence was dented he showed no signs of it. At his first press conference the 27-year-old betrayed all the self-belief of a man who knew exactly where his life was going. Jonathan Northcroft of the *Sunday Times* Scotland was there. He told the authors of his first impressions of Sutton: 'He came into his first press conference and – you are used to footballers being very bland and cautious – the first thing he said was, "Celtic are a bigger club than Rangers and I think we should start putting them in their place." Everyone thought he had a real arrogance and gallusness about him, but again that indicated the kind of personality O'Neill wanted at the club.'

Sutton played in Copenhagen in a game which ended up a 2–2 draw but, even in those early days, represented a small turning point for Celtic.

The opening paragraphs of the *Daily Record*'s match report indicate what grabbed everyone's attention: 'Harald Brattbakk finally showed the Celtic fans what he could do last night. Pity it was seven months too late and he was wearing another team's jersey.

12 JULY: FC COPENHAGEN 2 CELTIC 2
(Report by Neil Cameron: *Evening Times*)

In the first half of the match Brattbakk stole the show with two cracking goals as Neil Cameron, the *Evening Times* man at the match, remembers:

Harald was sensational and clearly out to bury some bad memories. This he did in 11 minutes, with a brilliant goal. He twisted one way and then the other to bamboozle Tom Boyd, then curled his left-foot shot just inside the post past Kerr.

However, he wasn't finished there. In 36 minutes, Todi Johnsson broke down the right and pulled his cross back across the six-yard box. Guess who was there, perfectly placed, to slide the ball in – the same man who once, while in Celtic colours, missed an open goal from two inches. Amazing, really.

The Norwegian's former team-mates and the couple of hundred travelling supporters looked on in utter disbelief.

Martin O'Neill carried out wholesale changes at half-time. Kerr, Hitzlsperger, Tebily, Riseth, Berkovic, Johnson and Lambert were replaced by Gould, Mahé, Stubbs, Petta, Larsson, Burchill and Petrov. The switches revitalised the team.

Bobby Petta, a player who had spent most of the previous couple of seasons in purgatory due to some woeful performances and a crippling lack of confidence which wasn't helped by the barracking he had received from the Celtic support, began to show signs that he was being reborn.

Mark Burchill, Celtic's youthful striker, got one back on 56 minutes as he moved swiftly on to a lovely trademark flick from Henrik Larsson, held off a defender and then rocketed a shot under the goalkeeper.

Celtic refused to lie down and with just ten minutes to go to the final whistle Larsson slid a lovely ball to Petta on the left and the Dutchman pinged a low cross through the six-yard line. Burchill met it beautifully, slotting home his second of the night and evening up the scores. Celtic could have won the tie when Johan Mjallby blasted a shot goalwards only to see it athletically saved by Michael Stensgaard.

Most reports, having naturally focused on Harald's revenge, took note of the way Celtic responded. Not all though. 'Not even Hans Christian Andersen, whose fairy-tale fantasies are a continued source of pride to the residents of Copenhagen, could have disguised the harsh reality which dawned upon Celtic in the Danish capital last week. If there has been a magical quality to Martin O'Neill's managerial career, his Midas Touch having lifted Leicester City and Wycombe Wanderers to new heights, this was his welcome to the real world.' (16 July, *Scotland on Sunday*)

Within days Celtic were on the move again, this time to savour the delights of the former East Germany where they would play the little-known Sachsen Leipzig. If the tour was a grind Martin O'Neill certainly wasn't showing it. 'It was done and dusted before I arrived,' he told the Scottish *Mirror* (13 July). 'But when I was a player with Nottingham Forest we once went to America and then South America for our pre-season. Compared with that, we are really just going to Edinburgh.'

The press certainly weren't happy about being dragged all around Europe to watch a series of rather underwhelming performances in poorly equipped stadia. At Sachsen Leipzig's third division and 'decaying' ground the facilities for viewing the match were far from perfect. Rob Robertson of the *Herald* remembers it clearly: 'The whole event was a bit weird. There was a pipe band on the pitch before the match playing at the same time as a local rock band. It was a racket. Then a sky-diver landed in the middle of the pitch.

'Nobody could see much of the game because the press-room was this little box with a few tables and chairs at the back of the stand. If you actually wanted to see the game you had to go into this tiny gantry which felt like it was going to collapse on to the park.'

The after-match facilities at the Alfred Kunze Stadium were not much better. 'We went into this basketball hall, which looked like it had been a beer cellar in another life. There were German fans sitting all around drinking and smoking away. Then Martin O'Neill came in and went down to the front to do the after-match press conference. The whole thing was broadcast throughout the hall on the tannoy while these people drank their beers, smoked their fags and carried on their conversations.'

The match itself hadn't gone to plan. Sachsen Leipzig had been going through a lean spell since they won the East German championship in 1964 and the East German Cup in 1967. They won 2–0. Only the appearance of Chris Sutton, in his first Celtic outing, lifted the gloom. The press, however, took into account the travelling and the fact O'Neill was trying a number of combinations and did not hammer the club too badly.

14 JULY: SACHSEN LEIPZIG 2 CELTIC 0.
(Report by Rob Robertson: *The Herald*)

Celtic managed to lose 2–0 and, although they did not play well, nothing too much can be read into the result, considering the lengths they went to even get here and the amount of changes that O'Neill made during the game.

It was yet another learning process for the Celtic coach, who conceded afterwards that his side had defensive problems that had to be addressed and that, tactically, the team needed fine-tuning.

'We have very obvious defensive frailties which we have to work on the best we can,' said O'Neill. 'The whole side needs improving all over the pitch and you have to defend from all over the pitch.

'One of the reasons why maybe they haven't done so well over the last year is because they haven't defended properly as a team and that's now quite apparent to me.'

O'Neill said he was pleased at Sutton's debut, although he conceded he was still lacking match fitness and only came on at half-time. He is also considering trying to fit in some more pre-season games, even if they are behind closed doors, so he can finally evaluate every player at the club.

When he came on, Sutton played up front with Henrik Larsson until Tommy Johnson appeared, which meant the Swede dropped back into the hole behind the front two. In the game, Sutton tried his best to use his physical strength to break down the German team's defence and indeed did quite well considering his time out of the game.

Overall the match was a good workout for Celtic, despite the result, although Martin O'Neill will clearly want to get some new players in to strengthen the squad which he has inherited, sooner rather than later in light of what he has seen in their three games so far.

In the first 45 minutes, Celtic were full of pretty touches from Henrik Larsson and Stilian Petrov but for all their invention they lacked any real bite to their play.

They got off to the worst possible start when Hagen Schmidt rose unchallenged in the box with central defenders Allan Stubbs and Oliver Tebily miles off him to head home after only nine minutes.

Just before the half-hour mark Celtic went even further behind when the midfield failed to shut down defender Jens Hartel who strode forward unchallenged before firing in a long-range effort into the top corner.

Included in the Celtic side last night was German teenager Thomas Hitzlsperger, who had hoped to win a contract with the Parkhead club, but he had a quiet game up until then and looked incredibly one-footed, which suggests his chance has gone of securing a deal.

'My abiding memory of the Leipzig game,' Rob Robertson recalls, 'was not what happened on the park but our return journey home. The whole thing was a day trip so we were all back at the airport in the middle of the night waiting to get on two tiny planes bound for Glasgow. I can remember looking at the Celtic squad, Larsson and Sutton among them, getting on this 24-seater in front of us and thinking, "My God – that's putting all your eggs into one basket."

'There was nothing glamorous about millions of pounds of talent trooping into a cramped little aircraft for a three-and-a-half hour flight home. The press had it worse. We had a separate 12-seater, for some reason we didn't travel with the team on that trip, and it was cramped. The meals were under the seats in front and there was no toilet.

'About halfway home one of the boys needed a pee and had to do it into this bowl. Then because the plane was bouncing about so much it started slopping everywhere and he got some plasticky cling-film stuff, covered it and put it on his lap. It wasn't first class.'

Celtic's week of foreign travel ended with the Sachsen Leipzig game. There were two more friendlies to play in Glasgow before a stiffer test of Celtic's mettle, Dundee United at the end of the month.

But the week of bouncing about all over Europe had given O'Neill a chance to spend some time with his players and the press a chance to cast an eye over him. Jonathan Northcroft was impressed: 'O'Neill was obviously a man to be reckoned with, who would and could make hard decisions. However, at first he did that without actually going into direct confrontation with the players.

'He was quite clever because he obviously knew he had to win over the dressing-room, so he was critical without mentioning individuals to the press. He was quite stand-offish in that first week. He just let the players do what they liked. He was basically observing how they would behave socially and so on. Of course he didn't have his backroom boys, John Robertson or Steve Walford, at that stage and so he looked like a man with an enormous task.'

The next game, then, was Bordeaux and Bordeaux was Martin O'Neill's homecoming. The friendly played against the French club in blazing sunshine at Celtic Park was also noteable for the Parkhead return of Henrik Larsson. Larsson, probably one of the finest strikers Celtic have ever played, had been out for much of the previous season after breaking his leg in a European match with Lyon. The footage of him looking down at his clearly snapped shin bone had been replayed over and over again during the previous season and the horror on his face was matched only by the slow realisation of what his absence would do to the club.

The dreadlocked Swede had been a revelation since signing for Celtic from Feyenoord three seasons before. His strength and grace on the pitch were matched only by his prolific goalscoring ability. He had started off at Celtic playing behind the front two but as his confidence grew so did his goalscoring. At the time of his accident he was Celtic's striker bar none. Such a break has finished many careers but Larsson was already legendary for his professionalism and dedication.

There were signs that he could have taken to the field again in May but it was in Euro 2000, to the delight of thousands of Celtic supporters, that he proved he was back in business. His comeback from injury had been amazing. His contribution to the coming season was to be truly astonishing.

So the hottest item on a baking Glasgow afternoon, as one commentator put it, was not sun cream but the Henrik Larsson masks worn by thousands of supporters.

But nobody had forgotten Martin O'Neill. When he stepped on to the pitch 47,224 supporters cheered like he had already won the league. His voice cracked as he addressed the faithful, though he later swore it was down to the poor PA system. And with some panache O'Neill finished off with a little joke: 'I hope I'm not getting booed by September.'

Ninety minutes later the euphoria had been reduced to a sobering silence as the team trooped off the park beaten 4–2 by Bordeaux. It may have been a friendly but Celtic's first match with Rangers was only a month away and the signs were not promising. Bordeaux, however, were no mugs. A side of silky quality, they were the champions in a country which had recently added the European Championship trophy to their cabinet to nestle alongside the World Cup.

22 JULY: CELTIC 2 BORDEAUX 4
(Report by authors)

Thirty-three minutes into the game a delighted Marc Wilmots found himself on the end of a lofted pass from Christian Dugarry courtesy of Celtic defender Oliver Tebilly, who had lashed out at fresh air as it passed him. The Belgian coolly slid the ball past Stewart Kerr.

Just before half-time the Celtic Park roof nearly parted company with its supports at the roar when Larsson slotted home a penalty awarded after David Sommeil had handled Eyal Berkovic's pass. It was Larsson's first goal in a Celtic shirt for more than ten months.

It was Larsson again in the midst of the action in 53 minutes when after skipping down the byeline he flicked a neat cutback at Mark Burchill allowing him to take Celtic's second with a diving header. A rocket of an overhead kick could have set the seal of the game had it gone in. But it was not to be. Bordeaux's Laurent Battles underlined how seriously the French were taking the game when he chopped down Eyal Berkovic in the 65th minute, then, furious at Berkovic's writhings, he kicked him. He was rewarded with the long walk to the dressing-room courtesy of a red card.

Celtic lost two goals in rapid succession. Laslandes' free kick bobbled out of Kerr's reach in the 67th minute for an equaliser. Substitute Pascale Feindouno compounded Kerr's misery when he lobbed him in the 86th minute. Then Jerome Bonnissel to slide past some weary tackles to bullet home a shot.

The cracks were there for all to see. *Scotland on Sunday*'s Andrew Smith likened O'Neill's new job to 'painting the Forth Road Bridge' and Rangers were only days away. Smith added: 'The absence of reliable wide players, the thinness of personnel for midfield and a similar concern in respect of O'Neill's attacking options suggest there is not a department in the side that it would not be justifiable to strengthen.'

O'Neill wasn't hiding either: 'We lost poor goals. It's my team now, and I've got to rectify the situation. If the same thing continues to happen, it would be a crisis,' he said in the post-match press conference.

The final warm-up game of the pre-season came against a West Ham side notable for the inclusion of yet another Celtic old boy. Irrepressible is the only way to describe the Italian whose time at Parkhead had been marked by stunning displays of individual skill, before he fell out with the club and headed off to the Premiership and notoriety.

A story doing the rounds in Glasgow at the time of his signing sums up his nature. Suited up and in the lift at Celtic Park on his first day, di Canio found himself accompanied by a couple of unsmiling club officials staring into space. Grinning, he turned to face them, undid his zip, pulled out his manhood and said: 'Whaddaya think of that, eh?' There is absolutely no reason to believe the story is true, but the warmth Celtic supporters felt for him was such that they certainly wanted it to be.

The West Ham game turned into a bit of a canter and, although di Canio was warmly received, the circumstances of his acrimonious departure had clearly cooled what had once been great affection from the supporters.

25 JULY 25: CELTIC 2 WEST HAM 1
(Report by authors)

Redknapp's men began as if they were going to sweep Celtic away and the home side did well to weather a storm which lasted for more than half an hour.

After just four minutes Kanoute won a high ball against Tom Boyd and then burst past Rafael as though he wasn't there and drilled a shot into the side netting.

Two minutes later Stilian Petrov was relieved to see his attempt at a clearing header from di Canio's free kick bounce off the crossbar and behind.

From the resulting corner Neil Ruddock rose unchallenged to head home but referee Stuart Dougal correctly chalked off the defender's effort due to Igor Stimac's foul on Boyd.

Celtic's first chance came in the eighth minute and almost inevitably Larsson was the provider. His perfectly timed and weighted through ball sprung the Hammers' offside trap and released Tommy Johnson but he pulled his shot wide from 15 yards.

Di Canio was off target with an attempted lob before a glaring blunder by Rafael presented the visitors with a golden chance to take the lead in the 25th minute.

The Brazilian's wayward pass from the left touchline missed its intended target, Boyd, by yards, Kanoute latched on to the loose ball and

Jonathan Gould had to dive low to his left to push the Frenchman's drive to safety.

Larsson remained Celtic's most inspiring performer, although he was often forced to come deep to look for possession. He may claim he has some way to go yet before he reaches peak fitness but his flicks, dummies and volleyed passes suggested that mentally he's as sharp as ever. It was hardly surprising, then, that he was the man who laid on the opening goal three minutes from the break.

Lubomir Moravcik started it with a 40-yard chipped pass from just inside the Hammers' half and when Ruddock failed to intercept Larsson was on to it in a flash. With only young Steven Bywater to beat he could have justifiably had a go himself but instead chose unselfishly to square the ball across the face of the goal for the on-rushing Johnson to blast home from six yards.

Celtic might have gone in at half-time two up but for a fine fingertip save by Bywater from Rafael's 25-yard lob.

Their confidence returned, Celtic looked the brighter side from the restart and increased their lead with another fine goal in the 52nd minute.

Bulgarian midfielder Petrov, breaking on the left, played a one-two with Larsson and nutmegged Bywater from six yards for a rare goal.

West Ham replied immediately with an equally fine strike courtesy of di Canio. Kanoute's cross was deftly knocked on by Frank Lampard for the Italian and his finish, curling his right-foot shot into Gould's bottom left-hand corner from 15 yards, was pure class.

Celtic brought on Alan Stubbs, Vidar Riseth, Eyal Berkovic and Mark Burchill for Boyd, Rafael, Petrov and Larsson on the hour and with the latter's withdrawal some of the snap disappeared from their play.

With Redknapp making a raft of substitutions of his own the match petered out into a training exercise.

The pre-season had ended on a bit of a high note although nobody but the most deluded supporter would have read any real significance into the result of the West Ham game.

With the friendly matches out of the way O'Neill was increasing the pressure to get his two back-room boys from Leicester, Steve Walford and former Scottish international John Robertson, up to Glasgow. The two had proved absolutely crucial to his success at Leicester. Without them Celtic were not getting the full Martin O'Neill treatment.

Robertson, one of the great Scottish players, had been O'Neill's team-mate in the double European Cup-winning Forest squad. Brian Clough used to joke about their respective talents. 'What's the point in giving you

the ball when there's a genius on the other wing?' he would say to O'Neill.
(9 September, *Daily Mail*)

The pre-season also ended with another meal. This time it was for the gentlemen of the press. Martin O'Neill invited the sports hacks to lunch just outside Glasgow. It was a convivial occasion with a lot of laughter but it had a steel edge.

O'Neill was obviously aware of the painful way the careers of previous managers had become mired in running wars with the press. He was keen to lay down the ground rules. 'He gave a short speech,' recalls Neil Cameron, now of the *Daily Record*. It was basically "I might look like a nice guy. I am not. I am a c★★t and I never forget." The new season was days away and there had been plenty high jinks with other managers before. He was warning us that he'd take his lumps when they were due, but if we crossed him we'd pay.'

Was it a style he'd learned from Brian Clough? Clough believes that O'Neill is the complete manager because he has come up the hard way through the managerial ranks. The two had an interesting relationship at Nottingham Forest where Clough bombarded O'Neill, who revelled in the dressing-room nickname of Squire, with insults about his university education. Occasionally when O'Neill would ponder whether he would be better returning to Queen's University, Belfast to finish his law studies Clough would bellow: 'Well f★★★ off back there then, because you're no bloody good at football.'

Yet the two occasions when Clough praised him have stuck in his memory as golden moments. The first came after Forest had been knocked out of the FA Cup at West Bromwich. 'I walked out of that dressing-room ten feet tall despite being sick at getting knocked out of a quarter-final.' (9 September, *Daily Mail*) And the congratulatory letter that Brian Clough sent to O'Neill after he won his first League Cup as a manager is framed and hanging on his wall at home. Indeed, Clough also advised O'Neill to take the Celtic job when the two met at a dinner function.

Clough, who was one of Britain's greatest managers, recalls spending time with O'Neill when he was at Nottingham Forest: 'After training, when I had been working with 20 players, Martin used to take up a lot of my time discussing the ins and outs of the game because he was that type, keen to learn.

'He drove me daft at times. But I never tried to discourage him from asking questions as I was always impressed by his desire to learn and put points he had picked up into practice. Martin has carried that desire to learn into management.

'Compared to the average footballer, and I am not being discourteous to us, he is pretty intelligent.' Laughingly, the two-time European Cup-winning manager added: 'I used to scream at players to stop the crosses and it took Martin two years to ask someone what it meant. When I explained to him that you don't have to be Einstein to work out that if you stop balls going into the box then you stop a lot of goals, he was quite happy. Now he employs the same thing at Celtic. I have seen him on TV, standing on the touchline yelling "Stop the crosses".' (6 June, *Celtic View*)

'He's got everything now – playing credentials at the highest level, precious knowledge gained from serving his time in the lower divisions, he speaks the players' language, he can be ruthless when necessary and he keeps the media sweet. And after working for me for a few years he's bound to have learned something about management.' (9 September, *Daily Mail*)

It was Clough, of course, who mischievously first lobbed the Messiah tag and Jock Stein prediction O'Neill's way. It's something the Celtic manager dismissed months later. 'Jock Stein is a god, no doubt about it,' he says. 'What he has done at this football club defied belief. While you would never, remotely, get close to it at all, at least you want to try to do your best and that means winning a championship.' (26 November, *Independent*)

Of course it was only July then and a ball had not yet been kicked in anger.

3.

INTO THE VALLEY

Celtic, Celtic that's the team for me,
Celtic, Celtic on to victory,
They're the finest team in Scotland, I'm sure you will agree,
We'll never give up till we've won the cup
and the Scottish football league.
They come from bonnie Scotland, they come from County Cork,
They come from dear old Donegal and even from New York,
From every street in Glasgow they proudly make their way,
To a place called dear old Paradise and this is what they say.

Chorus
There's Fallon, Young and Gemmell who proudly wear the green,
There's Clark, McNeill and Kennedy the best there's ever been,
Jim Johnson, Murdoch, Chalmers, John Divers and John
Hughes,
And 60,000 Celtic fans who proudly shout the news.

SOME FOOTBALL SEASONS are destined to be historic, others are best forgotten, but they all start with one thing in common: optimism. The season Martin O'Neill embarked upon as he and his players headed up to Dundee in the team coach was no different in that respect. Whatever had gone before, the sun shone through a cloudless sky and the squad were burning with optimism as they looked forward to their first real test under the new regime. An episode of *Chewin' the Fat*, the comedy series which had taken Scotland by storm, was playing on the video as it would before every match all season. The players laughed and joked. While they travelled north through the mid-afternoon traffic Celtic supporters all over the world were stirring to the same emotion and getting themselves ready to take in the game.

For Jimmy Johnstone the opening day of the new season evoked the kind of memories that few people are privileged to have. Jinky is a legend, emblazoned in every Celtic supporter's memory as a red-haired devil dancing through defences on the magical march to the European Cup. In Celtic terms he has seen it all, and for most of the really golden moments he was right there in the crucible of the football pitch. He was there too throughout 1969, in what for more than 30 years was to be Celtic's last Treble-winning season.

On 30 July, as always, his thoughts were with the Celtic team. And as always they turned to the opening days of his own great seasons in the sun. 'The first match of the season always seemed to be on a scorcher of a day,' he recalled. 'You could put the kettle on to the fact the weather would change just days before kick-off and we'd be sweltering.

'At the start of a season everything is new. The kit is fresh, the pitches are terrific. Great to play on. When you were going out at first on to the park the sprinklers would be on and the grass would be moist. I can remember just running backwards and forwards through those sprinklers just to cool down.'

The memory of matches played under the sun lingers with players long after the significance of the result has faded away. The Dundee United game that opened O'Neill's Treble-winning season was to be important for a lot of people because of the things they thought they saw in the team's performance. But there are other reasons why such matches seem unforgettable to those who are on the park.

'There are wee patterns,' Jinky adds. 'If it was a home match I'd have a long lie and get something light to eat in the house. If we were going away, say to Dundee, we would meet about nine or half-past nine and get on the bus.

'Sometimes we would stop on the way and the boys would have whatever they took, beans on toast, steak and chips or something like that. Often we would go to the Station Hotel for our lunch about 12, 12.30. We would all have the same thing to eat.

'Before the game I would stretch. I always stretched. I was a great one for it. Then I would have hot and cold baths. Slipper baths. I would jump in and out of them three or four times to loosen up. Then it was on to the table to get some oil. After that I would just get a feel of the ball, play it off the walls, just get it about me.'

Martin O'Neill's team arrived at Tannadice on the back of a pre-season tour that was hard and demanding. But in the '60s and early '70s participation in internationals and foreign jaunts before the season kicked off was virtually unheard of. Players were brought in for pre-season training fresh from weeks of uninterrupted leisure.

'I think it's crazy having these internationals and games,' Jinky adds. 'The players don't get any time away. When we were off, we were off. That was it. We left everything, tried not to think about football or touch a ball, just went on our holidays. Then when you got back for pre-season training and all the boys were in the dressing-room, it was great.

'I loved all the comradeship between the players, the banter and the jokes, the talk about who had done what when they were away. It brought you together. I have seen that attitude in Martin O'Neill's team. They are close.

'You needed the pre-season training to get the touch back. It's surprising how quickly the edge goes. The ball is a wee bit alien to you. Big Jock used to put us straight on to ball work from the first day. As you would be coming out the tunnel there was a ball waiting there for everyone. You just picked it up as you went past.'

While the sun really did shine over Scotland in Jinky Johnston's day – Britain sweltered through a series of scorching summers in the late '60s – some would have you believe that it always breaks out over Parkhead at key moments in Celtic history. Maybe, but it is not recorded what the weather was like during the most significant game in the club's history.

We do know it took place on a spring evening 113 years ago. The date was 12 May 1888, and 2,000 people paid at the rudimentary turnstiles to watch the Celtic players take on and beat Rangers. It was, as every supporter knows, the club's first-ever game in its first-ever season. It's fair to speculate that the result was the talk of the teeming districts which crowded around Celtic's new stadium off the Gallowgate at Parkhead.

The East End of a hundred years ago was remarkably different to the sparsely populated rundown area it has become. Then, families crammed into the tenements lining each side of London Road. Grubby, barefoot weans straight out of sepia-toned photographs ran wild on the pavements. Lives were played out in the open and tragedy, poverty and a growing sense of community in the face of adversity were the order of the day. Celtic's beginnings are well recorded elsewhere but they have such a major impact on the club today it's worth reconsidering them.

The Irish had started pouring into Scotland and especially Glasgow around the 1840s to escape the grinding poverty in their home country. As they found work in foundries and steelworks they called for relatives and friends to join them and successive waves had made the East End a boiling pot of Irish immigrants. In the late '70s a depression hit, banks collapsed and hundreds were thrown out of work. Against this grim backdrop the idea for Celtic Football Club was born. The guiding motive was, however, not entertainment but the raising of money for charity.

At the time the only really successful Irish club in Scotland was playing in Edinburgh. Hibernian attracted support from all over the country but the greatest numbers were based in Glasgow.

That was evident when Hibernian won the Scottish Cup at Hampden in 1887. Instead of getting on the train back to the capital the team party went to St Mary's Hall in the East End to celebrate. Amid the rejoicing their club president John McFadden stood up and dedicated the victory to every 'Irish Catholic' in Scotland. As a by-the-way he dropped a broad hint to the crowds present that it was time the Glasgow Irish started their own club.

As fate would have it, in the audience that evening were three men who were wrestling with the problem of trying to feed the many hungry children living in the area. They were Brother Walfrid, the headmaster of St Andrew's school in the city centre, Brother Dorotheus, the headmaster of St Mary's in the Calton, and businessman John Glass who ran a local building firm.

They already ran a charitable operation giving meals to the destitute children of the East End. At that time they were handing out literally thousands of free dinners every week. But the demand was insatiable. Food costs money and they needed to raise as much of it as possible in as regular a fashion as possible. Football matches were seized upon as a sure-fire winner to bring in a decent income.

They moved swiftly. At a meeting in St Mary's Hall on East Rose Street on 6 November 1887 Celtic Football Club was formally constituted. In that first match Celtic beat Rangers, albeit a reserve side, by the remarkable score of 5–2. A similar scoreline would resonate with Celtic supporters during Martin O'Neill's first season, although for different reasons. What was probably more important at the time was that the game proved that the club could raise significant amounts of money for charity. Celtic was in business. Raising money for charities still forms an important part of the club's ethos.

Today, the tenements that provided much of Celtic's support back then are all but gone and the strong Irish community long departed with them. But the links with that long-dead era are still there. They flow through the turnstiles at Parkhead at every game and through the doors of the Celtic Supporters Association on London Road before and after the matches.

On the morning Martin O'Neill's season started the double doors leading into the modern, squat building were swinging backwards and forwards as fans came in to meet friends before heading to their buses and on to Dundee. Some had come from the States, Australia and even more exotic places to collect their supporters club's tickets. Clubs from all over the world buy season tickets to leave in the London Road committee office so their members can use them when visiting Scotland.

Many in the association that day, as on every other, can trace their families back to those long-demolished tenements and that Irish community. Among them was Eddie Toner, the association secretary. His grandfather, Hughie Docherty, was for 30 years the groundsman at Celtic Park. 'I used to get in free to matches,' Eddie laughs, explaining how his lifelong devotion began.

His day began with his usual duties of sorting out buses, handing out season books and having a laugh with a few mates before heading off to the game around 11 a.m. 'There was a buoyancy about the place as there always is when we get the season starting off again,' he recalls. 'Okay, it was a season of rebuilding, but everyone was desperate to see how the team would look on the park.

'We weren't disappointed. Looking back, the United game was really important. I noticed something about the players as soon as they came on the park. Maybe it was the Martin O'Neill factor, but they were a different team from the one that had been there the season before.'

The London Road association is one of four representing supporters clubs all over the world. Nobody knows exactly how many there are but in North America alone 60 supporters clubs are registered. In Australia, where there are dozens of supporters clubs, the one in Perth has almost 2,000 members. Of course there are equally as many in Scotland, including one on Rangers' turf, Ibrox, and a pretty exclusive club in the House of Commons.

If you go through the London Road association's double doors, cross the hall past the desk with the big Celtic crest on it and go up the stairs to the left you will find Eddie Toner's office. It contains three desks, a computer and a trophy cabinet bulging with the fruits of Celtic Boys Club successes. It is a few weeks after the Treble win and Eddie, association president Gerry Madden, vice president Joe O'Rourke and committee member Brendan Sweeney are sprawled on various pieces of furniture trying to pinpoint the moment they realised that the season was going to be different.

'I was at Celtic Park on Martin O'Neill's first day,' says Eddie. 'I have been along there for the last six new managers. It was a standing joke in the work. They kid me on with "When are you going to get your day off to see your new manager, Eddie?"

'That first day he came out on the steps with a Celtic scarf and spoke to the supporters. There was no microphone so it was really hard to hear, but the gist of it was, "I'm really going to do my best for you boys."

'Then he did an unusual thing. He got down off the steps and walked straight in among the supporters, past the barriers, and started shaking their hands and talking to them. Celtic's security adviser nearly had a heart attack and pulled at him to come back in. I was impressed.'

The association is totally independent of the club and proud of it. It has owned its own premises since former Celtic Chairman Sir Robert Kelly gifted it to them some years ago. As well as the punters, through its doors have also marched the great and the good from the club's history. Often for bizarre reasons.

People still talk about the day Fergus McCann called. The Scots-Canadian millionaire bought Celtic in the mid-'90s and was out surveying his new empire which he had mistakenly assumed included the supporters association. 'Wee Fergus turned up outside the door with his bunnet on just a couple of days after he took over the club,' recalls Eddie. 'He just wandered up on his own and demanded to be let in. The guy on the door, I think it was one of the pensioners, said: "You're not a member. So you're not getting in." Fergus was furious. In his Canadian–Glasgow drawl he said: "Whaddaya mean I can't come in – I own this place."

'He was put right in no uncertain terms, but the message didn't penetrate. He got in and went straight to the bar where he demanded they switch the beer supplier to Scottish and Newcastle Breweries who had just done a deal to supply the function suites at Celtic Park.

'Once again he was told that we weren't part of the purchase price. Eventually the penny dropped and he left. He was never too keen on us after that.'

Fergus wasn't the only big name who dropped in on the association. In the dog days of the 1999–2000 season it became the focus of media attention when Kenny Dalglish, who was temporarily managing the club, decided to host pre-match press conferences there. Dalglish was involved in a bitter war of words with Scotland's sports journalists over the way they covered the club. In a bizarre bid to prove that they were spinning his words he decided to hold his press conferences in public so the fans could hear what he had really said. It was a public relations fiasco culminating in embarrassing headlines when senior *Sunday Mail* journalist Hugh Keevins was escorted off the premises.

'We all went down to watch the press conferences,' added Eddie. 'It was interesting to hear what the replies to questions were and to see what appeared in the papers the next day. But the Hugh Keevins thing wasn't a great moment.

'One of the committee members in the social club, a big bear of a lad, had taken a dislike to Keevins. He thought he was writing un-Celtic things and he asked him to leave. I told him. I said, "Look, this is a bad idea." But he wasn't having any of it. He didn't throw Keevins out. He just went over to him, tapped him on the shoulder and asked him to go. I think Keevins looked, saw the size of him and thought, "Right, I'm off." The story was headline news the next day and Dalglish was pilloried for it.'

And the papers had their revenge when the 'bouncer' was 'turned over', to use a newspaper term, for having the skeletons in his cupboard paraded in public.

Of course most of Celtic's supporters weren't even at the Dundee United game. There are far more season ticket holders than there are tickets available at away grounds in Scotland. The club conducts a ballot among those that want to go. And then there are those who can't even get a season ticket – there is still a huge waiting list. And finally there are those who are abroad.

The day the 2000–01 season began was a cause for celebration for the thousands of supporters who live in Australasia. That is, those who make up what is called the Southern Hemisphere supporters associations. And it wasn't just because a new manager and a new spirit of optimism beckoned. Until that day they had only been able to see to four live broadcast matches a year. They were traditionally the Old Firm games, colourful pieces of life-or-death football theatre, but not always title-deciders and never season-openers. Even that wasn't clear-cut though. The matches were only broadcast in Australia, for example, if there was no cricket on. And with cricket not only being popular Down

Under but also a game that tends to take a long time, it is always on.

Davey Paton's story is typical of the agonies fans go through when they have no choice but to follow a team which is 12,000 miles away. Davey suffered the unusual double blow for a Celtic supporter of being born and brought up in New Zealand – where only clips of matches are shown, often without warning and usually less than ten times a year – and then moving to Australia where things are marginally better. His tale is also curious because he started following Celtic, not because his family did – his father is a Hearts supporter – but because he was brought to Scotland for a holiday as a six-year-old in 1969, slap-bang in the middle of the last Treble celebrations. 'We were there chiefly for the ordination of my uncle and we were staying in a house full of Celtic supporters. All Mum and Dad have said is that I returned to NZ Celtic daft.'

Absence always makes the heart grow fonder as far as football is concerned and the club has become almost an obsession for him, as it has for thousands of others in similar situations. 'Until you have actually done it you cannot relate to a supporter who lives on the wrong side of the world,' Davey, now an accountant, admits. 'If you are daft, like I am, you will do anything to find out results and cannot relax until you know. What makes it worse is that matches are played in the middle of the night our time, and if you are up all night trying to listen to a commentary or watch a match on TV then it well and truly messes the next day up.

'It all changed at the start of the Martin O'Neill season when we got television screening of games. Until then it was a weekly ritual staying up until four in the morning on a Saturday night listening to the BBC World Service which only ever gave scoreflashes from the Celtic and Rangers matches.

'Often though, the final score may be 2 or 3 nil but the last update we had been given was at 1–0 and you would be left hanging on for news of a goal that had been scored maybe 15 minutes earlier.'

Davey's most emotional moment came at the end of the 1998 season when Celtic won the league under Wim Jansen after nine years of Rangers domination. 'It was Celtic v St Johnstone. We had to win or Rangers had ten. I think it was the longest week in my life. What made it worse was that there was no TV coverage at all. I had no internet access at the time so I sat at my desk at home listening to the BBC World Service.

'For some reason there were no English matches that day. The match kicked off at midnight our time. Of course the BBC had the world news headlines before crossing to *Saturday Sport*. I don't remember who the programme host was, either Paddy Feaney or Martin Fookes. Whoever it was spent the next five minutes telling us that they would be covering the usual assortment of sports from around the globe, but would concentrate on Scotland where Celtic were chasing the championship. He then said those never-to-be-forgotten words: "There has already been a goal at Celtic Park. Let's cross for commentary."

'It is very hard to describe the feelings that the next three seconds conjured up. Please make it be for us is the first thought, then just tell us for God's sake. Then you listen frantically to hear who is on the attack, since that is obviously the team who scored.

'I don't recall the actual commentary apart from "Larsson cuts inside, he's looking to shoot" and then absolute bedlam as the crowd drowned out the commentator. One goal was never going to be enough.

'At 1 a.m., just after half-time, the BBC World Service had a 15-minute *World News* report. Then the first five minutes after the sport comes back on it's a round-up of goals from around the country before going to the second-half commentary.

'That 20 minutes when I knew that the match was being played, but there were no updates, was hellish. We were then told it was still 1–0 and then crossed for commentary for the remainder of the second half of about 25 minutes.

'If you've never listened to football on the radio, take my advice: don't. Every opposition free kick is on the edge of your box, every opposition attack results in a shot with the keeper beaten, every player is out of position, every missed tackle is an important one. It truly is awful. St Johnstone nearly scored three times on radio, but never looked like it much later when it was shown on the telly. And then the words "Brattbakk must score".

'He did. I just cried. After momentarily cheering, the tears just came streaming down. I started singing along with the crowd through snuffles. Ten years of frustration, disappointment and under-achievement disappeared instantly. With the tears went the pressures of the last week.

'I was never worried for the remainder of the game. There was no way we would concede 2 in the last 15 or so minutes. After having a celebratory drink alone I went to bed sometime around 3 a.m. As I climbed into bed my wife said, "Well, did they win?" When I replied, "Yes!" she said, "Thank God!"'

Few people in Scotland would have thought as they celebrated this momentous victory that on the other side of the world lights were burning as thousands of fans sat glued to their radios.

The massive growth of the internet has meant that supporters all over the world can now get webcasts of matches as they take place. The internet is also vitally important for keeping supporters in touch with each other. Separate Celtic mailing lists for the Southern Hemisphere, Northern Hemisphere and another one covering Europe buzz every day with the latest rumours and news bulletins from Scotland. The European list delivers around 90 messages a day into the electronic mailboxes of supporters' computers. The debates that rage in pubs all over Scotland are mirrored there.

As the Treble season started Davey and other supporters were involved in a discussion of the merits of Martin O'Neill's appointment. 'Initially I have to admit I was sceptical of Martin O'Neill,' he says. 'To me he was an Irish Tommy Burns. Full of fire and passion, the kind of leader you want on your side – but I doubted he had the tactical ability to take us back to the top.

'I loved Tommy Burns. I was gutted when he was sacked, but had to admit that tactically he was found wanting when it mattered. I knew Martin had done well at Wycombe and Leicester but they were small clubs. This was different. All the talk of Guus Hiddink had me excited and thinking were Celtic at last looking at the big picture again. I felt deflated when O'Neill was appointed. I thought, here we go again – mediocrity. Needless to say I was wrong and it didn't take too many games for me to realise.'

Many were to later claim that all it took to realise that Celtic were a changed outfit was the Dundee United game. In the two days prior to the Sunday kick-off Martin O'Neill made two extremely significant signings.

First to arrive at last was Valgaeren for a reported £3.8 million and though it was widely speculated that his signing was too late for him to feature at Tannadice he boarded the team coach. 'Right from the start I had a great feeling about Celtic,' he announced at the press conference the day before. 'I had other options but I preferred to come here. It was pretty clear for me.

'I only played at small clubs in Belgium and Holland, and Celtic are a very big club,' he added. 'I came here because I think there is the chance to win prizes. I am a sportsman and I want to win things, so I will give 100 per cent to do that.'

Martin O'Neill had clearly shrugged off his misgivings about picking players based on a two-week sighting: 'He is a strong lad and is very competitive; he wants to win and I think he will be a big asset to us.'

(29 July, *Scotsman*) The manager brushed off suggestions that the negotiations to land Valgaeren had been especially complex. 'The days of making one phone call and getting a player on a plane are gone. But I'm really pleased I persevered, and that Joos wanted to come to the club.'

First-team coach Steve Walford was the second signing and although his arrival was low profile he was to prove just as crucial, if not more so, to the team over the coming season. The new coach was put to work immediately on Celtic's defensive set-up and he took a training session on the day he arrived. His arrival was greeted with one paper's joke that it would take magician David Copperfield to sort out the frailties of two of Celtic's defenders, Olivier Tebily and Rafael Scheidt.

But club captain Tommy Boyd said Walford had impressed: 'The manager obviously rates him highly because he has taken him everywhere with him and we have to trust his judgement. We must work hard to make sure there are no more silly mistakes. It's impossible for defenders to get to know each other's game so completely they can read their team-mates' minds. We can only try and develop as good an understanding as possible and hope a partnership can gel almost immediately. However, it might just never happen. But we'll try and get it right for the Dundee United match.'

Shoring up the leaks was a priority for the new manager. He said: 'We have to learn to defend as a team – the sooner that happens the better. Celtic did not defend well enough last season and lost games and goals as a result. Defending well is not a complicated thing to do – it really is as simple as preventing the man nearest you from doing something.

'We have to begin doing that starting tonight at Tannadice. The last thing I want is to lose games early on. If that happens losing can become a habit. I'd rather we were winning and enjoyed that habit.' (30 July, *Sunday Mail*)

Nobody can remember the exact details of the team talk before the match. But it was straightforward and to the point. Before starting O'Neill turned to Boyd and said: 'You'll have heard this a few times before.' Eight times in fact. Boyd was beginning his tenth season at Parkhead under his eighth manager. The line-up included Liam Brady, Lou Macari, Tommy Burns, Wim Jansen, Jozef Venglos, John Barnes, Kenny Dalglish and now O'Neill.

By that time O'Neill had impressed, as Boyd recalls: 'He was watching everything in the pre-season games and from that he knew what he needed to add in terms of quality and he did it. Before a game you get instructions from him. I want you to do this. I want you to do that. If you don't play to his style then it is changed, usually at half-time. That was a very strong feature throughout the season.'

Half-time is the crunch period for players in a Martin O'Neill squad, as the team had already learned. When the players come trooping in after 45 minutes they take their seats in the dressing-room and sit silently, waiting. 'Everybody is quiet, waiting until the manager speaks and wanting to hear what he has to say. You make sure you listen to what he says,' Boyd continues. 'He has been able to get the best out of players, not even in terms of one-to one, but in the terms of doing it during matches at half-time. It's just the truth. It's plain talking, oh God aye it's plain talking. But he gets everything right in what he is saying. And there are not too many people who can have too many comebacks.'

Can O'Neill be brutal? Boyd replies, 'When he needs to be, when he needs to be. Obviously for the most part he certainly tries to give encouragement, you know. Some players certainly need that as well. When you have to be hard on players he certainly comes down on them.'

Like the Rafael incident a month before? 'Not just him. Everybody has had it through the season with the exception of Henrik.'

Half-time team talks entered Celtic lore the season before when John Barnes 'lost' the dressing-room during the Inverness Caley Thistle game. It was the end for him. Barnes and his assistant Eric Black had come thundering in and attacked Mark Viduka for his lacklustre first-half performance. Goalkeeper Jonathan Gould then interrupted, saying if anyone should be blamed for not trying it was Israeli Eyal Berkovic. Viduka then took off his boots, threw them in a corner and refused to play on. The result is history.

O'Neill does not take any snash in the dressing-room, Boyd concedes. 'You look at John Barnes – maybe he didn't have the respect from others within the dressing-room. That is certainly something that can't be said of Martin. That's possibly something that happened in previous regimes. There would have been far more people answered back in John Barnes's time than there is now. There were certainly more arguments when Barnes was there.' Arguments? 'Oh, that happens with everybody. It is going on all the time. Often player to player, but sometimes player and manager. A bit of both. You can't go through a season agreeing with everything the manager has to say. The manager can, from time to time, get it wrong. Certainly players can get it wrong on the pitch. Occasionally you may have a difference of opinion. That is certainly something that can't be said of this year. The manager certainly got everything right, you know. There's been a couple of arguments, a couple of different things said, but that's for the dressing-room. You can't go through a season agreeing with everything the manager said.'

The match, which was televised live on Sky, kicked off at six p.m.

30 JULY: DUNDEE UNITED 1 CELTIC 2
(Report by Ken Gallagher: *The Herald*)

Celtic's record £6m signing scored his first goal in almost a year at Tannadice yesterday as he made his Scottish Premier League debut.

It ended a long and miserable period of the player's career as he was left out of Chelsea's first team and allowed to wither on the sidelines. The new Parkhead manager, Martin O'Neill, decided to throw the striker a lifeline and last night on Tayside he scored the goal that gave his new club victory after Dundee United had equalised in the opening minutes of the second half.

Before that, Henrik Larsson had given Celtic the lead eight minutes before half-time and throughout the game the Swede demonstrated just how superbly he has recovered from his leg break and also how hugely valuable he is to his club.

Sutton, though, after so long out of serious competitive action – and having suffered an ankle injury in pre-season training – was less impressive than his front-line partner, but when that scoring opportunity arrived he was there to take it and hand O'Neill a winning start to his managerial career with Celtic.

That was crucial, of course. O'Neill had talked of the Tannadice game for weeks now, ever-conscious of the need for victory and, perhaps, also knowing that it was at this ground early last season that the first cracks began to appear in the challenge which was being offered up by his predecessor, John Barnes.

He had taken Celtic to Tayside for his third game in charge and seen the tactical formation he had said he would rely on taken apart by the Tannadice team, who went on to win 2–1.

The last thing O'Neill needed was a repeat and, while he will remain concerned over the defensive worries which continue to haunt the team, he cannot have been happy to see a goal lost following a free kick with the aerial strength he has at the heart of his defence. That, though, is what happened and while in open play there was a more solid look about that area than there has been for some time, O'Neill will demand an explanation as to how the goal was lost.

Other than that, he had many things to keep him happy. He had the commitment that he always asks for from his teams. He had a balance about the side which augurs well for the future as he attempts to stamp his own trademark tactics on the side. Plus, above all, he had Larsson.

The Swede was at the heart of almost every attacking move which carried a threat and while he scored one goal that helped bring some relaxation to the team's performance, he might have had several others, curling dangerous shots in from various angles, watching some drift wide and others being cleared by the desperate United defenders. He offered a virtuoso display and O'Neill will realise that in the Swede he has a jewel of a player whose talents can shine at home and in Europe.

First of all, they had to be seen in the domestic context, of course, and in 37 minutes of this live televised game, the front man struck.

Referee Hugh Dallas, very intelligently, allowed the advantage to be played after Paul Lambert was fouled by David Hannah. Lambert kept his balance, surged forward, and released a forward pass towards Sutton. Jason de Vos cut the ball out but it broke to the Swedish international on the right-hand side of the box, who curled the ball delicately and accurately beyond Combe and into the corner of the net.

Hannah was booked during the Celtic celebrations and he was joined by Steve Thomson before half-time, while Neil Heaney had been cautioned earlier, all giving a clear indication of the side which was under the most pressure.

Three minutes after half-time, though, the picture had altered. Again the deep-seated problems in the Celtic defence surfaced, although Joos Valgaeren, the new signing from Belgium, had appeared to add the necessary strength and experience that O'Neill was looking for. When Jim Paterson, who had been fouled by Jackie McNamara to win the award out on the left flank, swung the ball into goal, it eluded Jonathan Gould and the three defensive stalwarts in front of him.

There was David McCracken, up in the opposing penalty box and able to force a header over the line from eight yards and suddenly Celtic realised that United were ready to offer up a meaningful challenge.

Before Sutton scored, another cross from Paterson out on the left brought trouble in the Celtic box and Thompson sent in a header which Gould finally held down low on the goal-line.

In 63 minutes, Eyal Berkovic went off to be replaced by Tommy Johnson and two minutes after that change the winner arrived.

Combe made a stunning save from a fierce drive from Lambert as

Celtic upped the tempo. The ball broke out to Stéphane Mahé on the left and the Frenchman fired in a vicious low cross which reached Sutton at the far post and the rangy striker hit the ball into goal and began the celebrations he has missed for so many months.

It was a sweet moment for him and one of relief for the Celtic support, who had wondered if victory had been snatched away from them yet again.

Jamie Buchan and Valgaeren were also cautioned in the second half but Dallas was firm and fair as he kept control of the match without resorting to histrionics.

Another former Lisbon Lion, Bertie Auld, watched the whole game and said it had left him with a spring in his step. To the *Evening Times*'s Neil Cameron he revealed: 'I saw more to encourage me in the first half on Sunday than I did in the whole of last season. The team did more good things in 45 minutes than in over 50 games – and that's the truth.

'The first thing which struck me was the running off the ball. The players didn't do that last season, but on Sunday everyone was making good runs and making themselves available. That allowed the ball players to have more options and opened up the play.

'In the first half it wasn't a case of Dundee United not getting forward, it was more that Celtic totally dictated the play. They played for each other and showed character, something which was lacking last season.

'When United scored Celtic didn't collapse or panic. Rather, they kept doing what they were doing and, as a result, got the second goal.'

Auld continued: 'There is a long, long way to go, but it was a good start and I was very pleased with what I saw. In fact, I got a wee lift when the game finished, I was so impressed. Even set-pieces were well executed, and they threatened every time from the free kicks they were awarded. That had been lacking for a couple of years, but Martin has obviously had them working on this part of the game.'

He said: 'Martin is a bubbly character. You could see that with the way he celebrated Celtic's opening goal. And his enthusiasm has obviously carried on to the field. The way the team played showed that. The skill and the passing was all there, but the passion was there as well. If the fans can see the team is giving their all, they will support them all the way.'

The performance from Henrik Larsson was one of the things to marvel at in the game. It was hard to believe the Swede had been out for so many months with a broken leg.

'Happiness' was the word that best summed up the supporters' reaction to the performance. It wasn't world-beating but it was solid and promising. Promising enough to raise expectations a little in the coming months. But before anyone could get carried away there was the small matter of a match with Rangers looming just around the corner.

4.

THE DEMOLITION DERBY

You are my Larsson
My Henrik Larsson
You make me happy when skies are grey
You can keep your Shearer
He's a ———
Please don't take my Larsson away

AS THE CELTIC TEAM limbered up in the dressing-room before the first Old Firm game of last season, shielded from the powder-keg atmosphere in the stadium outside, Martin O'Neill made a brief appearance. The new manager, who had made a point of preaching modest ambition in public, approached his players one by one and stared them straight in the eye.

'Are we going to win this championship?' he demanded with stern, yet controlled determination.

'Yes,' each one replied.

As he left the dressing-room he was approached by a Celtic director who asked him how he thought his team would perform. 'We're going to hammer them today,' he replied. (26 November, *News of the World*)

There are 756 games of senior league football played in Scotland every season. Most are forgotten about before the ink is dry on the back pages of the tabloid newspapers. Some linger in the mind longer, until considerations of the next important challenge occupy the thoughts of supporters. A handful remain in the memory over the course of the season, recalled as turning points, moments of particular significance. Some acquire a more enduring place in the collective consciousness because of an unexpected twist, a moment of poetry by an exceptional player or perhaps because of what's at stake: the Battle of Britain against Leeds United in 1970, the European Cup semi-final against Athletico Madrid four years later. Others are so memorable, they are recalled simply by the scoreline: Celtic 7 Rangers 1; 4–4 at Ibrox.

Then there is that Old Firm match at Celtic Park on 27 August 2000, a game that will live in the memory for decades because, for thousands of Celtic fans, it quite simply transcends superlatives. It is an unforgettable match for many reasons: Old Firm debutant Chris Sutton's double strike; Henrik Larsson's sublimely audacious lob. Celtic were 3–0 up after 11 minutes and 6–2 after 90 – the biggest winning margin in the tie since 1938 when Celtic won by the same scoreline. All that in O'Neill's first Old Firm encounter. It was, in the words of the T-shirt slogan, *the* Demolition Derby.

Yet just four weeks previously there had been little to suggest that the team would record such a momentous and historic victory over their oldest, bitterest rivals. After their indifferent pre-season displays and a hard-fought win in their league opener against Dundee United, the mood was of cautious determination rather than of bombastic optimism.

Despite the signing of Joos Valgaeren, the hawkish and mobile Belgian, to strengthen the centre of defence, O'Neill was still concerned about the fragility of his backline. The defence had received much of the blame for Celtic's abysmal showing the previous season, when the team finished a humiliating 21 points behind Rangers. The lack of a regular, coherent backline, awkward displays by Tebily and Mjallby and the continued presence of Brazilian Rafael Scheidt on the payroll were all sources of constant press ridicule.

O'Neill knew weaknesses also remained elsewhere in the squad. His fist signing had been Chelsea's physically imposing striker Chris Sutton, whom he acquired to protect his talismanic frontman Henrik Larsson. He now sought to buy in cover in the goalkeeping position and in the midfield, which he felt lacked a combative ball-winner in the Roy Keane mould. He also identified the lack of a player who could supply a plentiful supply of crossfield balls from the left side of midfield. After a few weeks in the job the manager was preparing to loosen the Celtic purse strings and top of his shopping list were Neil Lennon of Leicester City and Alan Thompson of Aston Villa.

'When O'Neill first arrived at Celtic, he watched tapes of their games from the previous season,' said Kevin McCarra, football writer for *The Times*. 'He thought they were quite nice but he didn't think they played hard enough or were well enough organised to get the ball back when they lost it. He thought the players just, more or less, stopped when they lost the ball. And he wasn't happy with the lack of power.'

McCarra added: 'He just broke it down to the basics. He looked at the tapes and thought well, they are not strong enough and they are not fast enough. He just broke it down to manageable problems that he would then solve rather than reeling in horror at the enormity of it all.'

Fans quickly realised that the so-called 'beautiful football' of the Barnes era, which had so dramatically proved the side's undoing the previous season, was being replaced with a more pragmatic, honest approach. Where Barnes had relied on the flamboyant skills of Mark Viduka or the all-too-fleeting inspiration of players like Eyal Berkovic, O'Neill opted for safety, strength and solidarity.

'John Barnes had various notions about tactical systems,' said McCarra. 'He would say, "That's the way Brazil play" and "That's the way France play", which is all very nice, except that France have fantastic players with which to flesh out that plan. O'Neill doesn't have any Utopian vision at all. He's a product of English football and the English nuts and bolts mentality. There aren't many visions.

'For the first time you began to hear people like Dick Advocaat talking about how physical Celtic were and how big they were. It was like a role reversal because that was always the kind of thing that was said about Rangers.'

O'Neill's philosophy was evident from the outset. Sutton, a traditional, powerful centre-forward who had fallen out of favour at Chelsea, scoring only three goals in the 1999–2000 season, and Valgaeren, an equally imposing centre-back who had impressed with his performances for Belguim at Euro 2000, were his first signings. O'Neill, a BBC analyst at the tournament, had vowed that he would not sign a player simply because he had had two good weeks for his country. 'He did the one thing he said he wouldn't do,' said McCarra. 'Valgaeren is a big, burly centre-back but he is actually quite mobile as well. You look at him and you think this guy looks very static and cumbersome but he isn't really. O'Neill has a good eye for that. He gets people with enough nimbleness about them.

'The Sutton signing wasn't regarded as preposterous. People thought he was a good player at Blackburn Rovers and who's to say it wasn't something to do with Chelsea that he didn't do very well, the way they played? The sports journalists were keeping an eye on him but there wasn't outright derision. People had already seen O'Neill and thought it was just as well to give him the benefit of the doubt.'

However, in his attempts to land Lennon, O'Neill was about to discover that nothing about his new job was going to be simple. What started as a transfer request quickly turned into a wrangle and then a saga and one which was doing little to foster amicable cross-border relations. The Irishman had left his previous club on reasonably good terms but that was quickly turning to acrimony as the Leicester board sought to frustrate the deal.

O'Neill was desperate to sign the player and Lennon clearly wanted to come to Celtic, rejecting a new contract offer from Leicester worth not far off £1.5 million a year. Lennon was O'Neill's type of player – solid, hard-working and, above all, a bad loser. The pair came from the same Northern Irish background and clearly had a close and productive working relationship.

O'Neill tested the water with a reported £6.5 million bid, but Leicester insisted they would not let him go for anything less than £8 million. Aston Villa were also known to have an interest in the player but Leicester chairman John Elson complicated matters further by placing an apparently arbitrary 48-hour deadline on all bids. Celtic, reluctant to enter into an unseemly haggle over the player, missed the deadline and, as far as the Midlands club were concerned, that was the end of the matter. They 'rewarded' Lennon with a new deal worth £30,000 a week which tied him to the club for the next four years.

For Lennon, saying no to Celtic was the most disappointing moment of his career. He had supported the club as a boy and was desperate to team up with his old boss. O'Neill too was devastated. He had missed out on an opportunity to sign someone he regarded as one of the best midfield players in the country. The episode had complicated relations with his former employers with whom he had always enjoyed a good understanding but, more importantly, it represented a major setback to his rebuilding plans at Celtic.

Forced to return to the drawing board, O'Neill improvised with existing players to meet the immediate challenges that lay ahead. In the subsequent months he would make a number of new signings and use existing players in new positions but none would fill the role he had devised for Lennon. It was a chasm in his plans that would be brutally exposed later in the season, forcing him to return to Filbert Street for one last try.

On 5 August Celtic played host to Motherwell in their first home league game of the season. Among the crowd was the pre-eminent keeper of the Catholic faith in Scotland, Cardinal Thomas Winning. His eminence (who was sadly to die shortly after the season ended) had been attending Celtic matches with his nephew through thick and thin. His love for the team was well known and his priests sometimes complained that he would spend only half the time at a meeting talking of business and the other half talking football. The Cardinal generally kept a pretty low profile at games but he did mention to his biographer how much joy being elevated from a bishop had meant to him. 'He told me that as soon as he became a cardinal everyone in the executive rooms at the club would stand as soon as he entered. "All the years I have been coming here nobody got off their backside," he laughed. "Then all of a sudden they're leaping out of their seats at Celtic Park." He loved it.'

The starting line-up for the Motherwell game included Tebily, in for the injured Alan Stubbs, and Stéphane Mahé, neither of whom would feature prominently in the manager's future plans. Danish stalwart Marc Rieper had just announced that his career was over at the age of 32 after a two-year battle against injury.

Motherwell arrived in confident mood, looking to continue their excellent record against Celtic which had included wins in two of their previous four encounters. The match began amiably enough with little to forewarn of the pyrotechnics that were to follow. Motherwell would end the tough-tackling, pulsating contest with ten men left on the park and Celtic with a man fewer after Chris Sutton and Jackie McNamara had been dismissed for second bookable offences. The home side held on for a 1–0 win with a gritty, determined display that would become characteristic of many more of their performances throughout the season.

5 AUGUST: CELTIC 1 MOTHERWELL 0
(Report by authors)

The breakthrough came after ten minutes with a strike from Celtic's Bulgarian midfielder Stilian Petrov. Though few among the 58,534 supporters knew it at the time, his swashbuckling performance was another portent of things to come.

His goal came after Paul Lambert collected a poor Motherwell clearance on the edge of the box. He fired the ball back in and, as the Well defence dallied, Petrov pounced to rattle a half-volley into the net.

The goal revitalised Celtic who continued to press forward. A long-ranged effort by Larsson was cleared by Goram and Celtic almost doubled their lead from the resultant corner when a Valgaeren header dipped over the crossbar. Motherwell were forced back under a barrage of pressure. Petrov almost grabbed his second when he connected with a McNamara cutback but his 20-yard effort skimmed over the crossbar. Sutton was booked for pushing Ged Brannan but the aggrieved visitors turned aggressors when John Davies was sent off. He had been booked after just five minutes for a late tackle on Petrov, and when the Celtic scorer slipped passed him in the 36th minute, the veteran defender hauled him down. Referee Alan Freeland produced another yellow and then a red card.

In the second half Celtic sought to exploit their advantage and Sutton came close when a shot inside the box took Goram by surprise, but the Celtic striker could only look on as his shot came crashing back off the right-hand post.

McNamara was sent off for two bookings in as many minutes. His first yellow came in the 65th minute following a reckless tackle from behind on Lee. And when he went in late on Kemble a minute later, referee Freeland had no option but to produce another red card. With 22 minutes to play, O'Neill replaced Berkovic with Mjallby in a bid to protect Celtic's fragile lead but 12 minutes later his plans were thrown into disarray when Freeland flashed red again, this time at Sutton who was judged to have pulled down his marker Greg Strong. Motherwell manager Billy Davies tried to exploit his side's numerical advantage by replacing defender Corrigan for frontman Elliot but time had run out for the visitors and Celtic held on for the win.

The match was an early indication of Celtic's new-found mettle but it was also the first real signal of Petrov's previously latent talents. By his own admission his early performances had revealed little of the promise the previous management team had waded through mountains of Eastern European red tape to expose. Still only 21, it was already evident that Petrov was experiencing a renaissance under O'Neill, whose footballing philosophy he obviously shared. 'Last season we tried to play beautiful football but now we must take the points,' he said after the Motherwell match. 'That is the most important thing.' (8 August, *Daily Record*)

It had been a battling, if unflamboyant, performance after which O'Neill predicted that Celtic would play 'much, much better' in the coming weeks. He knew they needed to if they were to match Rangers.

The next major league test would be against Kilmarnock at Celtic Park but, in the meantime, there was the distraction of a preliminary European tie against minnows Jeunesse Esch. The Luxembourg side wore strips like Juventus but that's where the similarity ended.

The first match was played away from home in the eerie surroundings of the Stade Josy Barthel where just 4,004 fans – most of them supporting Celtic – turned out to watch the spectacle. It was the sort of test which could so easily have presented banana skin potential in the past but on this occasion a solid, professional 4–0 win by Celtic turned the return leg into a formality. O'Neill gave first team challengers Bobby Petta, Johan Mjallby and Lubo Moravcik a chance to shine with Tommy Boyd, Eyal Berkovic and Stilian Petrov dropping out from the side which had beaten Motherwell. Celtic spent the first half sizing up their hosts before putting them to the sword with a Moravcik double and goals from Larsson and Petta.

The return leg a fortnight later was even more emphatic, Celtic running out 7–0 winners – 11–0 in aggregate. But not before the Luxemburgers had employed less than sporting tactics in a bid to unsettle their hosts. Jeunesse coach Eric Brusco claimed Celtic were not as good as Latvians Skonto Riga and predicted that they wouldn't progress far in the tournament. He went on to say that a 0–0 draw would be an 'enormous result' for his side at Celtic Park though, sadly, it was not to be.

The highlight of the return leg was Britain's fastest-ever hat trick, from Mark Burchill – three goals in three minutes, beating the previous mark set by Liverpool's Robbie Fowler against Arsenal in 1994 by 90 seconds. It was to be the striker's Celtic swansong as he spent the rest of the season on loan deals at Birmingham and Ipswich. A double from Berkovic and goals from Vidar Riseth and Stilian Petrov wrapped things up. All that was missing was a strike from man of the match Bobby Petta who limped off before the end with a leg strain.

Perhaps even more than Petrov, Petta was a player transformed under O'Neill. The former Ipswich winger had arrived on a Bosman deal under the previous regime as an understudy to Regi Blinker! That in itself was an indictment in the eyes of some supporters. Petta never became an object of ridicule among the Rangers support in the way that Blinker did, but that was only because he failed to register in their radar. Under Barnes and Dalglish he had made only a handful of appearances, largely as a substitute, and when he touched the ball he suffered the indignity of being mocked by his own fans. Harald Brattbakk and Darren Jackson had received similar treatment on the park but Petta suffered abusive comments from fans in the street.

'We have a love-hate thing with the supporters,' he admitted, sanguinely. 'They are so passionate and they are brilliant when things are going well but they can be hard when things are going badly,' he said. (12 August, *Daily Record*).

The Dutchman suffers insecurities about his own talents and thrives on the injection of self-esteem that only playing for the first team can bring. Intuitively O'Neill recognised what had escaped his predecessors and he reaped the rewards. Petta was reborn.

When he was included in the Celtic side to face Kilmarnock on 13 August, his first league start, eyebrows were raised among some fans. When asked about the possibility of buying wide players after Celtic's 2–1 win, O'Neill replied: 'I already have Bobby Petta.' Kilmarnock's tight marking did enough to inhibit the free-flowing movement on which Petta and Moravcik thrive, but the Dutchman was given enough room to show that his game was improving with every morale-boosting syllable that issued from O'Neill's lips.

For the second time in as many games Celtic posted notice of a new 'never say die' determination. Outplayed for much of the game, they still emerged winners with a spirited second-half fightback. They fell behind to a wonder strike by Andy McLaren but Henrik Larsson equalised after the break, before setting up Tommy Johnson for the winner.

The suspension of Jackie McNamara, following his red card against Motherwell, forced O'Neill to ditch his three-man defence for a back four. Celtic had scored nine goals in their previous two home games against Killie and, coming into the game on the back of three straight wins, they had reason to be confident. But it soon became apparent that this was not going to be a walkover.

13 AUGUST: CELTIC 2 KILMARNOCK 1
(Report by the authors)

After 17 minutes Andy McLaren, who had scored twice against Rangers the previous week, continued his run of form with a goal of exquisite quality. Collecting the ball 30 yards from goal, he carried it towards the retreating Celtic defence and, spotting a gap, he unleashed a shot from outside the penalty box which flew past Jonathan Gould and into the net.

One minute later Petrov had the chance to equalise, having found himself alone inside the Kilmarnock area but, from 12 yards and with only the keeper to beat, he struck his shot high over the bar. O'Neill's frustration was evident from his wild touchline gesticulations but Celtic's persistence was rewarded five minutes after the break when Larsson stepped up to equalise. The Swede shrugged off his marker and, with space in front of goal, sent his shot carefully beyond Marshall.

In the 73rd minute Celtic went ahead when Larsson turned provider. He sent a deft lob into the path of Johnson who, played onside by Gary Holt, found space to sweep the ball away from Marshall. As the game edged into injury time Christophe Cocard, a late substitute for Killie, guided a header just wide of the post. The Ayrshire side's sense of injustice was reinforced when Martin Baker was ordered off after an innocuous challenge on Moravcik with just ten seconds of the game remaining.

The smile had returned to Celtic Park. The team's performance had been less than emphatic but at least they had won. And for a Celtic support starved of success for so long, that was the most important thing. O'Neill's passion for the club was evident from the outset. His animated behaviour in the technical area during matches attested to his deep desire to win. In public he continued to set modest targets, insisting that Rangers were the benchmark team in Scottish football. Their dominance of the domestic game for more than a decade and their, albeit erratic, performances in the Champions League meant that they could rightly claim to represent the standard to which Celtic aspired.

Privately O'Neill was more ambitious. Quietly but efficiently he was laying the foundations upon which he hoped to build success. His attention to detail was impeccable. The team's training schedule was revolutionised. Training sessions became more inclusive, directions to players more explicit. Even the players' eating patterns changed, replacing their previous carbohydrate-fuelled diet with one that included more fruit and vegetables.

'What the players were eating was ridiculous,' said Professor Mike Lean, a nutrition expert at Glasgow University who was brought in by the club as an adviser. 'They were tucking into scrambled eggs and pasta covered in cheese and that was just before a match.'

For the players the most significant change in the way they trained was the five-a-side tournament that took place every Friday at training. Refereed by Walford and Robertson it pitted the first team's 'youngsters' against the 'oldsters'. It also featured the dreaded yellow bib bearing the words 'worst player'. Looking back, Ramon Vega remembers it was a little bit more than just a laugh. 'The tournament ran every week until the final Friday before the last league game. Then the team that had been best would get a big trophy. I was in the oldsters,' he laughs. 'Myself, Mjallby, Larsson, Tommy Boyd, all those players who were heading for 29 or 30.

'The team that loses always votes for the worst player. Your own team. You then have to wear the yellow top with "worst player" on it at training for a week. I have to be honest,' he laughs. 'I had it a few times. It is fun and also it is a little competition. But it is embarrassing if you get voted by your own team-mates as being the worst that day. Then you have to wear that yellow shirt around the club for a week. It is a good game and keeps the spirit up and makes you train properly as well if you want to be the best on the pitch and not the worst.'

Behind the scenes O'Neill was also working to ensure a harmonious approach. He wanted everyone involved with the club to be singing from the same hymn sheet. He introduced himself to all the staff, from the most junior upwards. He also ensured that he demonstrated due respect the club's history and traditions, inviting, as previously mentioned, the Lisbon Lions out for a dinner at Il Castillo restaurant in Newton Mearns. The event was not publicised and it was more than a simple gesture of respect.

'He took us to an Italian restaurant in Glasgow as a kind of getting-to-know-you,' said Bobby Lennox. 'He just sat amongst the guys while we had our dinner, moving up the table so that he had a chance to speak to us all. He paid for everybody and we all had a great night. He just mixed in like he was one of the boys. We swapped stories and everybody got to know him really well.'

Lennox added: 'As soon as Martin arrived the whole place changed. It was a happier place to be. Martin is bubbly and good to be with and he won't go by you, and he is just a nice guy. Everybody got a lift from that – players, people behind the scenes.'

And of course the early results helped to strengthen the bond of solidarity that O'Neill was forging among himself, the players and the supporters. 'As soon as you win two or three games the whole dressing-room gets a lift,' said Lennox. 'The supporters get a lift and people have smiles on their faces. It's easier to go training and it's easier to work harder if you are winning.'

However, O'Neill was also being forced to make some difficult decisions. The continued presence of Rafael Scheidt at the club was causing him some alarm. On a salary of £20,000 a week, Rafael was the most expensive defender in Scottish football and yet he had hardly featured in the first team since his much-vaunted transfer from Brazilian club Gremio. Reports about an alleged fraud investigation into the signing of players back in his native Brazil and revelations that neither Barnes nor Dalglish had actually seen him play before handing over £4.8 million of the club's money added to O'Neill's sense of frustration. A run-out in the second leg of the UEFA Cup tie against Jeunesse was enough to convince the manager that Rafael had no place in his team.

Eyal Berkovic, who was being paid a reported £28,000 a week, was also an unnecessary drain on the club's resources. The Israeli had been left on the bench for the club's last three matches and he did nothing to endear himself further to the manager when he told a newspaper that the best thing about playing for Celtic were the high wages.

In other areas of the squad, the manager knew he also had some decisions to make that would be unpopular. Goalkeeper Jonathan Gould, who had experienced an uncertain relationship with Barnes, would soon have competition for the first team. Despite glorying in the reflected success of a backline with strengthened resolve, it was clear that the goalkeeping pool should be strengthened. O'Neill was forced to drop his interest in Manchester United's second-string keeper Mark Bosnich after the Australian's wage demands proved prohibitive but few at Celtic Park were under the illusion that his search for a first-choice keeper would not continue.

Young striker Mark Burchill was also being forced to come to terms with the reality that he was not O'Neill's cup of tea. Burchill too had experienced an uneasy time under Barnes and, before him, under Venglos. Despite being a full Scotland international he was still a fringe player after three seasons at Celtic Park and it was obvious to anyone watching that he was no longer content to play the bridesmaid. 'I've never hidden the fact that I'm a Celtic fan,' he said. 'My family and friends are as well and it was always my dream to play for this club. But if I'm not playing for Celtic every week, I wouldn't get a game for Scotland.' (18 August, *Daily Record*).

When Celtic visited Tynecastle on league duty on 20 August Burchill had submitted a transfer request. The manager said he would be prepared to accept the request if a suitable offer came in. However, in the meantime, Tommy Johnson had suffered a thigh injury and O'Neill, needing cover up front, put Burchill on the bench. Elsewhere McNamara returned from suspension to replace Tom Boyd, who had started the match against Kilmarnock.

Sutton's £6 million price tag was already looking a snip as he grabbed a double in Celtic's 4–2 win. The visitors were three up by half-time, with

Larsson netting the other goal. Scott Severin brought the home side back into the game after the break but after Moravcik scored a fourth, Celtic never looked in any difficulty, even after Juanjo's late consolation.

19 AUGUST: HEARTS 2 CELTIC 4
(Report by authors)

Sutton's brace of goals came in an exciting four-minute first-half spell. In the 22nd minute Petrov charged through the Hearts defence but the ball appeared to be rolling harmlessly back to goalkeeper Niemi before Gary Naysmith needlessly intervened. The ball arrived at the feet of Petta who swung over an inch-perfect cross which was met by the diving head of Sutton.

While the Celtic supporters were still celebrating, Sutton charged a full 60 yards to win a corner. From the resultant in-swinger, the striker rose to head the ball high into the net for his second goal.

Hearts responded by pushing into Celtic's area but the defence cleared any danger and, in the midfield, Lambert and Petrov slowed down play until Celtic regained their composure. Their superiority was confirmed five minutes from the break when a low, powerful shot by Lambert from 25 yards was deflected into the net by Larsson.

After the break Hearts looked to be in even deeper trouble when Severin conceded a penalty for pulling back Sutton. However, in a unique lapse of concentration, Larsson blasted the ball over the bar. The home side continued to battle and they were rewarded in the 56th minute when Severin drove a short Cameron free kick from 25 yards low into the Celtic goal.

However any thoughts of a Hearts revival were shattered five minutes later when Celtic notched a fourth. Referee Willie Young played the advantage when Tomaschek fouled Larsson. The ball fell kindly to McNamara who played in Moravcik. The Slovak skipped past two defenders and drilled the ball high past Niemi from eight yards. Hearts pulled one back in 66 minutes when Juanjo volleyed home after Naysmith played in O'Neil down the left.

After the game Chris Sutton received a public endorsement from Henrik Larsson who said he believed their partnership would prove more prolific than the one he had enjoyed with former team-mate Mark Viduka who had left earlier in the summer in a big-money transfer to Leeds United. Viduka had angered his former team-mates when, in a parting shot, he claimed he had only had to play at 70 per cent of his ability to score a hatful of goals in Scotland and to win the SPFA's Player of the Year award. Larsson said. 'Chris has been a great signing for Celtic and I am not just talking about the goals he has scored already. He is better in the air than Mark Viduka and that is going to make it better for me,' he said. (20 August, *Herald*)

O'Neill also responded to Viduka's disparaging remarks, claiming that he was doing a disservice to Scottish football. It was an unwelcome distraction with less than a week to go until the first Old Firm match of the season and O'Neill's first major test as Celtic manager.

'Viduka is two things: a great player and bad medicine,' said football historian and BBC summariser Bob Crampsey. 'He will always be wherever he goes. It is just inherent in him. He will always be an intriguer and he will always have his own career very firmly in the spotlight. He will never stay anywhere very long because he has worked out that you make money in football by moving.'

Tension hangs in the air over Glasgow like a low frequency buzz in the days immediately before an Old Firm match. Nervous anticipation is palpable among the people as though they are preparing themselves for battle. Nothing in world football compares with the tribal ferocity of the encounter and in the August sun passions were simmering.

O'Neill knew that history favoured Rangers, who had perfected a solid habit of winning the season's opening derby fixture. They had won four of the last six such matches, giving them first blood and a vital edge for the rest of the season. The Ibrox side also had continuity on their side. Rangers manager Dick Advocaat had been in his post for the past two seasons, seeing off four previous Celtic managers in that time.

The combustible mood was fanned by some incendiary comments emanating from the south side of the city on the eve of the match. With more than a hint of self-conscious mischief, Advocaat announced that he could have signed Joos Valgaeren ahead of O'Neill, but had instead opted for the Dutch defender Bert Konterman. In another display of less than ingenuous pot-stirring Mark Hateley, the one-time scourge of Celtic defenders with eight goals in 22 Old Firm matches, said he thought it would be a good thing for Scottish football if Celtic won the tie.

In an admirable display of self-restraint O'Neill remained above the fray, refusing to be drawn into pre-match gamesmanship. Since becoming manager, his refusal to enter into any form of public discourse which was in the least controversial was partly a reaction to the way he had seen Barnes and Dalglish reviled by the Scottish press. But it also followed bitter personal experience. As Leicester manager he had been firmly rebuked by the Terence Higgins Trust after telling the *Daily Mirror*, with his tongue firmly planted in his cheek, that he had known Aids sufferers recover quicker than hamstring-injury victim Ian Marshall. On another occasion he entered into a tabloid slanging match with Chelsea chairman Ken Bates who had branded his Leicester side 'boring'. O'Neill retorted by describing Bates as a 'football cretin'.

'I did wonder what would happen to O'Neill in Glasgow if he was that combustible – would he go up in flames?' said Kevin McCarra. 'But he seems to have taken a look around him and made a very firm decision to moderate his comments. He became this very circumspect person.

'He's clever. Sometimes when people say that in football they mean he is not a dimwit. He's not really, really stupid. But I think he is just clever period. Irrespective of whatever field you put him in he would strike you as having a lively mind.'

It was fitting that the Old Firm game, when it came, was played on the Sabbath. Celtic's legion of longsuffering fans entered their traditional temple of worship and left believing they had witnessed a miracle. If divine inspiration were needed it came in many forms, most evidently from the Messiah himself, Henrik Larsson, who scored two goals, including one of the most craftily executed strikes ever witnessed within the hallowed surroundings of Celtic Park.

The victory was all the sweeter because it was accomplished with style and with a resolve which suggested it was not built on the flimsy foundations of the side's 5–1 win against the Ibrox men two years previously. Something permanent was finally happening at Celtic Park and it began on 27 August.

27 AUGUST: CELTIC 6 RANGERS 2
(Report by authors)

The home support had little time to lapse into their characteristic mode of introspection which tends to accompany spells in the game when the opposition have the ball. For after just one minute Sutton had put Celtic ahead. A clumsy challenge by Ricksen on Petta resulted in a corner on the left. The ball was swung in by Moravcik and it broke from the Rangers defence towards the edge of the penalty box. Larsson prodded the ball forward and Sutton, with virtually his first touch of the game, struck a low shot into the far corner of the net.

After eight minutes Celtic doubled their lead. Another corner from Moravcik swept across the penalty box and Stilian Petrov ducked low to direct a header beyond Klos. If the Celtic fans thought they were witnessing something special, more was to follow. Celtic continued to push upfield. Moravcik accepted a pass from Petta and dragged the ball to the byline. His cutback fell into the path of the onrushing Paul Lambert who drilled a shot from 20 yards beyond Klos. Celtic were 3–0 up after just 11 minutes as thousands of incredulous fans descended into frenzied delirium.

Paul Lambert limped off in 36 minutes and he was replaced with Johan Mjallby in the centre of defence as O'Neill sought to consolidate. However Rangers, by no means overrun despite the score, continued to press forward. With five minutes to go before the break the visitors pulled a goal back. Neil McCann sent Rod Wallace down the left and he beat off a challenge from Alan Stubbs before sending in a deep cross. Claudio Reyna was at the far post to head the ball towards goal and, although Jonathan Gould got to it, he could not prevent it crossing the line. Rangers had a glimmer of hope.

Five minutes into the second half Larsson provided one of the highlights of the season with a moment of improvised genius. Running on to a long clearance from Gould, he collected the ball on the edge of the Rangers box. With an almost imperceptible feint he passed Tugay and then Konterman before collecting the ball and, with Klos advancing, he chipped the ball over the keeper's head with delicate pace and pinpoint accuracy. The ball rose and dipped in a blink and, before it hit the net, the ecstatic Celtic support were on their feet voicing wild appreciation.

However the contest was by no means over and within four minutes Rangers had scored another goal. Stéphane Mahé brought down Wallace and Billy Dodds scored from the spot. However in a story which defied prediction and precedent Celtic had a few chapters still to write. Petta, who had tortured and tormented Ricksen with man-of-the-match-winning skills, swung a free kick in from the right and Larsson rose majestically to head the ball home.

Rangers midfielder Barry Ferguson, who had been cautioned in the 74th minute for a foul on Petrov, was dismissed nine minutes later for deliberately handling the ball. Rangers came close on a couple of occasions but Celtic delivered the coup de grâce in the closing seconds when Sutton poked home the ball from a low cross whipped in by Mahé.

For Eddie Toner, secretary of the Celtic Supporters Association, the result brought mixed emotions. It was one of only 20 games he had missed at Celtic Park over the past 30 years because he had been forced to attend a family christening in Manchester.

'I told my brother to phone me but only if Celtic scored. The christening started at one o'clock, at the same time as the game. I left my mobile on. The priest had just started the service when the phone went. Celtic had scored. I stood at the back of the church for a few minutes, ready to retake my seat when the phone went again. Everybody was turning round to see what was wrong. It was 3–0 before the christening was finished and I legged it into Altrincham and had to bribe a barman to put Sky on because some guys were sitting watching the Belgian Grand Prix.'

O'Neill could not have anticipated such an improbable start to his Old Firm career but he was predictably equivocal. 'We haven't won anything,' he cautioned. 'Euphoria of the highest order comes on the last day of the season or when you have won a cup.' (28 August, *Daily Record*)

Though the manager was not prepared to admit it, the game signalled the start of a paradigm shift in Scottish football. The balance of power still rested in the south side of Glasgow but he had taken the first steps in the reversal of that trend. Celtic had beaten their greatest rivals in emphatic style and, crucially, they had done so in the context of a genuinely impressive run of results.

'From that day forward it just seemed that here was a Celtic side who believed in themselves,' said former Celtic legend Charlie Nicholas. 'It was such a dynamic overhauling. That was the day Celtic fans said to themselves, "We have definitely got the right guy in here." O'Neill brushed Rangers aside as if to say, "Here we are, we are going to take you on this season."' Nicholas added: 'We have seen so often in the past the psychology Rangers seemed to have over Celtic when it came to the crunch games. Rangers didn't have to play that well, but they always got the result. How often did Tommy Burns' teams completely outplay Rangers and then fall to a sucker punch? The 6–2 game showed Celtic were a side capable of finishing Rangers off. It made an impression on Rangers that Celtic were ready for them.'

Events later in the season would prove that Celtic were not as ready as the scoreline suggested but, in the meantime, the fans enjoyed their moment of dominance. They knew from bitter experience that such occasions were few and far between.

5.

KEEPING THE FAITH

Oh! over and over, we will follow you,
Over and over, we will see you through,
We're Celtic supporters, faithful through and through,
And over and over, we will follow you.
If you go to Germany, you will see us there,
France or Spain it's all the same,
We'll go anywhere,
We'll be there to cheer you,
As you travel round,
You can take us anywhere, we won't let you down.
Oh! over and over, we will follow you,
Over and over, we will see you through,
We're Celtic supporters, faithful through and through,
And over and over, we will follow you.
If you go to Lisbon, we'll go once again,
In Zaire you'll find us there calling out your name,
When you need supporting, you will always know,
We'll be right there with you, everywhere you go.
Oh! over and over, we will follow you,
Over and over, we will see you through,
We're Celtic supporters, faithful through and through,
And over and over, we will follow you.

'I'LL TELL YOU WHAT being a Celtic supporter is all about,' says Adrian Cocozza, 'and this is a true story. There was a guy called Tommy, I won't tell you his second name, he died just recently. He was a merchant seaman and a member of the Pollokshaws No. 1 supporters club. He had a season ticket and he used to go to the games with us whenever he was in.

'A few years back his boat developed some sort of engine trouble and they put into New York to get it fixed. The crew were all given 48 hours off. Tommy immediately got on a plane to London, got the train to Glasgow and then came straight over to get the supporters' bus to Brockville, where we were playing Falkirk. Then when the match was over he got the bus back, the train to London and flew to New York. He made it. But he didn't have time to go home and see his wife and they just lived on the other side of Glasgow. You tell people that story, and it is true, and they say, "Ah, but he was obviously mad." But no, that's the way this club gets under people's skin. There are loads of supporters like that.'

Adrian Cocozza is a self-made man who has worked his way up to head a major construction company in Scotland. He started supporting Celtic when he was a boy in Govan during the '50s and has never lost the passion. 'Everybody was playing football then and we were all football daft. On a Saturday it was just something you did. You went to Parkhead and got a lift over the turnstiles.'

After both his parents tragically died within a short time of each other when he was in his early teens he went to live with his sister in Polmadie and started travelling to away matches. 'In those days if you were going to an away game on the bus, and I went with Pollokshaws No.1, it was a major expedition. Aberdeen would take four or five hours and if you went to a night game you weren't getting home until about three a.m.'

Fast forward 40-odd years and dark nights eating fish suppers on buses packed with singing supporters are just a happy memory. It is September 2000, Celtic has changed, as have the ways of supporting the club. For more than a decade Adrian has been able to pay Celtic back for some of the pleasure the club has given him. In the late '80s it was in the form of a small interest-free loan, then, after Fergus McCann took over, the loan was converted into shares. It has given him membership of a small group of investors who are entitled, twice yearly, to hear what the Celtic manager has to say and to quiz him on what's happening with the club. During recent years Adrian has been able to see Celtic's last four managers close up as they addressed a group of around 50 people in Parkhead's Jock Stein lounge.

He remembers Martin O'Neill's first encounter with them very early in the season. 'O'Neill's got presence,' he says. 'We could feel it, see it, when he walked in the room. I'll tell you something else. After the game, when we're in the lounges and everybody is drinking away and eating and talking there's a real buzz of noise. Usually the manager comes on the closed circuit television and is interviewed about the game. Now, normally nobody pays it much attention. You just think, "I'll watch it tonight on the telly." But when Martin O'Neill comes on everybody stops and watches. The whole of Celtic Park is silent when the guy is talking. Now I have never seen that happen with any manager before.

'Anyway, at the first executive club meeting he was calm and confident and answered everybody's questions well. He's canny too, saying things like: "This is a huge club" and "We have got a lot to do. I have only managed clubs like Leicester and Wycombe before." I asked him what he thought of refereeing in Scotland and he just smiled and said: "Referees are the same the world over." He's very, very professional but you can also tell he is a real Celtic man, through and through. It's a real passion.'

Other managers have found the experience daunting. Facing a powerful section of the club's support in a relatively small room can be intimidating. Add to that the fact that they are free to ask the manager any question they like and it is a heady mixture. When Martin O'Neill met the troops he was on a high. Rangers had just been despatched in such a magnificent fashion that there could be few questions over his ability. The club's support were also floating on a cloud of euphoria that would take weeks to disperse.

Not all managers have had such a successful beginning. 'Wim Jansen was nervous,' said Adrian. 'He was very nervous. You could put it down maybe to his English and having questions put to him in Glasgow accents. Wim was a lovely, lovely fellah. But he had a very hard time on the park when he arrived. There was huge pressure on him. I also remember feeling an undercurrent that he wasn't maybe getting on so well with Fergus McCann or Jock Brown (Celtic's general manager). I remember the first meeting Wim attended was the day they signed Harald Brattbakk. Jock Brown brought Brattbakk in to the room and not Wim. We thought that was unusual.

'Dr Joe was another nice guy too. But his English wasn't great and it was a bit difficult for both sides. You didn't really feel any presence with him. He was very, very knowledgeable, but maybe not someone who could make a room turn around.

'Of them all John Barnes was the most confident. And he could talk, boy could he talk. He talked like he could have been the manager of Brazil if he wanted. He didn't respond well to criticism, though. At that stage in his season things weren't going well and people let him know. There were a lot of questions about his tactics and he didn't really like that. You remember, he was running some 2–2–2 formation or something like that.

'In fact that season is the worst I can ever remember seeing at Celtic Park for as long as I have been coming. Worse even than the last days of the old board when the stadium was half empty, when the fans were protesting. That just wasn't a Celtic team.

'So I suppose the performance on the pitch has a lot to do with the way the manager seems. O'Neill, to be fair, was at that point going from strength to strength. Even from the Dundee United game.

'I think it was down to the way the team reacted to each other. I go to most of the foreign games on the team plane and you could see from the very first one that they were different. It was virtually the same bunch of guys who had been there the season before but there were no cliques, everybody was talking to each other and getting on well. You've got to put that down to Martin O'Neill.'

The Scotsman's Glenn Gibbons also noticed that the new man had an air of confidence about him and an ability to look ahead and avoid difficulties. 'When talking about managers it's difficult to see parallels between Stein and anybody. Jock Stein was such a huge personality. There are parallels in terms of impact though. I thought O'Neill's inaugural address to the media on the first day he arrived at Celtic was the most impressive I had ever seen. It's always a nightmare that first day because it is a circus. He was so impressive with them all, TV and radio and all the rest.

'Somebody asked him would he be looking at players when he was at the European Championships. And he replied, "I don't trust that. You can't judge a player on the basis of two good weeks for his country. I want to see him with his club in the environment he would play for us." And I thought, God, he's so right about that. There's many a poor player been signed like that. Of course he then signed Valgaeran. He actually admitted: "I've broken my own rule."

'There's something about O'Neill. He understands that he cannot allow the whole Old Firm thing to get to him. He's actually got the perfect combination for a Celtic manager. He has got a Celtic background. He is English-speaking and he understands it all, but remains aloof from it like the foreign coaches. Tommy Burns was consumed by it, they all are. Liam Brady couldn't handle it. I'm talking about the pressure. Every day people are tugging at you, not just the press, but everybody. Martin just said from the start, I'm not interested in that. He just stays away from it. It is one of his great achievements – to be able to come into that kind of thing and handle it. The foreigners manage it more easily. They are used to operating in a continental way and that's what they continue to do. Dick Advocaat doesn't see anybody except on appointed days. Fridays and Tuesdays for previews. Martin's the same. Jo Venglos could do it and wee Wim Jansen. Jansen could sit there all day and talk and really say nothing. Martin doesn't say much either, but there's a lot of it. Sometimes it's colourful and there are some nice witticisms in it.

'But for Martin to come from the tranquillity of Leicester and suddenly adapt was impressive. Amy Lawrence on the *Observer* told me she became very friendly with Martin when he was there. She would phone him and do interviews and all that, but she says she can't even get to him at Celtic, she can't even phone him. She will not be put through. For him to do it so quickly, to make that leap, shows foresight. You would have thought that in the first few weeks he would have said "Just come in and blether" and then realised it was too much. He didn't. He stopped it from the start. It's not a distancing, an approachability thing. It's just good management of his own lifestyle.'

September was to be a month of see-sawing backwards and forwards from the top of the league. Rangers were now behind, courtesy of that Old Firm victory, but Hibernian were technically the form team. Still, new managers traditionally do well in their opening days and all eyes were on Celtic Park, waiting to see when Martin O'Neill's squad would trip up.

There had been one good thing to come out of the last decade of underachievement. Celtic were seen all over the UK as the underdogs of Scottish football. What's more, O'Neill's arrival and, to a certain extent, the arrival of Barnes the year before had made the club sexy.

Chris Cairns, a Scottish journalist and Celtic season ticket holder, remembers sitting in a pub in Bath in September with a Rangers-supporting friend Graham Miller. 'It was a lazy Saturday afternoon and he was complaining that after O'Neill's move to Parkhead and things like that sugary romantic drama on telly (was it called *Glasgow Kiss?*) supporting Celtic was becoming the politically correct thing to do – especially down there in England. It was trendy suddenly to be a Celtic supporter. "Yeah, nobody likes us," he complained. "When I tell people down here I'm a Hun they look as if I've just told them I abuse wee boys." I was feeling all generous and ecumenical and was just trying to tell him he was just imagining it when Sky Sports on the pub telly flashed up the scores from Scotland – Rangers had lost and Celtic had won. And the whole pub raised a cheer. "See," said Graham sulkily into his beer.'

Before the month was really under way on the football field Celtic was in the headlines for other reasons. The surprise announcement that chief executive Allan MacDonald was to depart caught everybody on the hop. MacDonald had joined the club from British Aerospace 18 months previously, having made no secret of his passion for Celtic. He brought his friend and golfing partner Kenny Dalglish to Celtic and of course Dalglish brought John Barnes.

MacDonald said he found life in the Celtic goldfish bowl difficult. He had first-hand experience of the tightrope that officials of both Celtic and Rangers must walk when a newspaper attempted to brand him a bigot for a throwaway remark made at a supporters' convention in the US when he jokingly described some friends as 'huns'. But despite his obvious ability and affinity with the support he bore some of the responsibility for the previous season.

MacDonald also had to take some of the blame for the Rafael Scheidt affair. The Brazilian defender, whose performances in a Celtic strip had been less than stunning, had been signed for a reported £4.8 million without anyone from the coaching staff bothering to watch him play. With rumours abounding that the Brazilians were allowing inferior players to play in their national team simply to boost their transfer values there were dark mutterings in the East End about Celtic having been sold a pup. The truth was out there somewhere, but Scheidt had such a poor time at Celtic Park it hardly seemed to matter.

September was the month that Martin O'Neill introduced another change in the way players would prepare for matches. He had been impressed with the way the team bonded in the hotel the night before the Old Firm game. Taking Celtic players away before ties against Rangers had been a tradition for some years. Now O'Neill decided the team would stay together before every Saturday game, home or away.

'First off we started in Dunblane and moved to other hotels in Glasgow after that,' Tom Boyd recalls. 'We used to go away just for the so-called bigger games. He wanted to change all that. Prepare for every game the same way, so that's why we still went away for home games. The players got used to it. It's part and parcel of playing football. Probably every player would rather spend time with their families, in their homes, but these are the sacrifices you have to make for football. It works and you have got to do it. I have got no complaints. You would rather sleep in your own bed. It's something that has got to be done if you want to get everybody together and start thinking about the game. Put the other worries away.'

The routine now became training on a Friday morning, go home and pack up the overnight kit, then meet up in the evening when the team would have their meal together in the hotel. Dinner would be pPasta, fish, chicken. No chips', Boyd recalls. 'We would all sit together in two or three tables. It was a laugh. There is the usual dressing-room banter. There are certainly a few that like a wind-up. That's in every dressing-room. It's how you react that helps create a team spirit. If you can give it back that's fine. If you go into a wee shell and think, "Oh no, what's happening here," that's not so good.'

Chris Sutton was the wind-up merchant par excellence. Players who gave lengthy interviews would turn up to training to find them stuck to the dressing-room walls with a new headline inked in over the old. Pranks were Sutton's forte too. It wasn't long before his team-mates realised that it was best to gingerly put their hands into their pockets or their feet into their shoes while dressing just in case Sutton had left a little surprise.

September also opened Celtic's League Cup campaign with a tie against Raith Rovers. It was a stroll in the park for a squad who were already reaping the fruits of Martin O'Neill's management style.

5 SEPTEMBER: CELTIC 4 RAITH ROVERS 0
(Report by Iain Campbell: *Daily Mirror*)

Celtic effortlessly breezed through to the quarter-finals of the CIS Insurance Cup against ten-man Raith last night.

And while the performance never came close to reaching the heights of their Old Firm demolition of Rangers in their previous outing, it was still more than enough to destroy the hopes of the First Division side.

Two goals in two minutes towards the end of the first half did the damage – Chris Sutton tapping home from a yard in the 39th minute and Tommy Johnson adding a second from the penalty spot soon after.

And after Rovers' striker Alex Burns was sent off for dissent a minute after the restart, further goals from Johnson and new signing Alan Thompson completed the rout.

And the win was even more impressive given that boss Martin O'Neill could afford the luxury of leaving out Henrik Larsson, Paul Lambert, Stilian Petrov and Lubomir Moravcik.

However, Celtic were dealt a blow just before kick-off when Dutch winger Bobby Petta pulled his hamstring and was replaced by Olivier Tebily.

But the unusual change did little to unsettle Celtic, even if Raith did have the first effort at goal with four minutes on the clock – Burns driving high and wide from 25 yards.

The home side went close three minutes later when, after good work from Johnson and Jackie McNamara, Mark Burchill drove tamely at Guido van de Kamp.

Rovers were undone in the 39th minute when Celtic moved in front with the simplest of goals, with Thompson again causing all the problems.

His vicious in-swinging corner was helped on to the bar by the head of Valgaeren, but when the ball dropped on the line Sutton was on hand to blast it home.

And within two minutes the lead had doubled, when Johnson converted a penalty after being pulled back in the area by Kenny Black.

Hoops boss O'Neill brought on Eyal Berkovic for Sutton at the start of the second half.

And just minutes after the restart Rovers found themselves down to ten men.

Burns' frustration at a foul being given against team-mate Tosh spilled over into dissent, and having already been booked, he was sent packing by referee Dougie McDonald.

Celtic were quick to take advantage of their extra man, finding themselves 3–0 up after 55 minutes.

Johnston collected a pass from Thompson and sent a glorious 25-yard drive past van de Kamp as Celtic effortlessly slipped into cruise control.

There was even an appearance from Brazilian mystery man Rafael, who was introduced to the fray in the 58th minute for the injured Tebily.

And the defender almost instantly created a goal for Burchill, but van de Kamp did well to beat away the striker's effort after the Brazilian picked him out.

Man of the Match Thompson claimed a deserved debut goal as he cheekily backheeled into the net after the Rovers defence had made a hash of trying to clear a Johnson shot.

That the wheels were turning with ever greater efficiency behind the scenes at Celtic Park was no longer in doubt. O'Neill's backroom boys, Walford and Robertson, had fitted in well with the team and were beginning to work the old voodoo magic they had produced at Leicester. They had started the competition that was to become one of the key features of every player's training. In a few weeks the dreaded yellow bib was about to make its first appearance.

Martin O'Neill was also making his presence felt in all things Celtic. *The Scotsman*'s Glenn Gibbons told us: 'O'Neill is a hands-on man in every aspect. He's not just the head coach. He's a 12-hour-a-day man and gets involved in the running of the whole club. It's the old school. The same style Alex Ferguson has at Manchester United and Jock Stein was exactly the same. Martin is there all the time, maybe not on the training pitch, because he's got two top guys to do that, but he'll be somewhere in the stadium making his presence felt.'

The *Sunday Times*' sportswriter Jonathan Northcroft was fascinated by what the new backroom boys were doing. Looking back now he says the pattern was becoming increasingly obvious. 'O'Neill was putting-in on the training ground. But actually Steve Walford is the guy who designs a lot of the set-pieces. That was one of the most impressive things about Celtic. You saw the set-pieces which every team tries to work on and you think there would be no mysteries any more but Celtic consistently get goals out of them.

'At the start O'Neill had to be hands-on. At Leicester he was like a visiting dignitary on the training ground. He only turned up on one or two days a week and did so unannounced. That in itself kept the players on their toes because when O'Neill turned up that was suddenly a special thing. He kept an air of mystique about him.

'It was quite an effective psychological ploy because when he actually had them on a Saturday, they felt the extra need to impress him. At the beginning a lot of people said O'Neill had many attributes but he wasn't a coach. He disproved that in the early period at Celtic because he didn't have Robertson and Walford and he had to do things himself.'

The arrival of the Leicester duo took a great deal of pressure off Martin O'Neill and allowed him to delve deeper into the running of the club. They very quickly established themselves with the squad and played a major role in creating the new dressing-room atmosphere, free from bickering and petty jealousies.

'As soon as Walford came in,' adds Northcroft, 'O'Neill was able to relax and let Walford do a lot more of the training. Robertson is very important to him because he is the sounding board. It sounds like a very vague role but it is no less important for that. It's a bit like a politician's wife because when you have so many cares you do need someone you can trust and Robertson is the guy that Martin O'Neill can trust. Robertson does a little bit of work with the wingers, the attacking players like himself. What Robertson and Walford do is, they are much closer to the players than O'Neill. As people they are both good-time guys, jokey, avuncular, good, trustworthy blokes and the players come to them with their problems. Then they pass it on to O'Neill.

'John Barnes tried the same kind of thing with Terry McDermott. But that was such a naked attempt to install a guy in the dressing-room and it doesn't work unless the players respect the boss and the guy in the dressing-room. They didn't respect Barnes and that was a problem for McDermott.

'Walford is one of the best coaches in Britain, so they respect him. John Robertson has been a manager in his own right and he is also a legendary player and so he also had the respect. Also as people they are more effective. Training is a lot shorter and sharper than it used to be. The players feel that is important in them not getting as many injuries as in previous years. They tend to do less but when they do it they make sure it is more focused and competitive.

'To be fair to Celtic they have been extremely good for a number of years on the scientific side of things. When McCann brought in the general manager and coach system, sport science was identified as one of the major areas they wanted to look at. Their physio, Brian Scott, is absolutely superb and they have a very good club doctor in Roddy MacDonald. What O'Neill did there was an extension of previous policies.'

Hibernian, meanwhile, were limbering up for a match at Celtic Park which was to prove historic, if not for the game then for the result. O'Neill was continuing to play down his achievements as he had promised his players he would, and these were early days yet. But with eight match wins under his belt people were starting to sit up and take notice. The Hibs game would be O'Neill's ninth game in charge and a win would shatter Bill Struth's record for best opening run of any Old Firm manager. Disciplinarian Struth's record had been set back in 1920 and his Rangers team had gone on to win the championship by ten clear points. Was it a significant omen?

Celtic went into the game five points ahead of Dick Advocaat and Rangers, but Hibernian were the league leaders. The Edinburgh side had had a magnificent early run under Alex McLeish, displacing both sides of the Old Firm in a four-wins-and-one-draw canter. Hibs were, then, no pushover and were spoiling for the sort of gritty fight that could prove so crucial in later months. Victory for Celtic, on the other hand, would allow O'Neill's team to top the league for the first time in 13 months.

As 60,091 people squeezed into Celtic Park for the biggest match, in terms of attendance, of the season so far the buoyancy from the Rangers result was still evident. The euphoria ran through the crowd as songs rolled round the banked terracing of the ground from the minute the game kicked off. There was a bubbling enthusiasm in the air that had not been around since the days when songs for Van Hoojdonk, di Canio and Cadete used to be sung from the start of a match to the end. Rangers, who had travelled to play Dundee, were also still carrying the effects of the Old Firm game. They had to play without their captain Barry Ferguson, out of the match as a result of his red card at Parkhead.

But before kick-off Martin O'Neill had something else on his mind. Hearing that comedian Billy Connolly was in the crowd, O'Neill invited him into the manager's office for a bit of pre-match banter. Connolly had been given a seat for life at Parkhead as a thank-you for opening the Jock Stein stand and was to be a regular visitor.

This was the first of two encounters for O'Neill and Connolly that season. Although the second, which occurred after February's Old Firm game, would be more memorable for the two of them it was still interesting. A friend who was there when they met recalls: 'John Robertson and Martin O'Neill were in the office when Big Billy came in. It was a wee bit stiff at first until Martin said he and John had been to see Billy at one of his gigs at the Hammersmith Odeon. Quick as a flash Billy asked: "Did you pay?" They both laughed and said yes. That was the ice-breaker.'

The Big Yin then spotted the tactics board hanging on the back wall and in a jovial fashion offered O'Neill some of his own tactical advice: 'It's quite simple,' he said with a wave of the hands, 'Lambert gets the ball and passes the ball to Moravcik. Lubo crosses the ball over for Henrik to head a goal.'

And that's exactly what happened.

9 SEPTEMBER: CELTIC 3 HIBERNIAN 0
(Report by Stephen Sullivan: *Celtic View*)

Super Swede Henrik Larsson turned in a vintage performance to inspire Celtic to come up trumps in the battle of the greens and leapfrog Hibs in the title race.

'We shall not be moved!' was the deafening cry at the end, and there is no doubt that table-topping Celtic will take some shifting if they continue along their current path . . .

For, while this was far from their best performance of the season,

Martin O'Neill has instilled a gritty determination in his side that will make them a very tough nut to crack.

Hibs couldn't manage it, and although Celtic's play was patchy, they had a backbone of outstanding performers through the middle of their team.

There was Jonathan Gould, who pulled off some vital saves, the composed and uncompromising Joos Valgaeren, Lubo Moravcik, as inventive as ever, and, of course, Henrik Larsson.

The fans' hero looked lively from the moment the game kicked off, and as well as scoring twice and having a hand in the third, the Swedish internationalist put in his usual incredible workrate to ensure that the Hibs defence never had a quiet moment.

Celtic started the game brightly, and with only three minutes on the clock they were denied a penalty when referee John Rowbotham waved away Paul Lambert's claims that he had been bundled over the box by Tom Smith.

At this stage, Jackie McNamara was a real threat on the right, and just five minutes later he took advantage of some good set-up work from Lambert and Stilian Petrov to cut inside and fire in a left-foot shot that went just wide of the post.

Then, after some neat interplay between Lubo Moravcik and Alan Thompson, Celtic's veteran Slovak sent in a 30-yard rocket that Nick Colgan did brilliantly to tip over the crossbar.

It was all Celtic at this point, and with 17 minutes on the clock, the deadlock was broken.

Tom Boyd launched a long ball deep into the Hibernian half, and when the ball was knocked on into the path of Alan Thompson, he won the race to reach it before Colgan and was clattered by the Hibs keeper for his troubles.

Rowbotham had no hesitation in pointing to the spot, and when Henrik Larsson placed the ball, there was only going to be one outcome.

He duly drilled the ball low into the net, and Celtic were on their way to the top of the league.

Ever since last Sunday's demolition derby, the Celtic support had been eagerly anticipating this fixture, and the punters weren't disappointed as the match flowed from end to end.

Before this match kicked off, Hibs had conceded just one goal in six games, but having already doubled that tally, Henrik Larsson duly tripled it in first-half injury time with a real classic.

The Hibs defence might have thought that the danger was over when

Lubo Moravcik's corner was lobbed clear, but Paul Lambert met the ball first time on the volley to play the pass of the season back to the Slovak.

Moravcik then measured a perfect cross on to the head of Henrik Larsson, and the Swede finished off a fantastic move by bulleting the ball into the top corner.

Alan Thompson was enjoying his first taste of the SPL deputising for the injured Bobby Petta in the left wingback position, but the former Aston Villa midfielder was given a more central role in the second half and appeared to thrive on his new-found freedom.

Just seconds after the restart, he pinged a vicious 20-yard drive that fizzed inches wide of the target, and minutes later he lined up a free kick from a similar distance and again came within a whisker of scoring a spectacular goal.

Celtic had lost a little momentum, but as the 60,091 crowd were boosted by the news filtering through that Dundee had equalised against Rangers, the pace began to pick up again.

After 58 minutes, a fantastic free-flowing move involving Joos Valgaeren, Henrik Larsson and Stilian Petrov ended with the young Bulgarian being denied by a brave stop by Nick Colgan.

Then the excellent Chris Sutton controlled a long ball from Jackie McNamara on his chest and knocked the ball over his head to play in Larsson, who was only prevented from completing his hat trick by another point-blank save from Colgan.

At the other end, Jonathan Gould made sure that the Celtic support would be spared a nerve-wracking final ten minutes by making a similarly superb stop to block a close-range effort from Mixu Paatelainean.

A goal-line clearance by Frank Sauzee then denied Chris Sutton what would have been a well-deserved goal, but the Frenchman's efforts to keep the score at 2–0 were to prove in vain as Celtic claimed a third in injury time.

Larsson's defence-splitting through ball put Paul Lambert in on goal, and in a typical show of unselfishness from the Scotland midfielder, he squared the ball for substitute Mark Burchill to calmly slot the ball into the unguarded net.

Rangers had drawn 1–1 at Dens Park and Celtic were surfing the top of the table with the team and fans on the crest of a wave of euphoria. The performance may not have been of the swashbuckling type dazzlingly played out by Tommy Burns' sides in the mid-'90s, but the results were right. In the players' lounge after the match the mood was one of quiet optimism.

The lounge is a peculiar part of Celtic Park. It sits underneath the main stand and has no bar, only a few tables and chairs. A water cooler stands by the door, packets of energy bars lie on a small table and a television set is built into the wall at head height. It's a small wood-panelled room where players' families and friends wait after the match for them to return. As part of the new regime under Martin O'Neill that wait had got longer. Players could sit down for a post-match meal as the club capitalised on the latest developments in sports science which suggest that the quicker lost energy is replaced the faster recovery will be.

Brian Wilson, an agent and Celtic supporter, has been in the lounge many times. 'There is a slightly different atmosphere than outside. It's not the same level of euphoria you get with the fans. It's more restrained. It's very small. There are maybe 40 people standing shoulder to shoulder. There are wives and girlfriends and of course the children of the players. Their parents will sometimes be there. The players all tend to arrive in bunches and mingle about chatting. Then they go home or out for dinner or whatever.'

Wilson was in the lounge during the previous season when a young Bulgarian player's discomfort had been plain for everybody to see. He said: 'Stilian Petrov was the club's first really young player bought for around the £2 million or £3 million mark. He was 19 and didn't speak English. The club was geared up to deal with more mature players who had come on big salaries. They usually come with families and friends and Celtic just leaves them to get on with it, having sorted out their necessities. Stilian was totally on his own and he was kind of left that way. I used to see him in the lounge just standing by himself and got chatting to him. He wasn't very happy in Glasgow.'

The Petrov who left the players' lounge after the Hibs game was a totally different person and a totally different player from the year before. He was already playing a key role in the team and was one of the players whose careers had turned around. As we shall see, he had no doubt whatsoever over who to thank for it.

Looking back, Billy McNeill sees the change in attitude of the side at such an early stage in the season as absolutely crucial for what was going to follow. 'The early performances were dogged and determined. There was no immediate turn-around when everything was put right on the training ground. The biggest thing that he instilled was an appetite for success. I remember going up to the first game against Dundee United at Tannadice and it was anything but an inspiring performance. But we got the result through an appetite that had not been evident in the previous season and bit by bit you started to feel a better relationship between the players. After the 6–2 game you started to see the confidence gush out from the players and there was a determination and unity. All of a sudden the team had a different look and a different shape and it showed that they had a gaffer who was very positive.

'A whole lot of players who had been under-achievers the previous season started to have a confidence and a belief in their own ability that Martin had helped to stimulate and encourage. Bit by bit the team got better but it took a long time before results absolutely flowed.'

With Hibs out of the way, for the time being at least, there was a collective sigh of relief at Parkhead. But the month was to throw up tougher tests.

First, though, there was the Annual General Meeting to be dealt with. One of the great achievements of Fergus McCann's stewardship of the club was to bring the ordinary fans in as shareholders. It added a vibrancy and enthusiasm to what was an otherwise dull occasion and brought the supporters much closer to the people who ran the club.

The enormous size of the Celtic family was apparent at the meeting which 2,500 shareholders attended. The club, the directors believed, had to move on from its reputation as the sleeping giant of European football and tap in to the enormous fan base. There were 250,000 fans registered across the world, a staggering figure for a club based on the periphery of Europe in one of Britain's most northerly cities. The proposals to feed the monster and give supporters, wherever they lived, the chance to have a ringside seat at the action was top of the agenda. Celtic wanted, said chief executive Allan MacDonald, to provide 24-hour news streaming and video footage of the club's exploits through the internet.

The thorny issue of television revenue was also raised. Despite the enormous hunger for everything Celtic, the club trousers a mere £2.5 million a year through broadcasting revenue. The income is less than half that earned by the lowliest English Premiership clubs and a fraction of what the top performers earn. The problem was, and is, the bottleneck of the Scottish League. With a limited market across the world and a fairly predictable diet of grim matches in unglamorous circumstances Celtic's only hope of hitting superstardom, said outgoing chief executive Allan MacDonald, was to compete with more glamorous opponents. For that reason the club would be backing the proposed new Euroleague which would comprise teams from Holland, Belgium and Portugal. The suggestion was, however, to be stillborn after the footballing authorities made it patently clear that any such restructuring would be resisted vigorously.

MacDonald's point was well made, but it is an issue that will be almost impossible to resolve for a variety of reasons including the fact that Scotland has its own separate national squad. If Celtic and Rangers were to play in the English Premiership, surely the most accessible and attractive league, the arguments for Scotland to compete in the World Cup and European Championships as a stand-alone country would be undermined.

Interestingly, at around the same time as the AGM an independent academic study into Scotland supporters showed that the number of Old Firm fans following the national side was in decline (23 September 2000, *The Herald*). A mere 38 per cent of them were also Scotland supporters. The decline had not, however, come from the Celtic side. Rangers supporters, who had traditionally made up the backbone of the Tartan Army, were losing interest. A survey published in 1995 had already shown that most Celtic fans were also supporters of the Republic of Ireland. Despite the decline, support for the national team continues to be healthy from outside the central belt of Scotland. The large body of Scotland fans will probably always ensure that the country retains its own independent squad.

On the playing side Celtic were paying out £19 million a year in wages, added Mr MacDonald, about exactly the same as the club took in ticket sales.

Herald reporter Chris Starrs, who attended the AGM courtesy of his family's shares in the club, remembers that MacDonald also faced criticism from the shareholders over his performance and his appointment of Kenny Dalglish. MacDonald told them: 'If you wanted my head you got it.' The outgoing chief executive later received a standing ovation from the shareholders as he wound up the meeting.

Out in the world of the football park, fixture congestion was becoming evident as Celtic dealt with their European commitments by squaring up to HJK Helsinki on 14 September. It was to be a sticky and slightly unconvincing performance, but the result was the right one.

14 SEPTEMBER: CELTIC 2 HJK HELSINKI 0

(Report by Ian Paul: *The Herald*)

They should make it through to the second round of the UEFA Cup all right, but Celtic harked back to some bad old times when they made life hard for themselves after looking like tearing apart the Finnish visitors.

It seemed certain, after Henrik Larsson had put them two goals ahead by the interval, that Celtic would run up a score that would have made their trip to Helsinki a pleasant jaunt. Instead, from being far superior to HJK, they slipped into complacency as the Finns gathered confidence and on more than one occasion threatened to snatch the away goal that could have made life very uncomfortable indeed for the Parkhead side.

The 40,454 on site had been in benevolent mood as their side had taken control, scoring with the two best attacks they had mounted during that spell. However, their patience grew very thin as they watched a sloppy, lazy show after the interval.

They could have been made to look very foolish if the Finns had been even marginally more penetrating than they proved.

The chances are that HJK will be more aggressive at home in Helsinki but a two-goal lead ought to be enough to see the Parkhead men through, especially as they have the players capable of snatching a goal or two over there.

That would have been totally unnecessary had they done the job properly last night.

Manager Martin O'Neill did not accept that his side had taken their foot off the accelerator in the second half. 'That was not the case,' he said. 'At half-time I was very pleased with the 2–0 score and thought we had done very well. I'd have settled not to lose a goal against a team that was dangerous on the break. There were uncomfortable moments, especially in the second half, but I told the players before the game to forget the idea of scoring four or five goals. There was a certain amount of tiredness in the second half, and I think it was that, and that alone, that prevented us from going further ahead.'

The manager pointed out that, while the team had scored a lot of goals this season, 'It doesn't always flow. What was vitally important was not to lose an away goal. Now it is in our favour. They have some quick, talented players and I did not expect to dominate for the whole game against a decent side.'

The HJK manager, Jyrki Heliskoski, was pleased that his team had put up such a gallant performance. 'We had problems at the beginning because we are not used to that speed of game. Our players were eager

81

but also a little nervous, but it was a very fine experience for them. Our biggest problem was Larsson, but little by little we got better.'

The return leg on Helsinki's home territory promised to be a more testing and dangerous experience.

By the time Celtic played their next game against Dunfermline on Monday, 18 September, their lack of league activity over the weekend had seen them lose the top slot once again to Hibs, by a point. Rangers were two points behind, but the Pars match was Celtic's game in hand and a victory would put them first again, as well as reaffirming the gap between them and their most powerful rivals.

The tie was to be memorable for another fighting performance from Celtic, this time a comeback and a last-gasp winner. Once again the fans were sent home happy, but this time with the reassurance that Celtic were winning matches they would definitely have lost the previous season. It was the old cliché: championship contenders must be able to grind out results. Not that O'Neill had yet cracked a light over his real ambitions. After the Hibs game he had pointed out that Celtic were 'not the finished article' and raised the point that the team might be winning but they were not yet flowing. Unusually for Scotland, the pundits were waiting for two bubbles to burst. With Rangers bouncing along in third place many expected both the Hibs and Celtic trains to hit the buffers anytime soon.

The Dunfermline game was also memorable for an incident in the penalty box when Celtic, instead of being on the receiving end of questionable decisions, appeared to have benefited from one. Paul Lambert had to endure a storm-in-a-teacup claim of diving but it was soon forgotten.

19 SEPTEMBER: DUNFERMLINE 1 CELTIC 2
(Report by Robert Martin: Scottish Mirror)

Henrik Larsson shot Celtic back to the top of the SPL but Dunfermline were left fuming at the penalty decision that helped keep Celtic's 100 per cent record under Martin O'Neill intact at East End park last night.

The Pars players pointed the finger at Paul Lambert for taking a dive in the box to earn his side a spot-kick a minute after Stevie Crawford's own penalty had given the home side the lead.

Henrik Larsson converted the kick, and then went on to notch the winner four minutes from time to give Celtic all three points.

But Pars midfielder Ian Ferguson raged: 'I saw it on Sky TV and any contact was outside the box.

'I was disappointed at the way Lambert went down. It was as if he had been hit by a truck.

'It changed the course of the game and I think that he will be embarrassed when he sees it.'

Celtic boss Martin O'Neill, meanwhile, hailed the attitude of his players.

He said: 'I don't think we played at all well, but the team performance and in particular the lads at the back were excellent. We could have chucked it when we went a goal down, and accepted it just wasn't going to be our night, but our attitude got us through more than anything else.'

The importance of the game and of Henrik Larsson's performance stuck in the memory of Martin O'Neill. Looking back at the end of the season he remembers Larsson's last-minute goal as one of his key strikes of the season. Larsson had taken the ball around a defender, back-heeled it to Thompson then moved into position to receive the pass back from him. With two touches he skipped around the Pars keeper before sliding it into the back of the net.

'I think it showed just about everything Henrik has got,' O'Neill said. 'Remember in that game we have got an equaliser. We're in the last four or five minutes of the match and we're still desperate for a win. He receives the ball magnificently. There's a little turn of pace and he remembers Thompson is behind him, a little back-heel and there he is in front of goal.

'Even so, Henrik Larsson has finished that off with minutes to go, in a match that is of prime importance to us, as though it were a training game. The goalkeeper helps him a little by going down a bit early, but even so he still has to finish.

'All the centre-forwards I have seen that have been very good perhaps would have been inclined to think he has got the opportunity to left-foot this and perhaps volley it over the bar and still go into the dressing-room and say, "It doesn't really matter. The chance just fell to me." Henrik was prepared to take that extra touch at that stage of the game.' (from the video *Tongue In Cheek: 100 Great Larsson Goals*)

But, despite the beauty of Larsson's goal, was Martin O'Neill's charge to the top of the league in perilous danger of coming unstuck as the Dundee game loomed? In the last game, although Celtic had taken the points, their performance had been far from convincing. Dunfermline were still smarting over the defeat and the grumbles over Paul Lambert's penalty-box tumble had dragged on all week.

Dundee had not won at Celtic Park for 12 years, the sort of statistic that allows Celtic managers to sleep soundly on the evening before a match. But the Dens Park team were on the up and up and bore little resemblance to the side which had dipped in and out of the Premiership. Italian Ivano Bonetti had restored pride and passion to the team and they were playing some nice football. It was already clear that Bonetti, who had played for Juventus and Sampdoria, was a manager of some quality. He had filled his team with players who had a significant track record, including Artero (Real Madrid) and Nemsadze (Grasshopper Zurich). Argentinian striker Juan Sara had hit the headlines by celebrating every one of his goals by baring his T-shirt with the legend 'Jesus Loves You'. Alarmingly for the Celtic support he had done it three times in mid-week during the Dundee derby. Dundee had also held Rangers to a welcome draw at Dens Park a few weeks ago. Now it was Celtic's turn to feel the heat. As the match day began there were a few butterflies fluttering around the stomachs of the more pessimistic members of the Celtic support.

23 SEPTEMBER: CELTIC 1 DUNDEE 0
(Report by authors)

If there were any doubts in Celtic minds over the potency of this Dundee side then Sara wiped them away on six minutes as he rose to meet Bonetti's corner and was only denied by the crossbar.

Celtic took the hint and Lubomir Moravcik and Chris Sutton both underlined Rab Douglas's talents when they forced the Dundee keeper into two top-notch saves within a minute. The Dundee keeper then excelled himself with a stunning save from Sutton in the 18th minute.

Alan Thompson showed how well he is settling into his side with an exquisite cross which picked out the former Chelsea striker. Only the athleticism of Douglas, who dived majestically to push it past the post, stopped a goal being recorded to the home side.

Dundee defended heavily throughout the match, clogging up the Celtic attacks and frustrating their forward surges. In a half of few up-close encounters with the Dundee goal only Henrik Larsson's tantalisingly scooped shot seemed capable of breaking the deadlock. Alas, although it bypassed Douglas it ended up on top of the netting. Thompson served up two more opportunities on the left thanks to his blistering pace, but his shots were not up to the task.

In the second half Jackie McNamara slipped a ball on to Sutton at the edge of the box in the 56th minute, but the rangy striker's left-foot shot was thrashed back by Douglas. The rebound was whipped off Larsson's toe by the lanky legs of a Dundee defender.

It wasn't all blood, sweat and snotters. Larsson pulled back to pick up the ball and cleverly fed Thompson on the left. The former Aston Villa man delivered a perfect cross for Petrov, surely one of O'Neill's born-again players, to crash a header past Douglas.

After the match the Celtic manager paid tribute to the skills of his squad, but picked out the Bulgarian midfielder Petrov for particular praise: "During the summer I probably was not completely aware of exactly what he could do," he said. "But I did speak to him and told him that all good sides have a goalscoring midfield player. He's doing very well, and he can score goals."'

Five days later the Celtic team was boarding a plane to play HJK Helsinki in Finland for the second leg of the UEFA Cup tie. Following Celtic abroad is one of the most enjoyable aspects for the supporters and the team always brings a massive support. Among the thousands who went to Finland was Graham Lynn, 42, a computer specialist from East Kilbride.

The idea is to have as much fun as possible while following the team and, along the way, get to meet new and interesting people – or something like that. Graham started to find out what was on offer in the way of entertainment before he left Glasgow to join his brother-in-law Stephen McCirmmon, 26, in Helsinki.

'When I was at home I saw the Helsinki site on the internet and got an e-mail conversation going with this Helsinki supporter, Marco. He suggested we organise an 11-a-side match between the Helsinki fans and the Celtic fans a couple of hours before kick-off. He even thought he might be able to get it on telly.

'I thought, "Aye, okay." I decided just to tell guys going over and spread the word amongst the fans. But what with the long journey and having a few drinks and all that stuff the fans' game kind of went out of my mind.

'On the day of the match we went to the Irish pub, Molly Malone's. That's the first thing you do when you're on these trips, you find the Irish boozer. There's always one. Except this was an Irish pub with a difference – it had a Rangers fan behind the bar, an English bloke. He wouldn't play the Celtic tapes on the bar's stereo. I suppose it wasn't really your typical Irish bar. It was a bit upmarket with folk music and all that.

'The bar was heaving and there were guys going up to the barman all the time saying "Put this on, mate" and he just refused. Then one Celtic fan just stood up and shouted: "This b*****d won't put the music on so let's gie him some songs." The whole place just erupted.

'The barman was going mad at the noise and then he promised to put the tapes on if we'd stop singing, but it was too late.

'Anyway my brother-in-law and I decided it was time to get out and went wandering up towards the stadium. I had taken a few bottles of Buckfast to Helsinki with me, it was a special request from my brother – he doesn't live in Scotland any more so it was a bit of nostalgia. Anyway, we were well on.

'When we get to the stadium we find this wee pub and it was just full of Helsinki fans. We were sitting down beside this Finnish guy and I noticed he had a bag full of footballs. I said, "Do you like a wee bit of football, big man?" He said "Yeah, but they're for the supporters' game." I just thought, "Oh, no."

'So he asked me and my brother-in-law to go down with him to the game. What could we do? We thought, okay, we'll go and watch. When we got there the Helsinki lads were all there in full kit, with water bags, sponges, fans, the whole thing. There was also a camera crew from the local tv station waiting to film it.

'Marco was there and when I introduced myself he said, "The e-mails?" I said "Yeah." I could see him looking at just the two of us and I said: "This is our team."

The game went ahead after they gave us half their side, but I don't think they filmed it. There was only one other Celtic fan, a guy we'd met from London who just stood on the touchline roaring "Get intae them." The whole thing was weird.

'We had another laugh before we went back to Scotland. We had got asked to leave the hostel because there was too much singing and we were staying in this posh hotel. We got talking to this Finnish girl and asked her where the nightlife was in Helsinki. She said: "I'm meeting a friend tonight and you can come along and I'll show you the good areas to go." We both thought, "Oh, ho."

'We met her pal at this bar and she introduced herself. Her name was "Minging". I kid you not. We started giggling and then we couldn't stop. We were roaring. And that was the end of that.'

It was a month of six matches and, counting European games, the Celtic squad had notched up 12 wins before taking to the field against HJK Helsinki. 'Field' was probably the most accurate description of the pitch. Tina Turner had held a concert on it the week before and, to the Celtic squad's dismay, it looked more like the Somme.

28 SEPTEMBER: HJK HELSINKI 2 CELTIC 1

(Report by authors)

Celtic's winning bubble was well and truly burst at the 13th attempt when they found a Finnish side far tougher material than their fans, at least, had anticipated.

However, it could have been a great deal worse had it not been for the goal struck by £6m striker Chris Sutton in 17 minutes of extra time which will certainly have gone a fair way to repaying his transfer fee.

Two goals ahead from the first leg at Parkhead against the Finnish side, Celtic managed to toss away that advantage in the chill of the Helsinki air and they came close to going out of the UEFA Cup.

The two goals they lost will not be remembered with any relish by the defence, in particular goalkeeper Jonathan Gould, who seemed at fault on both occasions, nor substitute defender Vidar Riseth, whose error led to the second goal.

Celtic had played well enough for a while in the first half when they were almost in complete control, but with five minutes left, HJK's smart striker Paulus Roiha shot with the first of his two goals and that left Celtic's confidence waning fast.

They became very tentative indeed, and when they lost the second goal in 75 minutes they were on a slippery slope to another early exit from Europe. Sutton's goal in the 107th minute saved the blushes and put his team into the second-round draw this morning.

One serious setback last night was the bad knee injury suffered by captain Tommy Boyd midway through the first half.

Producing a surprise in the line-up for European contests seems to be the fashionable tactic these days and it was manager Martin O'Neill's turn to defy the predictions when he left out Lubo Moravcik and brought in Eyal Berkovic, who has spent most of the season on the bench and under consistent speculation that he would be leaving Parkhead.

With Alan Thompson ineligible, it was a welcome return, too, for Bobby Petta after a three-game absence through injury. It was Petta who immediately caused heartache in the Finnish defence with a superbly placed free kick that needed only a touch to put his side ahead.

However, although Celtic took control right away, they were given a warning that HJK could break dangerously when Kopteff did precisely that and sent over a cross, or maybe a shot, that hit the top of the bar and went behind.

Celtic suffered a severe blow in 33 minutes when Boyd was carried into the dressing-room with a knee injury after a clash with Saarinen, although the injury may have been caused by his studs catching on the turf.

Vidar Riseth replaced him but the incident interrupted the momentum, although Larsson did chest down a neat ball for Berkovic, who just could not get a foot to it from about ten yards. Berkovic tried a hopeful effort from outside the box but hit it much too high.

The unthinkable then happened with five minutes of the first half left. After all their possession and all their attacking Celtic went a goal down. A long ball forward was chased by Roiha and Valgaeren, but as they reached the penalty area, Gould also came rushing out and the Finn stretched out his foot to steer the ball past the goalie into the empty net.

The Finns made a change at the start of the second half, with Jussila coming on for Rami but it was goalscorer Roiha who caused Celtic a fright, outwitting Mjallby on the left and shooting for the near post where Gould got down to grasp the ball.

A better move by Celtic involving Sutton and McNamara ended with the wing-back's shot being blocked and Larsson's outstretched touch going straight to the keeper.

The 5,000 or so local fans were beating the drums, literally, with greater gusto now and their side seemed also to be growing in confidence as shown when Saarinen tried an ambitious volley and was not far off target.

There was a scare for Celtic in 63 minutes when the defence was left in a tangle and Saarinen gave Kallio a simple chance from close range. Somehow the Finn placed the ball outside the post.

HJK then replaced Kopteff with Hannu Haarala before Lambert came very close to equalising after Larsson laid the ball into his path 20 yards out. He hit it well, too, but the keeper also did a good job to beat out the ball.

In 75 minutes, the stadium was rocking as the Finns levelled on aggregate. Riseth slipped, allowing Haarala a straight shot at goal. Gould made a wonderful stop and the damage seemed to have been avoided until the keeper lost the ball and in ran Roiha to hit it into the empty net. Celtic were now seriously in trouble as the Finns went for a victory they had not believed was possible. Lambert tried to save the day again with a fine volley that cannoned off a defender and went for a corner from which Healy shot past the post.

It was then into overtime. Celtic brought on Moravcik for McNamara but it was Petta who set up a great chance in four minutes for Larsson who touched the ball past a post from a few yards. But luck was really out for Moravcik a couple of minutes later when his right-foot shot came off the post.

However, in 17 minutes of extra time, Celtic climbed out of the hole they had dug for themselves. Moravcik tried a volley that went along the front of goal and Sutton steered it past the keeper.

Celtic went through on aggregate, but the result was a little bit of a fright for the support. Bordeaux beckoned in the next round, but first there was the question of just how long Celtic's unbeaten league form could continue.

6.

HOORAY HENRIK

Henrik Larsson, Henrik Larsson
Henrik Larsson is the king of kings
Henrik Larsson, Henrik Larsson
Henrik Larsson is the king of kings

THE CELTIC SQUAD were in Finland for the second leg of their European tie against Helsinki when Morten Wieghorst realised something was not quite right.

The popular midfielder had just returned from a long lay-off following a knee injury and he was looking forward to first team action for the first time in four months. His injury could not have come at a worse time, coinciding with the arrival of the new manager. Since the start of the season he had been restless and eager to prove himself as he watched his team-mates help Celtic storm to the top of the league. But he knew you couldn't rush these things. Push yourself too hard and the injury is exacerbated and then you're back to square one. He would have to bide his time. Take the treatment, visit the physio, get as much rest as was necessary.

By late autumn he was back in serious training and close to full fitness. The Monday before the Helsinki game he had played a reserve match in Glasgow and he had come through that first test with no apparent recurrence of the injury. Things were looking up. His knee felt strong and healthy and he had a positive mental attitude.

But when he arrived in Finland, ready to train with the first team, his body didn't seem to be co-operating. After so much rest he should have been feeling sharp and alert but instead he was stiff and lethargic. Something was wrong. He didn't know what but he knew something was wrong. He put it down to a mild bout of flu – none of the foreign players ever quite got used to the damp, demoralising Scottish climate, the way the rain seeps through your skin and chills your bones. After the training session Morten felt drained. He figured that he couldn't have been as fit as he had imagined and he resolved to put in an extra effort before the weekend. If only he could summon the energy.

The result of the match added to his sense of despondency. Celtic won the tie courtesy of Sutton's extra-time strike but it had hardly been the emphatic victory the team had hoped for. The Scandanavian players in the Celtic team always liked to put on a good show when they were in the Nordic countries; show them how good Scottish football really could be. But they had not done themselves justice. Helsinki were a tricky outfit but Celtic should have beaten them more convincingly.

On the journey back to Glasgow after the game, Wieghorst began to notice other symptoms which convinced him there was something wrong with his health. During the flight he felt a tingling sensation throughout his body, like a bad dose of pins and needles. When he arrived home to his wife Anna, it was three a.m. and he barely had enough energy to say hello before collapsing into bed.

It seemed like his head had barely hit the pillow when it was time to get up again for early-morning training. By the time he arrived at Celtic Park he was too tired to train. He excused himself and returned indoors to the players' television room. He lay down on the floor and slept.

By Friday morning he felt worse. He woke with excruciating back pain and, when he tried to walk, he found that he kept losing his balance. His limbs were weak and he barely had the energy even to sit in a chair. Enough was enough. He had kept this to himself for too long. He called the club doctor Roddy Macdonald and told him he was worried about his health. Macdonald gave him a thorough examination. The doctor said he thought he knew what was wrong but he couldn't be sure. He told Morten to go home but to keep in touch over the weekend if things got worse.

By Sunday morning Morten had a diagnosis. He was suffering from Guillain-Barre Syndrome. Being able to put a name to his symptoms helped but he was still none the wiser. Like most people, he had never heard of Guillain-Barre Syndrome. He was told it was a potentially fatal neurological condition which affects one in every 100,000 people. The condition occurs when a bug invading the body bears the same characteristics as the body's nerves. The antibodies which fight infection become confused and, as well as attacking the bug, attack the nervous system. The nerves lose contact with the muscles and paralysis sets in. Nine out of ten sufferers recover but some become severely paralysed, unable to walk, and a small proportion never recover.

For the moment Morten was able to remain at home but the doctor told him that the situation could change if his condition worsened. By Monday evening he had lost all feeling in his legs and arms. Slowly, his body was turning numb. At eleven p.m. he was rushed to the Southern General Hospital in Glasgow's south side and admitted to the intensive care unit. Half an hour later Macdonald arrived at the hospital with Martin O'Neill.

'I'm not a natural crier but I cried then,' said Morten. 'That was when it first hit me that something was terribly wrong. That's when it sunk in. It can kill you.' (22 December, *Daily Mail*)

It wasn't long before the newspapers were on to the story. 'celtic player admitted to hospital with mystery brain bug' ran the headlines. The story generated a tremendous amount of public goodwill. Get-well messages flooded into Celtic Park. Morten – who had signed from Dundee for £600,000 five years previously – was one of the most popular members of the Celtic squad. A key member of the championship-winning side in 1998, he provided a link with the Jansen era. There was admiration and respect when he earned a deserved place in Denmark's World Cup squad in the same year. And there was sympathy when he suffered a cruciate knee injury, forcing him to miss the last nine months of the 1998–99 season before coming back – only to be injured again.

For the players there was a sense of *déjà vu*. Morten was not the only Celtic player to have fallen victim to a serious illness. In 1998 Darren Jackson was sidelined for three months after undergoing major surgery for the brain condition hydrocephalus. He made a slow but full recovery and was able to continue his career. The following year Alan Stubbs was diagnosed as suffering from testicular cancer. He also made a full recovery after a successful operation.

As news of Morten's condition emerged over the course of the weekend, the mood in the Celtic dressing-room dipped. In time his strength and determination to overcome the illness would galvanise the players, instilling within them a determination to do what he would want them to do – win football matches. But when the players travelled to Pittodrie on Sunday, 3 October the mood was predominantly one of deep concern. It was perhaps no coincidence that they dropped their first league points of the season on that trip.

Not for the first time, it was left to the predatory instincts of Henrik Larsson to salvage Celtic's unbeaten record.

Aberdeen's recent performances against Celtic had been less than inspiring. In their last four encounters they had conceded 23 goals, scoring only once. But it was the Pittodrie side, brimming with confidence and with 6 players under the age of 21, who took the game to Celtic, outplaying their more experienced rivals in the first half.

Sutton had suffered a broken nose against Helsinki and declared himself unfit, leaving the Celtic attack lacking his potent strength. In midfield the more industrious Alan Thompson replaced Berkovic. But it was the defence that was to prove the weakest link. From the start, the back three of Mjallby, Boyd and Valgaeren struggled against the pace of Aberdeen's attack.

1 OCTOBER: ABERDEEN 1 CELTIC 1
(Report by authors)

Boyd, who had suffered a leg injury against Helsinki, was lucky to stay on the park following an inept tackle on Winters on the edge of the penalty box after 13 minutes.

Mackie was giving the Celtic defence a torrid time. On one occasion he left Valgaeren for dead, testing Gould with a low shot. When he was subsequently left free to deliver two dangerous crosses into the box O'Neill decided it was time for a tactical change. He pulled Jackie McNamara from midfield into right-back, switched Boyd to left-back and paired Valgaeren and Mjallby together in central defence.

After 37 minutes he was forced to reshuffle his pack further when Thompson left the field with a hamstring strain. Stéphane Mahé took over, but the enforced change did little to improve Celtic's rhythm.

They paid the price in stoppage time when Aberdeen's in-form striker Robbie Winters recorded his seventh strike in six outings. The goal, which followed a speedy exchange of passes between Eoin Jess and Derek Young, left the Celtic defence stranded.

For the first time in the season Celtic greeted the half-time whistle with a sense of relief knowing that, but for a combination of luck and a lack of composure by their hosts, they could have been further behind.

A toe injury prevented Lambert emerging for the second half and he was replaced by Moravcik. And it was the substitute who was to provide the telling contribution that led to Celtic's equaliser. In the 81st minute the Slovak whipped in a cross from a short corner and Larsson rose unchallenged to head the ball home decisively to record his 13th goal of the season.

All of Celtic's good work could have been undone by Petta who was dismissed for a second bookable offence with just seven minutes remaining but the side hung on for a point they really didn't deserve.

The result meant Celtic stayed at the top of the league, two points ahead of Hibs and three ahead of Rangers. O'Neill's public response was, as ever, supportive of his players but he knew they would have to improve if they were to meet the challenges that lay ahead.

Larsson's late strike provided enormous relief to the fans, not only because it earned the side a necessary point, but also because it was the first goal of the striker's new post-dreadlock era. Supporters had been stunned by his freshly shorn look when he emerged from the tunnel at Pittodrie. He had sported his trademark dreads ever since he burst on to the international stage at the 1994 World Cup in the USA. The eight-inch strands were the team's lucky totem and the more superstitious fans feared their removal could result in a Samson-style loss of strength. They needn't have worried.

There were some casualties of the new look, not least the thousands of fans who had purchased Henrik face-masks adorned with his distinctive hairstyle which was now decidedly passé. One firm had produced thousands of dreadlocked Henrik dolls which they knew would now be as difficult to sell as Christmas cards on Boxing Day.

Prestwick air-traffic controller and season ticket holder Annette Toal retains a lingering guilt that she was responsible for the now infamous Henrik haircut. Annette had always harboured a 'thing' for Henrik – an admiration not limited to his goalscoring ability. Never having met him, and never anticipating such an event, she was resigned to worshipping him from afar. That is, until she and her husband found themselves booked on the team's flight to Helsinki for the UEFA Cup tie. There was the object of her undying fantasies less than ten feet away, and there was she, with nothing but a scrap of Larsson wallpaper in her handbag just begging to be autographed. After plucking up the courage, she finally sidled up to him and asked him to sign it. He was more than happy to oblige.

Returning triumphantly to her husband Steve, she immediately regretted not asking him to sign something better. Steve fished out a copy of the poster which had come with one of the Celtic videos he had bought and Annette grabbed it and ran back to Henrik and the Bhoys. 'Sorry, could you sign this as well?' she pleaded with her most seductive smile.

'Oh, it's you again. Certainly . . . welcome.'

On the return journey Annette was waiting to board her flight at Helsinki airport when, again, she spotted her idol and immediately felt pangs of regret that she hadn't been photographed with him. So she approached the now more-than-a-little-bemused Henrik again, thrust a camera into the hands of a bystander and instructed him to push the button. Larsson, being the perfect gentleman, did not object while his image was captured for posterity next to the now familiarly beaming visage of Annette.

The following day, back in Glasgow, Annette was at Celtic Park to collect tickets for the beamback game against Aberdeen the following Sunday when who should she see trotting out of the training ground but the now familiar object of her desires. Having been castigated by her nieces for failing to procure individual Henrik signatures for them, she resolved to remedy the situation. When Henrik spotted her approach out of the corner of his eye, his trot broke into a canter and then something approaching a mild sprint but he knew resistance was futile and, as he nervously shuffled with the keys of his Mercedes, he felt the bundle of memorabilia again being thrust under his nose.

Henrik had now been confronted with this same grinning woman 4 times in just over 12 hours but, being the consummate professional that he is, he dutifully obliged with his signature. The following day Larsson's haircut was revealed to the world and Annette can't help thinking that it was a desperate attempt to avoid the attentions of persistent stalkers like, erm, herself.

Larsson was fast becoming a national icon. His excruciating leg-break the previous season had precipitated a period of national mourning. It wasn't just Celtic's title ambitions that took a battering in that crunching tackle in Lyon, it was the country's collective psyche. Larsson provided cosmopolitan character in an otherwise drab footballing environment. With him out of the picture, it was a bleak landscape. Yet from his first kick of the ball on his return to action in Euro 2000 it was obvious the injury had done little to diminish his extraordinary talents. He was the linchpin of the Swedish side, scoring a wonder goal against Italy.

Now he was back to his very best, rattling in goals at an alarming rate, he captured the public's imagination more completely than any player in living memory. His dreadlocks and his hallmark extended tongue are among the most distinctive images in the Scottish game. In the UK only Manchester United's talismanic star David Beckham could rival him for star quality.

'I was born in the 1960s and my big heroes were Jimmy Johnstone and Bobby Lennox,' said Eddie Toner, secretary of the Celtic Supporters Association. 'I had pictures of them all over my walls when I was at primary school. When I started taking a keen interest in football, Kenny Dalglish was my hero. But Larsson is a bigger star than any of these guys. Whether he is a better player, I don't know, but he is Celtic's biggest ever superstar.'

When Larsson signalled his desire to remain at Celtic Park until the end of his career his place in the pantheon of club legends was secured. He took hagiology to new heights. 'He's not just a great player, he's a great Celt,' said Lisbon Lion Jimmy Johnstone. 'He takes a great interest in the history and traditions of the club. John Clark, who played in Lisbon, is our link with the club. As well as being one of Martin O'Neill's backroom staff, he's also a sounding board for the players. No one talks to him more than Henrik. He's fascinated with the Celtic teams of the past and he wants to know all about them.'

Interest in all things Henrik was soaring. Two brothers decided to cash in on his celebrity by selling Larsson tongues at £1-a-piece. The *Daily Record* obtained one of his dreadlocks from the West End hairdresser who had removed them and offered it as a prize to a lucky reader. Sales of Henrik merchandise were booming – including hand-knitted Larsson dolls from Texas – Swedish flags fluttered appositely alongside tricolours at Celtic Park and he even had his own signature tune, the theme music to the film *The Magnificent Seven*, which was played after every goal he scored. Replica strips appeared bearing the number seven with 'God' emblazoned across the back. In a spirit of ecumenicalism one fan had 'Allah' printed on the back of his shirt.

No one was arguing. Well, almost no one. Journalist and football observer Phil Miller recalls being collared by one Celtic supporter in a Glasgow pub who insisted Larsson was, in fact, the Son of God, and, like all good, deranged conspiracy theorists, he had an archive of spurious circumstantial evidence to prove it. 'He genuinely believed that Larsson was Jesus Christ,' Miller explained. 'What struck me was the coherence of his argument. He had a number of facts which he felt proved the validity of his case. Some were purely interpretive, like Larsson was the saviour of Celtic whose career had been resurrected. And he looked vaguely Middle Eastern. But there were other points that were more specific. He was the son of a fisherman, his wife was called Magdalena – similar to Mary Magdalene – and his son was called Jordan, after the country where Christ was baptised. He also pointed out that whenever Henrik scored he extended his arms in a crucifix position. The guy was clearly a bit of a zealot but he was totally convinced.'

Larsson, though, was happily confining his miracles to the football field and determining that Celtic would not easily surrender the lead they had established at the top of the league. 'We've played a lot recently and sometimes you just slip off top form,' he told the Celtic website. 'We're still on top and we'll make sure we stay there.'

Celtic's next league test was against SPL newcomers St Mirren on 14 October, but in the meantime there was the distraction of World Cup qualifiers for a number of the club's international players. Jackie McNamara was included in the Scotland squad for their double-header against San Marino and Croatia and Larsson joined the Swedish squad, scoring in a 1–1 draw with Turkey.

O'Neill had been forced to publicly deny that he would be leaving Celtic to become the next manager of the English national side. Several London-based newspapers had linked him with the job following the shock resignation of Kevin Keegan. Refuting claims that he was leaving Celtic was an uncomfortable and unfortunate chore that was to occupy much of O'Neill's time in the coming months.

Another tedious burden that was to prove all-too-routine in the season ahead was being asked to react to the bullish observations of Rangers' imperious German midfielder Jorg Albertz. On this occasion Albertz dismissed Celtic as 'lightweights' and insisted Rangers would cruise to their third title in a row. 'Celtic are doing well but let's see how they last over the full season,' he said. 'They are ahead now but they'll drop off as the season goes on. We're a better team and will prove that by becoming champions again.' (12 October, *Daily Record*) On this occasion Celtic decided that the best response was dignified silence. They would do all their talking on the park.

14 OCTOBER: CELTIC 2 ST MIRREN 0
(Report by authors)

The game started with a minute's silence for Donald Dewar, who died earlier in the week, and that set the tone for a distinctly funereal atmosphere at Celtic Park. St Mirren were never likely to beat stronger, slicker, more technically gifted opponents but at least they were prepared to have a go, playing three up front in an effort to win. For a spell in the second half, when the score remained at 1–0, following Sutton's first-half strike, they performed well, with Ricky Gillies directing operations in the midfield, supported by Iain Nicolson down the right and striker Maikel Renfurm. But any uncertainty as to the result was removed with Larsson's exquisite free kick.

It was a moment of genius in an otherwise quiet Larsson performance, squandering a series of gilt-edged opportunities. Lubo Moravcik too had an unusually ineffective game, missing three clear chances in the first half.

Paul Lambert returned to the side following an operation on a poisoned toe, but Celtic were without Mahé, McNamara, Stubbs and the suspended Bobby Petta. Didier Agathe made his competitive début and he was arguably the best player on the park.

In the first ten minutes Celtic had created three clear openings but failed to convert them. Larsson headed an Agathe cross over the bar and then provided a brilliant diagonal ball from 40 yards which Lubo Moravcik shot inches over the bar. Seconds later, Thompson's long ball forward was nodded on by Sutton into the path of Larsson but Scrimgour was off his line quickly to make the block.

By the mid-point of the first half Agathe was starting to exert an influence with his electric pace on the right flank, creating two clear openings that should have been converted by Larsson and Moravcik. Sensing the Frenchman's increasing danger, St Mirren manager Hendrie made a tactical switch in 27 minutes, replacing Lee Sharp with Baltacha.

With Saints under siege, Sutton made Celtic's superiority count in the 33rd minute when Moravcik's dipping corner was met in front of goal by Sutton whose backward header ended up in the net. Celtic came close again before the break when Larsson's header from a Petrov cross landed on the roof of the net.

After the break Celtic continued to dominate and within 3 minutes Thompson rattled a 25-yard drive wide of the post. Larsson missed again in front of goal after being played through by Petrov but again Scrimgour was quickly off his line to block his shot.

St Mirren posted notice that they weren't out of the game yet with a couple of decent chances. Nicolson fired a long-range effort over the bar while Gillies latched on to a Nicolson cross but his effort was gathered by Jonathan Gould. Celtic pressed forward in an effort to find a second goal that would make the points safe. They should have scored midway through the half when Larsson played a cute back-heel into the path of Agathe. The Frenchman rounded the keeper but, incredibly, faced with an open goal, his shot struck the inside of the post and rebounded to safety.

However, with just minutes of the game remaining, the Celtic fans were finally able to breathe a sigh of relief. Celtic won a free kick on the right-hand side of the box from which Larsson curled a shot into the far corner of the net.

The following day Rangers lost 1–0 to Hibs at Easter Road, courtesy of a David Zitelli strike. Advocaat blamed poor refereeing for the loss. The result left the champions trailing Celtic by six points and third in the league behind the Edinburgh side. For the first time in three seasons Celtic were installed as SPL favourites and bookmakers were unequivocal about who had made the difference. 'It is a reflection of what Martin O'Neill has done for the club over a short period of time,' said Tote spokesman Jeremy Scott. 'Even when Celtic thrashed Rangers earlier in the season all the firms were reluctant to alter their odds. However, the results over the weekend have persuaded us to reassess the whole situation north of the border.' (17 October, *Daily Record*)

There was more good news when O'Neill finally managed to land a new goalkeeper. Despite public pronouncements that there was still competition for the position, few doubted that Rab Douglas, a reported £1.5 million signing from Dundee, would be his first-choice keeper. His signing left incumbent keeper Jonathan Gould in an invidious position. He had been a regular in the Celtic side for the past two seasons, where he had equipped himself admirably. His performances under O'Neill were solid if unspectacular and yet he still found himself on the fringes. To his credit he remained cheerful about his position and, rather than seeking an escape route, he resolved to remain at the club to fight for his position.

'Although O'Neill is quite ruthless about getting rid of people, he is also a pragmatist so he would keep someone as long as he needed him before bumping him,' said Jonathan Northcroft. 'O'Neill had been sounding out agents about goalkeepers and everyone knew he was going for a goalkeeper.

'Gould went to his office halfway through that period and said, "Look, gaffer, this is really unsettling me, there's no smoke without fire. You're in the paper all the time denying you are going to sign goalkeepers but there's still speculation. I am not stupid." O'Neill said to him, "Jonathan, you're a hell of a man. You make things really difficult for me. You just keep playing so well that it's very difficult for me to bring in a replacement. You have had such a great season." Gould left his office on cloud nine until he got halfway down the corridor and realised that, despite the flattery, O'Neill hadn't actually offered him any reassurances at all. He was still going to be replaced. And it's interesting that someone like Gould has actually fallen into line and accepted the contract.'

Celtic travelled to play St Johnstone the following Tuesday. On a dark and wet October night there was a moment of radiant surrealism for one group of Hoops fans. Members of the geographically challenged Ibrox Celtic Supporters Club set off for Perth in a bus which was an unfortunately brisk shade of orange. As they pulled up at a set of traffic lights in deepest Govan they were surrounded by Rangers fans making their way to Ibrox for Rangers' Champions League tie against Galatasaray. In the confused darkness several Rangers fans mistakenly sensed common cause with the supporters in the bright orange bus.

'One Rangers fan made the big "T" sign, asking for tickets,' said Ibrox CSC member Jason Henderson. 'Most of the guys on the bus had their jackets done up so he obviously didn't realise we were a Celtic bus. A few of the boys jokingly signalled that they had two tickets. The bus pulled away and the Rangers fan started running after us like a gazelle. He chased us down the road, through a roundabout and another set of traffic lights. We were almost on the motorway when he eventually caught up with us. He chapped on the window and asked if he could buy one of our tickets. Everyone on the bus was in hysterics. We had to politely but firmly point out that we were unlikely to have any Rangers tickets because we were all Celtic supporters.'

Celtic's win was overshadowed by St Johnstone boss Sandy Clark's post-match accusation that Johan Mjallby had provoked debutant Stuart Malcolm into throwing a punch which earned him a red card. The win was secured with goals from Joos Valgaeren and Henrik Larsson, extending Celtic's lead at the top of the league. The Belgian defender rose to head home Alan Thompson's 40th-minute free kick while Larsson grabbed their second from the penalty spot in the 86th minute after Alan Kernaghan brought down Bobby Petta.

A last-minute hitch prevented Douglas from making his debut in goal and so Gould kept his place. The combination of unyielding rain and a stodgy playing surface was never going to be conducive to attractive football. Celtic deserved the win but their midfield dominance was such that the scoreline should have been more emphatic. St Johnstone had few efforts on goal throughout the 90 minutes and never really troubled Jonathan Gould.

17 OCTOBER: ST JOHNSTONE 0 CELTIC 2
(Report by authors)

Celtic's first goal came after 40 minutes following some sterling work by Petta, the Glasgow side's best player on the night. Petta, who had replaced Moravcik in the Celtic starting line-up, found space on the left and was brought down by Malcolm. Valgaeren scored from the resultant free kick.

Malcolm's sending off was a sad moment for the youngster who was making his debut for the home side. He was dismissed eight minutes from time after throwing a punch at Johan Mjallby in the box as Celtic were waiting to take a corner kick. Referee Rowbotham had no option but to send him off and, despite Clark's protestations, he clearly had to go.

Celtic's second came from a penalty when Kernaghan was judged to have body-checked Bobby Petta in the box. Larsson stepped up to send Alan Main the wrong way from the penalty spot.

With just eleven league games played, Celtic were already nine points clear of rivals Rangers and five clear of Hibs, who were maintaining a robust challenge in second place. With Rangers not due to play until the following Sunday, Celtic were in a position where a win against Dundee United the day before would put them 12 points clear. Such a gap in the East End side's favour had not existed for a generation and comparisons were already being made with the club's Double-winning side back in the centenary season of 1987–88.

The parallels were striking. Then, as now, Rangers were led by a free-spending, rumbustious manager. Celtic were led by a charismatic figure in his first season at Celtic Park. Then, as now, Billy McNeill had made a series of inexpensive, pragmatic signings who proved better value for money than the conspicuously costly signings being made across the city. Limited but effective talents like Andy Walker, Billy Stark and Mark McGhee were brought in while McNeill's one extravagance was Frank McAvennie, bought from West Ham for a record-breaking £750,000 to lead the attack. O'Neill was similarly budget-conscious. His signings ranged from the inexpensive – Valgaeren, Thompson and Douglas – to the downright cheap, a mere £35,000 for the precociously gifted Agathe. Again the frontman, Chris Sutton, was O'Neill's one lavish purchase. Then, as now, Celtic had adopted a utilitarian approach where winning was more important than winning well. The centenary season had been characterised by single-goal wins often scored in the latter stages of the match. In addition Celtic had lost the title to

Rangers the season before and were quietly determined to wrest it back.

As the players prepared for their next match, there was bad news from the Southern General Hospital where the condition of Morten Wieghorst had worsened. Doctors had been forced to perform a lifesaving tracheotomy, feeding a ventilator tube through his windpipe to help him breathe. He was effectively paralysed, only able to move his eyes and mouth. 'I was going off my head when Anna couldn't make out what I was saying. I couldn't speak for eleven days,' he said. 'Anna was amazing. I was lying there with tubes sticking out of me, all over the place.' (23 December, *Daily Mail*) During that crucial period his life hung in the balance. Doctors performed a procedure called plasmapheresis, which cleans the blood, and that helped contain the infection. But he needed enormous reserves of inner strength to pull through.

The news cast a pall over the Celtic dressing-room. There were also other problems which threatened to disrupt O'Neill's velvet revolution. Mark Burchill had already left the club on a loan deal with Birmingham City and now it looked as though Eyal Berkovic was about to follow suit. The little Israeli's position was hardly improved when his lawyer wrote to Celtic demanding to know why he was being left out of the team. The letter, signed by Yoel Goldberg and passed to an Israeli newspaper, demanded to know why Berkovic had started just 3 out of O'Neill's opening 16 matches, when he was patently the most gifted player at the club. If his relationship with O'Neill had been cool beforehand, that letter finally ensured that he had no future at the club.

'You always knew that Martin O'Neill was a guy who likes team players, guys who work hard, guys with a physical presence and he just made plain from the start the sort of Celtic dilettantes who would be kicked out,' said Iain Campbell of the Scottish *Mirror*. 'Burchill's big problem was that he was up against the best strike partnership in the country. Sutton and Larsson were surpassing everyone's expectations.'

Berkovic was, unsurprisingly, absent from the squad the following weekend. Jonathan Gould remained in goal, despite the arrival of Douglas earlier in the week, and Agathe kept his place after his electrifying display against St Mirren. McNamara was left on the bench. Celtic did indeed race 12 points clear of Rangers with goals from Larsson and Thompson on either side of half-time. A late own goal by Lambert gave the visitors hope but Celtic hung on for a deserved win.

United did not deserve to have been even challenging Celtic. Anchored at the foot of the table, they had seen chairman Jim McLean resign in disgrace the week before following a violent incident involving a BBC reporter. Even history was against them – they hadn't scored more than one goal at Parkhead in the past 13 years.

21 OCTOBER: CELTIC 2 DUNDEE UNITED 1
(Report by authors)

Celtic carved out their first opening after ten minutes when Petta slipped a defender on the wing and delivered an inviting ball across the face of goal, but Sutton was a split-second late in making contact. Midway through the first half United player David Partridge almost put Celtic in front when he headed a Thompson corner off his own bar.

However it wasn't long before Celtic were on the attack again. Petrov found Petta with a long cross-field ball and the Dutchman raced down the wing, lobbing in a cross which was met by Sutton, but keeper Combe made a comfortable catch. Moments later Larsson connected with a Thompson corner but his header crashed off the post.

The breakthrough for Celtic came in the 34th minute when Petrov hooked in a corner from the right and Larsson found space to dive in and head beyond the keeper. The Swede could have doubled Celtic's lead moments later when he picked up a Sutton knock-down in the box. However, with too much time on his hands, he tried to curl it into the far corner with the outside of his foot and the ball rolled harmlessly wide.

United thought they had an equaliser on the stroke of half-time when Petta cleared an effort by Licina off the line. Referee John Underhill ruled that the ball had not crossed the line and he stuck to his guns despite being surrounded by angry United players in the tunnel after he whistled for the break.

Celtic could have been two up a couple of minutes into the second half when a Larsson back-heel sent Sutton free inside the box. But Combe was quick off his line to make a brave save at the feet of the big Englishman. United boss Alex Smith replaced Gustavo Fuentes with Cameroon striker Mvondo Atangana in an effort to pull something from the game. However it was Celtic who increased their lead soon after. Agathe crossed from the right onto the head of Sutton who nodded the ball down into the path of Thompson. From 12 yards out he fired the ball beyond the reach of Combe.

Valgaeren almost made it three when he slid in at the back post just too late to latch on to a Thompson free kick.

Smith made another change in 72 minutes, replacing Anastasios Venetis with Stephane Leoni and his adventurousness paid off when

United pulled one back in the 77th minute, albeit from an own goal. A harmless ball into the Celtic box looked to pose little danger but confusion among the home defence allowed John McQuillan to press forward. Sensing the danger Lambert went for the ball, but sliced it into his own net.

Celtic's next challenge was against Bordeaux in the second round proper of the UEFA Cup. Supporters were typically sanguine about the team's prospects. In light of Celtic's most recent European performances, being involved in the competition at all by October was a triumph in itself. For the generation of Celtic supporters most associated with European success in the 1960s and '70s, a rich folklore had been established around overseas trips. From the tavernas of Montevideo to the bordellos of Amsterdam, tales of louche debauchery, lost passports, missed flights, stolen romantic assignations and the bonding of lifelong friendships had accompanied Celtic whenever they travelled abroad.

Among the richest veins of Celtic lore are tales of fans' efforts to make it to Lisbon for the 1967 European Cup final, of supporters willing to cash in their life savings, sell their cars, miss their own parents' funerals in order to make it to the game. Some hitch-hiked to and from the Portuguese capital, so determined were they not to miss the biggest day in Celtic's history. One fan famously refused a lift on the return journey because the car that stopped was only going as far as Coatbridge and he lived in Dennistoun.

Bordeaux was another opportunity for Celtic fans to evangelise the club message abroad. Among them was David Norrie, a 23-year-old software engineer from Glasgow, and 5 of his mates who, in the long tradition of Celtic supporters abroad, gave absolutely no thought whatsoever to their travel arrangements beforehand. They included contractor David McCarron, 23, Anthony McGill, 24, a software engineer, Paul Mackle, 24, a project manager, and students Kevin McShane, 22, and Jeff Meechan, 23.

'It wasn't exactly a paragon of forward planning,' admitted David. 'In fact there wasn't any planning at all. We arrived in Paris on our way to the south of France to discover there was nowhere to stay as the whole city was full. The train station also happened to be shut. We ended up sleeping on the streets of Montparnasse in the rain. When the station opened at five we moved in there to sleep in a locker room until the gendarmes woke us up by blasting their whistles. Charming.

'The return journey was unbelievable. We didn't start to plan it until after the game when we were sitting in a little bar in Bordeaux getting slightly puggled. The waitresses were giving us free drink and trying to look up our kilts. We decided to sleep in the station and catch the 5.14 a.m. to Paris. The trouble was this station was full of homeless people. Big Davie came looking for us just in time to find a North African-looking guy going through Paul's bag. Not that it mattered. Paul had already lost his camera and phone anyway.

'We made sure we didn't miss the train by going to sleep on the freezing platform. But there was a small technical problem. We arrived back in Paris less than two hours before our plane left from Beauvais, 62 km outside the city. We grabbed a taxi, but didn't arrive at the airport until 10.25 a.m., just in time to see it taking off.

'We weren't alone though. There were around 60 people left at the airport, which is just a collection of small buildings in the middle of nowhere. The railway station is seven miles away and the next plane was not for five days. We didn't panic. Instead we got the local taxis to take us all to Calais for £30 each. It was about this time that Kev, who had spent most of the day playing his newly acquired bongo drums with Jeff, started to worry he might miss his girlfriend's 21st birthday party in Glasgow that night.

'I called my brother in London to see if he could organise a flight. No answer. He was stuck on an underground train. We then got a bus to London for a tenner and got the last six places on the Glasgow bus at 10 p.m. that night. We got home at 7.30 a.m. the next day and Kev missed his girlfriend's 21st.'

Celtic gave themselves an excellent fighting chance of making it through to the third round of the UEFA Cup with a spirited performance in France – and once again it was charmed striker Henrik Larsson who provided the inspiration.

The Swede's 24th-minute penalty earned the visitors a well-earned draw after they had fallen behind to a Christophe Dugarry header. It meant Celtic would entertain Bordeaux at home a week on Thursday with a vital away goal, knowing that the fate of the tie was in their own hands.

In fact Celtic should have taken more from a game which they dominated for long spells, outplaying their hosts. Larsson, in particular, gave the French a torrid time with assistance from Moravcik, Petta and Agathe. In defence, a solid display by Valgaeren, Boyd and Mjallby nullified the potent threat of World Cup star Dugarry.

O'Neill was forced to play Larsson as a lone striker after Sutton ruled himself out because of a lingering ankle injury. However it didn't take Celtic long to show their adaptability.

26 OCTOBER: FC BORDEAUX 1 CELTIC 1
(Report by authors)

After just 30 seconds a Moravcik throw caught the Bordeaux defence napping. Petta latched on to the ball and swung in a cross which defender Alain Roche only managed to head skywards. Larsson beat keeper Ulrich Rame to the ball but was unlucky to see his header loop just over the bar. In the ensuing clash the Swede received an accidental punch in the face from Rame, for which he required treatment.

Bordeaux felt they deserved a penalty in the 11th minute when Portuguese striker Pauleta was brushed off the ball by Mjallby in the Celtic area but the referee waved away their claims. Two minutes later Celtic almost took the lead when a Rame punch from a Moravcik corner fell into the path of Lambert on the edge of the penalty area but his low shot was cleared off the line by François Grenet. Celtic's confident display was rattling the French and their lack of composure was demonstrated with a yellow card for Lassina Diabate for a high challenge on Petrov.

But all their hard work was undone in the 22nd minute when they found themselves behind to a Dugarry goal.

Bordeaux won a corner and when Grenet's cross came in Dugarry was the first to react, taking advantage of a momentary lapse of concentration in the Celtic defence to nod home at the near post.

Celtic responded immediately, drawing level from the penalty spot two minutes later after a typically ingenious passage of play by Larsson. The striker saw defender David Sommeil dally in the Bordeaux penalty area and raced in to rob him of the ball. Sommeil upended Larsson as he tried to repair the damage he had caused and Norwegian referee Tom Henning Ovrebo pointed to the spot. The penalty was converted with characteristic panache by Larsson himself.

Moravcik could have put Celtic ahead on the half-hour mark when he lobbed a pass from Larsson over the bar. At the other end of play Feindouno challenged Gould with a dangerous header and Dugarry continued to look threatening.

And when the teams emerged for the second half, it was Bordeaux who took the initiative. Only a vital intervention by Mjallby prevented Lilian Laslandes having a clear shot at goal. The big striker then tested Gould with a header as the French began to impose themselves for the first time in the game. Laslandes was the second Bordeaux player to be booked after 59 minutes for a foul on Larsson.

As the game progressed, however, Celtic settled into a comfortable pattern of play with the French failing to seriously threaten Gould. Agathe was booked after 62 minutes for a clumsy tackle on Dugarry a couple of yards outside his own box and from the free kick Gould only just managed to scramble Laslandes' low-driven shot away.

Bordeaux pressed forward in the dying moments but their only real chance came from a powerful Dugarry header in the 92nd minute. Fortunately for Celtic his effort came rebounding back off the upright.

By the time Celtic travelled to Fir Park for their final match in October, it was clear that Morten Wieghorst was going to survive. A black cloud lifted from Celtic Park. The doctors were able to remove the tube from his throat where there was now a hole the size of a ten-pence piece.

'The doctors had to give me a plug to fill the hole so I could talk,' he said. 'Anna came in. I just said, "Hello, love, I can speak." It was a great moment.' (23 December, *Daily Mail*)

News of his recovery was announced at Celtic Park where the relief was palpable. Morten's illness had weighed heavily on the players' minds. 'It would have a devastating effect in the dressing-room,' said former Celt Charlie Nicholas. 'Not all the players are pals. Some players don't get on at all. But when something like this happens it's very difficult, mentally, for the players to get over it and it's bound to have an effect on the way they play. Happily it seems to have brought them closer together and it formed a bond between them. Even if they were not great mates they had seen one of their own pull back from a life-threatening illness. It would put football into more of a perspective. The players would look at someone like Morten and then they would think of their own grievances about a wee injury or being left on the bench, or the fans having a go at them for missing a tackle and it would show that there are more important things.'

Iain Campbell, chief sports writer at the Scottish *Mirror*, said: 'Wieghorst's illness was an important reminder to the players that football was not as important as life and death. It was a motivating force and it was obvious that he was in everyone's thoughts.

'Wieghorst is extremely popular. He is one of the most likeable guys at Celtic Park and one of the most popular guys with the players. He has a very easy-going manner. It's quite strange for a Dane. He is Celtic's Jorg

Albetz in that he started speaking English with a Scottish accent rather than a Danish accent. When O'Neill said Wieghorst would have another year on his contract, it was an important gesture.'

Six goals, plenty more action besides, yet the main talking point at Fir Park was a Johan Mjallby 'goal' that escaped the eyes of referee Hugh Dallas and one of his perfectly placed assistants, Graeme Curr. More accurate officiating would have taken Celtic 15 points clear of their Old Firm rivals but the 3–3 draw against Motherwell put Martin O'Neill's men a win ahead of second-place Hibernian and opened even more daylight between themselves and the defending champions.

Afterwards, the manager refused to criticise Dallas or his seemingly unable assistant for failing to see the Swede's sliding shot in 59 minutes cross the line by two feet, and preferred instead to praise both teams for providing an evening of high entertainment for the Sky audience and the 10,800 fans who braved the conditions.

29 OCTOBER: MOTHERWELL 3 CELTIC 3
(Report by Darryl Broadfoot: *The Herald*)

Mjallby opened the scoring in 14 minutes but Derek Adams and Lee McCulloch hit back for Motherwell only for the pendulum to swing in the visitors' favour courtesy of strikes from man of the match Joos Valgaeren and Jackie McNamara. A 77th-minute penalty from Ged Brannan earned Billy Davies' men a point.

Davies saw no need to meddle with his winning formula after two straight wins, so the fit-again Scott Leitch and Jamie McLean were only afforded seats on the substitutes' bench.

Alan Thompson, Celtic's only change from midweek in place of Lubo Moravcik, was heavily involved in the first chance of the match, stabbing the ball in the direction of Didier Agathe but the Frenchman's shot was collected then spilled by Stevie Woods. Larsson heeled the ball back to the Geordie but his net-bound shot was deflected to safety.

The breakthrough came amid a 13th-minute penalty-box mêlée. A deep Thompson corner was headed back towards the danger area by Larsson and as the defence struggled to scramble clear, Mjallby barged through a ruck of bodies to send the ball into the roof of the net at the second attempt.

'Well quickly regrouped and the home crowd did not have too long to wait for the restoration of parity.

John Spencer received a long, looping ball on the left-hand side in 22 minutes and although his first cross rebounded back to him, his headed return was met full-on by Derek Adams, who nodded past Jonathan Gould. Motherwell almost took the lead six minutes before the interval but Spencer's stinging shot was beaten away by Gould.

While Northern Ireland winger Stuart Elliot became more and more involved for Davies' side, keeping McNamara in defensive mode throughout the first 45 minutes, Celtic's chief creators, Bobby Petta and Agathe, were shackled closely by Martyn Corrigan and Steven Hammell respectively. The importance of Chris Sutton is only truly apparent in his absence, and without his link-up skills and predatory instincts, his Swedish partner received insufficient support.

O'Neill sought to remedy the situation for the second period, with the adaptable Agathe taking a more advanced position alongside Larsson, but it was Motherwell who went ahead after a swift 51st-minute counter-attack.

A poor pass from McNamara was intercepted by Brannan and, without hesitation, he sent Adams scampering clear down the left with a piercing pass. His shot was deflected for a corner and McCulloch found space at the near post to convert Spencer's set-piece.

Celtic's response was swift, however, and within four minutes they were back in the see-saw match thanks to Valgaeren. Thompson's free kick was headed into his path by Larsson and from close range the Belgian found the net to the delight of the visiting support, who only minutes later were left cursing that dreadful refereeing decision.

Mjallby slid Thompson's cross over the line, with Corrigan hooking the ball away from at least two feet inside the net, but as the Swede wheeled away in celebration, neither referee Dallas nor his far-side assistant signalled a goal.

The sense of injustice was forgotten in 71 minutes when McNamara capitalised on Celtic's period of sustained domination. The full-back played a neat one–two with Larsson and, although he appeared to miscue his strike from just outside the area, he did enough to stab the ball beyond the reach of Woods.

Still, the drama was not over and Motherwell were handed a lifeline in 77 minutes after Mjallby's clumsy challenge on Motherwell substitute Don Goodman inside the box. Brannan converted the resultant penalty to ensure a grandstand finale to a pulsating match.

Celtic should have won but the draw was important as it took them into November 13 points ahead of Rangers, a gap not even the most optimistic of supporters would have anticipated at the start of the season. It had been a deeply disappointing month for the Ibrox side who had lost three league games and were languishing in fourth place behind Hibernian and Kilmarnock. But if the 6–2 game against Rangers had sparked an important psychological shift among the Celtic players, making them believe that they could take on their strongest rivals and beat them convincingly, the Motherwell game also had important lessons. Iain Campbell of the *Daily Mirror* said, 'The Motherwell game was a signal that the old Celtic Park paranoia was disappearing. When things went wrong in the past, like when they had a perfectly good goal by Cadette chalked off against Rangers, there was a feeling that the world was against Celtic. That game was an indication that it wasn't easy in football and sometimes you have to battle and grind and that's something Celtic did the whole season. Martin O'Neill brought that Premiership work ethic to them where, instead of feeling sorry for themselves, they just buckled down.'

7.

STUBBSY

When you walk through the storm
Hold your head up high
And don't be afraid of the dark
At the end of the storm
There's a golden sky
And the sweet silver song of the lark
Walk on, through the wind, walk on, through the rain
Though your dreams be tossed and blown
Walk on, walk on, with hope in your heart
 And you'll never walk alone
You'll never walk alone
Walk on, walk on,
with hope in your heart
And you'll never walk alone
You'll never walk alone

STILIAN PETROV had arrived in Glasgow the season before in a huge fanfare of publicity. The midfield potential in a boy his age was said to be enormous. His transfer price reflected it. But within months of arriving he had serious misgivings. Unable to speak English and left largely to his own devices, he was homesick and feeling some major regrets. He was also being played out of position as a defensive midfielder and he despaired whether he would ever make his mark. Bulgarians are shy by nature and Stilian's reticence was making things difficult. On his first day at the club, in the midst of a strange country in a strange city, he had even been unsure how to get to the house that was provided for him from Celtic Park.

The problem was partly due to his age. Unlike other players signed on a relatively large transfer fee he did not have a wife or family to support him and he arrived in Scotland knowing nobody. Eventually he was taken under the wing of football agent Brian Wilson's family. They fed him, transported him to and from training and helped him with his English.

We catch up with him a year later as he is driving to Sofia in Bulgaria on the way to take a flight to Bali for his honeymoon. The five-hour car journey with his new wife Paulina and his brother gives him time to reflect. 'I was very, very unhappy in Glasgow,' he says. 'The food was strange, the language was unusual for me and I felt a bit lost. I was being asked to play in a position that was difficult for me. I knew last season when I was in the team a lot of supporters thought I wasn't worth the money and some people at the club wondered why I was getting a game. At the start of the new season I wasn't looking forward to returning. I sat in Bulgaria and thought I would be coming back just to leave Celtic.

'But Martin O'Neill spoke to me well. He told me to lose a bit of weight, which I did, and he told me he liked his midfielders to score goals. He then asked me what position I wanted to play in and said he would let me play there so there could be no excuses. I have not looked back.

'The atmosphere in the dressing-room had changed as well. Everybody now talks to everybody else and there is no more sitting in small groups. I couldn't say when this happened. Nobody said anything. When Martin O'Neill came it just seemed to change.'

Petrov is highly superstitious and insists on placing the tongue of his boot under his laces before playing in a match and wearing three red-and-white laces around his wrist before starting a game. One of the laces fell off before he took to the pitch in a game against St Johnstone at McDiarmid Park last year. It was a match in which he was to break his leg.

Despite the serious injury which left him confined to his Clydeside flat for weeks, Petrov was to go on and pick up Scotland's Young Player of the Year award. It was an extraordinary turn-around in fortunes in such a short space of time. Not everything had changed though. He was lying on the beach in Bali during his honeymoon when he picked up an English newspaper and noticed a report saying Ramon Vega had turned down £25,000 a week to stay at Celtic. '£25,000 a week,' he was saying to a friend on the phone five minutes later. 'What's going on?'

Petrov's growing form was one of the key factors in Celtic's resurgence. Others, including Bobby Petta, were also playing out of their skins. The omens were good as the team entered November, a grim month of miserable weather, with a clutch of tough matches on the horizon.

None were harder than the one awaiting the team at the end of the month. Rangers stood barring the entrance to Christmas and the winter shutdown like avenging angels. The second match between the two sides would take place at Ibrox, or Castle Greyskull as fans jokingly named it, and it was unlikely to be a pushover.

For all the delight at the 6–2 win everybody who followed Celtic was only too aware of what had happened to Dr Jo Venglos's side after they crushed Rangers at Celtic Park in the season's first fixture. Then the result had been greeted with enormous rejoicing in the East End because it had been so unexpected. Supporters had gathered at Parkhead fully bracing themselves for a real turning over at the hands of a clearly capable Rangers squad. Lubo Moravcik's stupendous opener and the four that followed were then a bolt from the blue and one that had the fans dancing in the streets. But those who took it to mean the Celtic revival was fully up and running were cruelly put right in the rematch at Ibrox and the subsequent withering of Celtic's title hopes.

Anyway, November was to be a historic month for Celtic as Rangers stuttered and stalled their way through their league campaign. The first game of the month was in the CIS Cup against Hearts at Tynecastle. Celtic produced a gutsy performance and ended up with a scoreline that flattered slightly given that the match went into extra time. It was a great victory all the same, and made better by Martin O'Neill's gamble in playing a trio of young players – Crainey, Smith and Healy, who all managed to get on the scoreline. With a seven-game month beginning, O'Neill had decided to rest a couple of key players for a cup competition he had reasoned was not a priority.

1 NOVEMBER: HEARTS 2 CELTIC 5
(Report by Robert Martin: *Scottish Mirror*)

Holders Celtic kept a firm grip of the CIS Insurance Cup at Tynecastle last night – but only after they were made to fight all the way after a gutsy performance from Hearts.

Goals from Stephen Crainey, Jamie Smith, Colin Healy, Lubomir Moravcik and Jackie McNamara justified boss Martin O'Neill's faith in his younger players, even if it took extra time to kill off the capital club's challenge.

In normal time, Colin Cameron's 35th-minute penalty had put Hearts in front, only for young full-back Crainey to level with a low drive three minutes before the interval.

Another of O'Neill's babes, striker Jamie Smith, then put the Hoops in front just before the hour mark, with Cameron again beating Gould from the spot ten minutes later to send the game into extra time.

But Celtic finally came through in the 98th minute, when Antti Niemi, who had been in superb form throughout, could only turn Johnson's header onto the post, and Healy was on hand to turn the ball home from all of six yards out.

A further two goals in the dying minutes by Moravcik and McNamara resulted in a misleading scoreline.

It was rough justice on Hearts, who did much to restore pride around Tynecastle after being embarrassed by derby rivals Hibs ten days earlier, and who showed a commitment in their play that was sadly lacking on that occasion.

In his choice of players, O'Neill was as good as his word after admitting he would rest several of his top stars in a competition he described as the least of his side's priorities this season, despite their status as holders.

Both Henrik Larsson and Paul Lambert dropped out of the squad altogether, while Johan Mjallby, Bobby Petta, Tom Boyd and Stilian Petrov were all afforded places on the substitutes' bench.

Rangers were now lying in fourth place in the league with an unthinkably large gap of 13 points between them and Celtic. There was Treble talk on the streets of Glasgow and Martin O'Neill's carefully constructed plan to keep the pressure off by playing up his opponents was becomingly increasingly hard to stick to. But O'Neill wasn't one to be carried away by the heat of the moment. He reacted swiftly to the growing euphoria by holding a press conference at Parkhead and blasting it out of the water.

O'Neill insisted that winning the Treble was a far-fetched notion and beyond his team's capabilities. He said: 'The thought of doing the Treble doesn't even enter my head. It's absolute nonsense. Indeed we know that a crisis is just waiting around the corner for us. That's not just me being ultra-pessimistic, that's just what happens in football. It will happen to us, of that there is no doubt. We just have to be strong enough to know it's coming.'

He was right.

Before all the fun started at the end of the month there were a few equally important games to be dealt with. The next Scottish Premier League match was at Kilmarnock. Rangers had already stumbled there and Kilmarnock were expected to be no mugs.

5 NOVEMBER: KILMARNOCK 0 CELTIC 1

(Report by Iain Campbell: *The Mirror*)

Martin O'Neill's Celtic showed once again that their nerve is unlikely to fail them in their bid to recapture the title from arch-rivals Rangers for the first time in three years.

The league leaders succeeded where the champions failed when they came away from a clash with Kilmarnock with three valuable points last night.

An inspired goalkeeping performance from Gordon Marshall, ironically a former Celt, threatened to slow the Parkhead club's championship surge.

And with Killie always liable to score on the break, particularly in the second half, there was plenty of danger to contend with.

But an Alan Thompson goal just after the hour was enough to give O'Neill's side another crucial win at a venue which has been a graveyard for them in the past.

The truth is that Celtic should have won more easily than by the single goal which separated the sides, but the heroics of Marshall and some sloppy finishing from Henrik Larsson meant the visitors had to endure some worrying moments in the closing stages as they held on to their lead.

The Gers' return to form and movement closer to full-strength placed just a bit more pressure on the leaders at a noisy, passionate Rugby Park but if they were nervous they didn't let it show.

With the first-choice striking partnership of Chris Sutton and Larsson happily restored to the delight of the sizeable travelling support as well as the thousands who watched live on TV, the leaders took an early stranglehold on the match which they rarely looked like losing.

Even the loss of key midfielder Paul Lambert, who looked less than fit throughout, shortly before half-time, hardly upset the momentum of a side which seemed well prepared for the threat an in-form Killie offered.

In fact, Lambert's replacement Didier Agathe hardly affected the balance of O'Neill's side and offered something different when the elusive opener refused to come.

It was the former Raith star who finally opened up a Killie defence well organised by Marshall and Freddie Dindeleux with a superbly judged pass which eluded both Larsson and Sutton but was finally met by Thompson who gratefully tapped the ball past a keeper who had looked unbeatable up till then.

With absent powerhouse Gary Holt badly missed in midfield, the home side had been forced on the back foot for much of the game, but Marshall was more than capable of handling just about everything his old mates could throw at him.

His first-half save from a powerful Sutton header which was ripping into the corner of the net bore more than a passing resemblance to Gordon Banks' stop from Pele at the 1970 World Cup finals.

Then he bravely came off his line to put Larsson off when the Swede threatened to grab the breakthrough just before the break.

Marshall defied Sutton again from point-blank range just 60 seconds into the second half and the danger wasn't properly cleared before he had to turn a Stilian Petrov shot around the post.

Ironically, Celtic's goal came at a time when Killie were finally beginning to threaten Jonathan Gould's goal after finding it virtually impossible to get anywhere near it in the first half because of Celtic's control in midfield.

Young Jamie Fowler got free from two markers to send Christophe Cocard into the penalty area.

The Frenchman's cross swept right across the Celtic area but there was no Killie player on hand to convert the chance, with Johan Mjallby being forced to adopt desperate tactics and play the ball out for a corner.

Goal hero Thompson, described by O'Neill as 'masterful', admitted that he was happy to be able to take some of the pressure off strikers Larsson and Sutton by hitting the winner.

He said: 'It's nice to get a goal because it takes some of the onus off Henrik and Chris who are expected to score all the time. It may have looked an easy chance but I've seen people miss them.'

Larsson should have had the game tied up with two later chances but seemed to want to walk the ball into the net.

Lambert's injury was to prove worse than first expected, putting him out of the team for some time and adding an extra pang of hunger to Martin O'Neill's desire to bring midfield dynamo Neil Lennon from Leicester.

But something happened after the game that indicated to many supporters that Martin O'Neill was no ordinary manager. Instead of taking his players back to Parkhead O'Neill took them to the Royal Concert Hall in Glasgow where the Celtic Supporters Association were holding their 55th annual rally. Celtic managers and players have always attended the night of bands, speeches and Celtic songs, but not for a long time had the full squad turned up. Indeed in previous years the organisers had had to deal with the embarrassing sight of rows of seats earmarked for club personnel lying empty.

The year before John Barnes hadn't even bothered to turn up. It had been the first time in living memory that the Celtic manager had not been present.

It was Guy Fawkes night, Kilmarnock had been put to the sword and as 'Mr Las Vegas' Hugo Straney bounded on to the stage he was able to welcome the full Celtic team on with him. To tumultuous applause they trooped on one by one before taking pride of place in the front rows and settling down to listen to the 'fabulous' Patricia Ferns and the 'sensational' Smackee. By the time the evening closed with the traditional roof-raising rendition of 'Hail, Hail' the organisers were more than impressed with O'Neill's commitment.

CSA President Gerry Madden said: 'It was all down to Martin O'Neill. The year before we'd had about eight or nine first team players. They're people you can always count on to come. The Tommy Boyds of this world. Old professionals. But this time we had the whole squad, backroom boys, the lot. It was tremendous.'

Joe O'Rourke, CSA vice-president, added: 'Sometimes the younger ones slip away. They go to the dancing at Victoria's or places like that. You can understand that. This time Martin O'Neill made sure beforehand everyone was going to be there. Only one player said he didn't want to go, and we'll not name any names, but he is on loan to Blackburn now, and he was told by Martin that if he didn't show up then he would be fined a week's wages.'

Partying aside, the month's first real potboiler was the second-leg tie with the classy French side FC Girondins de Bordeaux. A draw in France in October should have been enough to put Celtic through – after all, Parkhead always rises to the European occasion. True to form, on the night of 9 November it may have been cold enough to guarantee brass monkeys stayed indoors, but the atmosphere in the stadium was boiling.

Celtic had good reason to expect success. Four months earlier when the two sides had met in a friendly the Celtic defence had been woeful. The mix-ups, an embarrassed Alan Stubbs explained later, had been down to language difficulties. Partnered by Brazilian Rafael and Olivier Tebily from the Ivory Coast, the language of football had been no substitute for a smattering of English. In the intervening period Rafael and Tebily had drifted out of the picture and the defence had hardened significantly.

As the crowd settled into their seats the club's master of ceremonies,

Tony Hamilton, cranked up the atmosphere with a showman-like introduction of the team: 'Henrik . . .' he bawled then waited theatrically until the crowd roared back: 'Larsson.' Once again he roared 'Didier . . .' and the reply came roaring out of the stands: 'Agathe.' By the time the whole squad had been welcomed in this fashion the stadium was jumping. On the tannoy the unmistakable sounds of the latest big hit, 'Who Let The Dogs Out', was blasting into the cold night air. The lyrics, of course, were subtly changed by the fans to include a few less than complimentary lines about Rangers. Then it was a full volume rendition of 'The Boys are Back in Town' by Irish rockers Thin Lizzy before the crackling strains of 'It's a Grand Old Team' announced the teams were taking the park. It had started, as many great European games have started at Parkhead, as a wonderful night of Euro-optimism – but it wasn't to be.

9 NOVEMBER: CELTIC 1 BORDEAUX 2
(Report by Rob Robertson: *The Herald*)

Celtic crashed out of the UEFA Cup last night after Bordeaux gave them a lesson in how to take the few chances which occur on vital European nights. However, for all their opportunism, it was a win the French side scarcely deserved in what was an enthralling Parkhead encounter.

Martin O'Neill's side, apart from a ten-minute period in the second half of normal time and a few minutes of the second period of extra time, dominated proceedings in this second-round, second-leg tie.

If anything, they have only themselves to blame for not taking advantage of the midfield superiority they enjoyed and the chances they created.

Even the after-match statistics illustrated Celtic's dominance, with the French side only creating three real chances in the 120 minutes of football, two of them resulting in goals.

The finishes of Lilian Laslandes, the first 12 minutes before the end of normal time and the winning goal five minutes before the end of extra time, had to be admired.

They also put in the shade the efforts from the Celtic strikers, who showed a lack of composure, with the main culprits being substitute Tommy Johnson, who squandered two good chances, and Chris Sutton, who missed a first-half header, although the Englishman's physical presence made him the Parkhead club's best player on the night.

For Bordeaux, David Sommeil was lucky to escape with a booking for a dreadful tackle on Henrik Larsson, while Lassina Diabate was guilty of a shocking challenge on Jackie McNamara in 27 minutes.

The midfielder soldiered on till just before half-time before coming off. Even the enforced change did not disrupt Celtic's pattern of play, and Colin Healy slotted in well to their formation.

Certainly, all through the game it looked like the Parkhead club, who had drawn the away leg 1–1, would cruise into the third round of the UEFA Cup for the first time in 17 years.

The confidence of the 51,000-strong crowd was based on the constant pressing game that O'Neill had adopted and which seemed to be paying off.

Certainly, they had successfully nullified Christophe Dugarry, who was the main threat to Celtic's chances of progressing.

With Dugarry sulking around the park, it meant Celtic were the side that looked to have the inspiration to win the game, but they failed to make their dominance pay.

Henrik Larsson and Stilian Petrov both came close in a first 45 minutes in which Bordeaux could only boast a header from Pauleta that sailed over Jonathan Gould's bar.

In the second half, Celtic continued to press, and, in 53 minutes, Ulrich Rame had a great save from a Larsson free kick, and two minutes later the breakthrough came.

Bobby Petta beat two players on the left-hand side and played in a bad cross, which Alain Roche made a real hash of. The defender did not know whether to head or chest the ball away and succeeded in only pushing it out into the path of Moravcik, whose shot beat Rame low down at his right-hand post.

That served as an understandable wake-up call for Bordeaux, but apart from a ten-minute period of pressure they never looked like they would breach the Celtic defence, in which Joos Valgaeren was outstanding.

However, 12 minutes from time, Laslandes got the first of his two goals when Laurent Battles crossed, giving the striker the easiest of tasks to score.

It was a tense affair from then until the end of normal time, as was the 30 minutes extra period. Even then you would have put your money on Celtic as they pressed forward looking for the winner.

As it turned out, with five minutes of extra time left substitute Bruno Basto put over a tempting cross to Laslandes, who volleyed the ball into the roof of the net, although Gould seemed to get the faintest of touches.

At the end, substitute Eyal Berkovic went down looking for a penalty when it looked like he had a chance to stay on his feet and round Rame to score.

The ball then fell to Tommy Johnson, who had all the time in the world to at least hit the target, but he screwed the ball wide, his lack of composure in front of goal summing up Celtic's disappointing evening.

Certainly their second defeat of the season will be a bitter pill to swallow for Martin O'Neill, but the lessons for him to learn are clear.

Looking back now Billy McNeill thinks it was perhaps not too bitter a pill to swallow. It may even have been a blessing in disguise. 'I didn't think the European issue was particularly important in the first year. It would have been nice to progress, but it might well have interfered with what happened domestically. I felt the domestic situation was the most important. I always felt it was possible to win the league in your first season. I did it on two occasions. Wim Jansen did it. It's something that is eminently possible and that, to me, was the most important aspect to the season. The very fact that, not only did he win the league, he took cups as well, makes it even more sparkling and more special.'

His comments make sense when it is remembered that Celtic went into the European tie on the back of that gruelling 120-minute CIS Cup game with Hearts. The match 8 days before would have taken its toll.

The relentless pace of the month swept on and Celtic were given almost no time to catch their collective breath before being plunged into yet another potentially difficult league challenge. Both sides of the Old Firm were playing when Celtic met St Johnstone at home on Sunday, 12 November. It was to be Rab Douglas's debut as a Celtic keeper and also an opportunity for the Hoops to slide a further wedge between themselves and Hibs if they won. The five-point gap at the top of the table that was on offer was tantalising. But St Johnstone are no mugs. The Perth side have been one of Celtic's bogey teams and even at Parkhead they could prove to be a handful. Despite the misgivings, though, it all came right on the night:

12 NOVEMBER: CELTIC 4 ST JOHNSTONE 1
(Report by authors)

Henrik Larsson struck twice for Celtic yesterday to ease their European hangover with a 4–1 home win over St Johnstone which puts them 5 points clear at the top of the Scottish League.

First-half goals from Chris Sutton, Larsson and Lubo Moravcik, plus a second from the Swedish international after the break, softened the pain of Celtic's midweek UEFA Cup exit to Bordeaux.

Larsson took his total for the season to 19 goals and pushed Martin

O'Neill's unbeaten team to 41 points from 15 games and widened the gap on second-placed Hibernian.

Sutton put Celtic on track after 13 minutes at Parkhead. Stilian Petrov's run into the box appeared to be halted by a foul, but Sutton pounced and curled a right-foot shot past keeper Alan Main. Larsson made it 2–0 in the 35th minute when he gathered a pass from Moravcik and slid an angled right-foot shot past Main.

Then Moravcik got on the scoresheet on 39 minutes with a dipping shot past Main from near the corner flag. Larsson's second goal was a delightful 59th-minute lob from Alan Thompson's pass before Craig Russell scored a consolation for St Johnstone.

Hearts, smarting from their painful exit from the CIS Cup, were next up in this run of three home games. Celtic had eight from eight in their home league games, a remarkable record, and with the prospect of another victory on the cards they would have the best home league results in Britain. It was getting hard to ignore the fact that the planets seemed to be aligning for a Martin O'Neill glory season.

Then something dreadful happened. Alan Stubbs, 29, a fit and strong defender, a young man in the prime of his life, a father with young children, was struck down for the second time in the space of a year with cancer. Stubbs had been treated for testicular cancer the season before and, after having been given the all-clear, returned to the squad. Now, on the eve of the Hearts game, at a routine visit to his specialist he had been given the terrible news that the cancer had returned. A growth had been found on his bowel which would necessitate an operation and chemotherapy. Treatment was to begin immediately. He was readmitted to hospital.

Celtic issued a terse statement on 17 November. 'Alan and his family will receive the highest level of support from Celtic Football Club,' it said. 'The club appreciates that Celtic supporters and the general football public will be concerned at this development. However, the club would like to request that the privacy of Alan and his family be properly respected by all.'

Looking back months later Stubbs said: 'My wife Mandy was there when I saw the specialist and I could see she was bitterly upset, but that made me realise I had to be even more strong for her and the children.

'When I knew I was going to get chemotherapy I thought: "Let's get it done." If it meant me being healthy and not playing football again, I didn't have a problem with that. Football wasn't relevant to me then.

'I spoke to Heather [his four-year-old daughter] when I was first going for chemotherapy and I said: "Daddy's going to have to go to hospital." She asked why. I told her I had a lump inside which needed to go away and the treatment I was going to get was going to make my hair fall out.

'She looked at me very strange, as if I was having a joke, then she asked if I would look like her uncle who has got a skinhead. I just started laughing because it was such an innocent remark.' (29 April 2001, *Sunday Herald*)

Once again real life had put football in its place.

18 NOVEMBER: CELTIC 6 HEARTS 1
(Report by authors)

Cameron showed his quality by firing his team into a wholly undeserved lead after 14 minutes when he carved a path through a static Celtic defence, exchanged passes with Scott Severin and clipped a shot on the rise from the edge of the area that floated beyond the reach of Robert Douglas.

From this point, only Antti Niemi was given the opportunity to impress. Which he did and then some. Midway through the first half, he blocked close-range headers from Henrik Larsson and Johan Mjallby in quick succession. The latter save, in particular, was a corker, with the Celtic defender placing his knock-down seemingly out of the Finn's reach only for the goalkeeper to claw the ball from behind his body somehow while at full stretch.

By this stage it was 1–1, with Joos Valgaeren equalising in the 15th minute courtesy of an artful effort from 18 yards, his clipped shot possessing both perfect curl and flight on its way to the net. It wasn't until the 35th minute that Celtic edged in front, a twist from Lubo Moravcik at the edge of the area, followed by a poked effort that nicked through a packed area and over the line low at the near post. Two minutes later, the contest was ended when Agathe slipped the ball through to Larsson and the Swede drove the ball against Niemi before scooping the rebound over the grounded goalkeeper.

On the stroke of half-time, a downward header from a Moravcik cross allowed Mjallby to make it 4–1 and, after a lull, Celtic hit a further 2 goals inside 2 minutes, a Larsson tiddler squeaking under the body of Niemi in the 81st minute before Stilian Petrov bundled the ball over the line after a neat cutback from Agathe.

All the games during November shrank to mere sideshows when compared to the one standing astride Celtic's path to the championship. Countless managers throughout the years had repeated the mantra: there are merely three points at stake. The same as in every other match of the season. Nobody has ever believed it.

How can you describe Old Firm encounters? Searing passions, unbelievable pressures and enormous levels of desire to win, not just from the players but the fans too, combine to ensure there is no such thing as an ordinary Old Firm match.

Over the years there has been tragedy. At Ibrox on 5 September 1931, Celtic's young goalkeeper John Thompson was fatally injured in an accidental clash with Rangers' Sam English. English was letting rip with a shot from Celtic's penalty area when Thompson bravely dived for the ball. His head was struck by English's knee with maximum force. He died at the Victoria Infirmary on Glasgow's south side that evening.

On 2 January 1971 the most tragic Old Firm fixture ever took place. Celtic were leading from a Jimmy Johnstone goal with just a minute remaining as Rangers fans piled out of the ground on stair 13. With 15 seconds left Colin Stein equalised and as fans began to turn and look back at the pitch to join in the celebrations people began to tumble on top of each other. In the ensuing crush 66 people died and 145 were injured.

There were, then, some extremely dark moments. But other games were just bizarre. The Old Firm match at Parkhead on 2 May 1999 was one played under a mountain of intolerable expectations for both players and fans. A win would give Rangers the title on their opponents' home ground. Three players were sent off. The referee was floored by a coin thrown from the stands and seconds later awarded a controversial penalty which Rangers scored, giving them a 3–0 victory. In the mêlée one fan tried to invade the pitch from the top tier of the stand and plunged onto the supporters below. Remarkably, neither he nor the startled supporters below were badly injured.

The baggage that everybody trailed behind them as they went into these encounters was more of a camel train. The last time the two sides had met at Ibrox was at the tail end of the last season on 26 March. Celtic were demoralised and in disarray. Dick Advocaat's players polished them off with a 4–0 win that set the seal on their championship season. Unusually, given Celtic's form in recent years, this upcoming game was vitally important for Rangers. Lose it and they would lose the championship. It was an incredible thought so early on in the season and one that focused the minds of Advocaat and his players.

Celtic went into the match full of confidence. But Martin O'Neill, as always, was preaching caution. At a testimonial dinner for Tommy Boyd held during the month the mood was one of boundless optimism as the championship seemed to be within reach of Celtic's outstretched fingertips. O'Neill stood up, took the microphone and calmly told the audience that Rangers were the club to beat, whatever the points gap.

Celtic went into the game undefeated domestically for months. A win would have meant 17 games without a loss, one better than Jock Stein's team achieved in their European Cup year. Not surprisingly the point was made to Martin O'Neill. He responded with his, by now, customary attitude: 'Look, there's only one way of going one better than Stein. That's winning two European Cups.

'I was a member of the Forest team that went 42 league games unbeaten. And I played in 38 of those. As I told Clough, not so long ago, not only that but I was the leading goalscorer. Clough said to me, "I would never remember that, son. I don't even remember you."' When the laughter subsided O'Neill added: 'Actually he didn't say that. I just made it up. But he would have said that. I didn't give him the opportunity.' (November 26, *Independent*)

There were good omens for the game though. Peter McCullagh from Port Glasgow had walked into his local betting shop prior to the previous Old Firm encounter and put money on Celtic to beat Rangers 6–2 three months before. For good measure he also had a double on Sutton to score first. His reason for this crazy bet? He had had a dream which foresaw the whole match. Of course Sutton scored first and Celtic matched the result. This time the Tote bookmakers had offered him a free £25 bet to have another go. Peter hadn't had a dream but he kept seeing Henrik Larsson scoring first and Celtic winning 2–1.

Peter said: 'Almost every day I get people asking me for tips. They still talk about my 6–2 bet and that was an amazing day. Funny thing was when we went 3–0 up I knew we would win 6–2. I was at the game but if I'd been in the bookies I'd have been trying to get more money on 6–2. I've had a few dreams since and a couple of weeks ago I saw Celtic beat St Johnstone 4–0. However, in the game proper Saints scored a late goal to lose 4–1. I keep seeing Larsson celebrating and 2–0 seems right but I'll also be having £1 on 7–1.' (25 November, *Daily Record*)

Rangers had cranked up the pre-match pressure in the way that only they can – by spending a fortune. On the eve of the game they had burst the Scottish transfer record to sign Premiership striker Tore Andre Flo for a staggering £12 million. As the papers pointed out, it was not the first time a Norwegian had been signed as the clock ticked down to an Old Firm encounter. The year before Kenny Dalglish had paraded Vidar Riseth with a similar motive of unsettling the opposition in mind. It hadn't worked.

In what was a reminder of the deadly serious side of Old Firm rivalry Rangers had invited young Cara Henderson to be their guest at the game. Cara had been the girlfriend of schoolboy Mark Scott who was horribly murdered by a Loyalist bigot as he walked home from a match through Bridgeton. She had started an anti-bigotry charity called Nil-by-Mouth. Describing going to her first Old Firm game, she said it was 'like facing the inner demons' she had felt since 16-year-old Mark's death 5 years before. And, in another sign that even at the tensest moment there was something in common between the clubs, Rangers fans unfurled a huge banner at the start of the game wishing Alan Stubbs every success in his battle against cancer.

26 NOVEMBER: RANGERS 5 CELTIC 1
(Report by Ian Paul: *The Herald*)

Just as many of his Parkhead predecessors have had to learn, Martin O'Neill discovered that Ibrox is an unwelcoming place to spend an afternoon when you are manager of Celtic, even, or maybe especially, if your team arrives in the Govan district of Glasgow brimful of confidence.

The words 'egg' and 'face' come readily to mind in these situations, yet Celtic were entitled to confidence after their splendid form of the season to date, with 16 unbeaten matches in domestic competition behind them, including a 6–2 thrashing of their rivals in August.

Their supporters turned up in ebullient mood but, like the team, were sent home to think again. The O'Neill side is simply the latest permutation of Celtic hopefuls to suffer depression on this ground. Not since 1994 have they beaten Rangers in their own backyard and they never really looked like doing it this time, either.

Even so, there was not a Rangers man among the 50,083 who anticipated a reverse thrashing of this magnitude to soothe their troubled souls.

There should be no doubt, either, that the scoreline was fully justified. Certainly, Celtic midfield player Alan Thompson did not aid the cause when he was sent off after 64 minutes following 2 yellow cards for fouls on Barry Ferguson. At that point the score was 2–1 and Celtic were still in with a chance, although the fact is that they had been outplayed for most of the game.

Rangers had looked worth more than the Barry Ferguson goal in 34 minutes that had put them in front and, even after Celtic equalised through Henrik Larsson five minutes after the break, they remained in the ascendancy, especially after they went ahead again through their £12 million man, Tore Andre Flo, shortly after. Once Thompson went off the possibility of a going-over for the away team was there and it was duly forthcoming. Rangers, like a boxer seeing an opponent with a cut eye, went all out to earn vengeance for the Parkhead defeat. Ronald de Boer headed in their third, Lorenzo Amoruso their fourth, and substitute Michael Mols finished off a fine move for the fifth.

Three of their goals came from corners, a fact that did not enchant O'Neill, but they all came after the loss of injured Johan Mjallby at half-time.

Ferguson was superb for Rangers, as were Claudio Reyna, back after an eight-game absence, and Amoruso, but failures were undetectable in this refreshed side that bore out their manager's insistence that they would resume normal service once the missing players returned.

Flo found the pace of the game hard to handle, which is hardly surprising since he had not been a regular in the Chelsea side. His goal will have done him a lot of good and he will clearly improve a great deal with match practice.

Even so, few players get the chance to become an instant hero in an Old Firm debut. That did happen for the Norwegian, who could scarcely have imagined that inside a minute he would have a glorious opportunity to score his first goal for his new club.

Reyna did some brilliant work on the right, cut inside and delivered the ball to Jorg Albertz. His pass inside the box for Flo to run on to was well measured, but the

Norwegian, challenged by Tommy Boyd, slid his shot wide.

Incredibly, Rangers missed another chance three minutes later when Celtic made a dreadful mess of things. Mjallby seemed to be about to clear an overhit ball from Amoruso when he suddenly ducked to leave it to keeper Robert Douglas.

Presumably the Swede had heard the keeper shout, but at any rate the ball bounced off Douglas's chest and went to de Boer, who shot over.

Reyna was booked for a foul on Bobby Petta and then Boyd had a brilliant tackle on Flo to avert what could have been a very dangerous situation. Celtic's first opportunity came from a free kick after Bert Konterman knocked down Larsson from behind. Thompson's free kick was too high, but a little later he delivered a fine free kick into the area where Larsson chested it back to Joos Valgaeren, whose shot went past the post.

The Belgian internationalist then had his name taken when he fouled Ferguson and it was 23 minutes before Celtic had a serious attack which ended up with a shot on target. A superb run by Didier Agathe left a couple of players stranded and he pushed the ball to Larsson who laid it on for Chris Sutton. It needed a good block by Amoruso to divert the Englishman's effort for a corner.

The breakthrough came, deservedly, for Rangers in 34 minutes when Ferguson scored. The move began with a free kick taken by Arthur Numan from a spot that O'Neill, judging by his protests on the sideline, reckoned was a long way ahead of where the foul took place.

When the ball reached Reyna on the right, he sent in a quick pass for Ferguson to pick up at speed and fire past Douglas from about the penalty spot.

They nearly made it two when Albertz rode a tackle by Agathe and cut the ball back at such pace that it came off the feet of Boyd and, happily for the Celtic captain, went straight to Douglas.

Thompson was shown a yellow card after he brought down Ferguson, who recovered quickly after some treatment.

The second half began in familiar Old Firm fashion when three players were booked inside four minutes. Firstly, Scott Wilson fouled Petrov, and then Amoruso and Sutton were shown yellow cards after some shenanigans off the ball at a free kick.

Rangers were almost caught out by a fine Bobby Petta cross over Konterman to Thompson, but Numan saved the day, sending the ball for a corner.

However, he couldn't do much to help when Thompson's corner found the Ibrox defence flat-footed and there was Larsson heading firmly out of the reach of Stefan Klos to level the scores.

Three minutes later, the singing Celtic choir was silenced in mid-note when Rangers went in front again. This time they did the damage from a corner, taken by de Boer and headed back on to the bar by Albertz. When the rebound came to the far post, Flo flicked it into the net.

Michael Mols then came on for Kenny Miller and Celtic were on the back foot again and were in further trouble when Thompson was sent off in 64 minutes after fouling Ferguson for his second yellow card.

Three minutes more and the day was heading for a bleak end for the green and white brigade. Rangers scored again, once more from a corner, this time by Albertz on the right, which found de Boer at the far post outjumping everybody to nod it down and over the line.

Mols then brought out a good save from Douglas, but Rangers made it four in 76 minutes with another Albertz corner catching Celtic dithering as Amoruso raced in to head past a bewildered Douglas.

McNamara illustrated the Parkhead frustration as he was booked for a tackle on Ferguson, but there was worse to come for Celtic. With five minutes left, Albertz sent the ball inside to de Boer who laid it in front of Mols at speed, but the Dutch striker calmly steered it into the net. The deed was done.

The result sent shock waves through the Celtic support. Had the bubble really burst? Rangers were now 12 points behind and they had a game in hand. All of a sudden keeping that gap open was looking more and more difficult as the wide open spaces of the rest of the season reappeared. For Celtic fans heading back into work the next day was difficult. Weeks of growing success as Rangers appeared to be sliding into oblivion had disappeared at a pop. There was some tough ribbing to be taken and the prospect that the 'forces of darkness', as Rangers were jokingly known, were stirring. The backlash that followed was predictable and painful. But O'Neill had consistently warned that there were tough times ahead. Everything he said had come to pass.

On the internet, the Celtic Mailing List, a forum for hundreds, if not thousands of Celtic fans from all over the globe to communicate with each other, was buzzing. The mood was one of disappointment but there was also an urge for calmness. One e-mail posted the day after the match by Jason Henderson in Glasgow eloquently sums up the position: 'On Sunday we got a severe rodgering – make no mistake about it. We can go on about the two stonewallers and Amoruso for his persistent fouling. We can even highlight Ferguson, who never even received a booking. Yes, he could have gone into the box at the Chapel and taken confessions – that's how much he got away with. Everything that could have gone against us did – much the same way that everything went for us in the 6–2 humping. I'm sure there are people on the list who are screaming murder at Martin O' Neill and handing out more than just level-headed criticism. All I can say is calm your horses there.

' I recently saw the film *On Any Given Sunday* with Al Pacino and this couldn't be closer to the truth. It's about American football and how on any given Sunday *any* result can happen. This is what happened on Sunday. This is what happened to Alex Ferguson on more than one occasion as well. Also, for anyone still punting the name of Hiddink, you'll find he is taking on the job of managing those giants of South Korea – end of story.

'All I can say about Sunday is that, in my opinion, we weren't beaten by a better footballing side, but by a side with the greater hunger. Again, exactly the same as happened in the 6–2 game. Maybe it's just me but I didn't see them play outstanding football – the difference was that they were first to every ball and we played no football at all. At 1–1 there was NOT one Tim in Ibrox who did not think we could do it – even from the start till de Boer's goal they were as quiet as I've ever heard them.

'However, at 3–1 I was sitting with my hands over my ears – yes, that's how bad it was. I was just hoping the ref would blow the whistle and we could escape with some dignity. If we came away with that score then we would not have all this hysteria on the list. The fact that we didn't means that we can apportion some blame to the tactics of Martin O'Neill. At 3–1 and with a man down all we were looking to do was shut up shop – Bobby Petta was in Reyna's pocket and should have been substituted for Colin Healy to give us some grit in the centre of the park. That didn't happen and that's where the final goal came from.

'With the exception of the first and last goals the rest were ALL defensive errors – however there's no point going over and over them. Just like there is no point lingering on this game for too long. For once in a few years we are in a position where the league will not be decided by the Old Firm games. It's our reaction to this result that will ultimately determine how far we have come. Maybe someone with the stats can show us the sort of run they need to go on to equal our wee run after the last Old Firm game.

'The fact is that even though we've all been optimistic – and rightly so with the way the team are playing – we ALL know that the team is not complete. We still know we need that dominant midfielder and an extra forward. If we sign them before Christmas then we'll romp away with the league. If we don't then there is always that glimmer of hope for Rangers.

'They need players if they are going to catch us. That's why it's up to Celtic to take the initiative and lead from the front. Starting on Wednesday night we must go out and blow Hibs away. If we do this then the doubt immediately swings back over Govan way.

'On a final point, it was pleasing to see every Celtic player, to a man, turn towards the support and applaud them at the end. They knew they received a tremendous backing and from their reaction I'm sure that they *will* pay us back. The best laugh has to be from Advocaat: "I wanted more goals so we could bring out a video." Well, here is some advice – see once your editing department has finished with it, send over the footage and we'll sling it in our own video – *The Championship Season*.'

29 NOVEMBER: HIBERNIAN 0 CELTIC 0
(Report by Iain Campbell: *Daily Mirror*)

Martin O'Neill brought his Celtic side to a blustery Easter Road looking to put Sunday's 5–1 mauling at the hands of Rangers firmly in the past and his title dreams back on track.

But after 90 minutes of effort – in a game in which the Hoops seemed to be suffering from an Ibrox hangover – Celtic returned to Parkhead with a single point, as the match ended scoreless.

The visitors were still 12 points clear of their arch rivals at the top of the Scottish Premier League going into the game and were also looking to increase their lead over second-placed Hibernian.

But O'Neill was without midfielder Alan Thompson – sent off at Ibrox – and into his side came Jackie McNamara, while Lubo Moravcik made way for highly rated youngster Colin Healy.

French winger Didier Agathe was also in for a hot reception from the home crowd after leaving the Edinburgh outfit for Parkhead back in August.

Hibernian, however, have been this season's surprise package – and beat Rangers here earlier in the campaign – and had the chance to close the gap on Celtic to just four points with a victory.

The windy conditions were tricky for both sides, and in the ninth minute the Hibernian defence hesitated and gave Henrik Larsson the opportunity to shoot. But his effort flew just wide after taking a deflection off Sauzee.

From Healy's corner Johan Mjallby fired the ball home from close range after a goalmouth scramble. But the referee ruled that goalkeeper Nick Colgan had been fouled and the goal would not count.

In the 17th minute Agathe could have rubbed salt in Hibs' wounds when he crossed from the right to Chris Sutton, who headed on to Larsson – but the Swede was unable to get his effort on target.

The home side forced their first attempt on target in the 28th minute when Paul Fenwick fed the ball through to Mixu Paatelainen in the box, but the Finn drilled a shot straight into the hands of Robert Douglas.

Celtic were temporarily reduced to ten men on the half-hour when Bobby Petta went off to have stitches in a leg wound after a crunching challenge from Sauzee.

Hibernian created a good chance in the 33rd minute when Mjallby let a long ball from Gary Smith run across his body in the area and Paatelainen hit a shot over the bar.

Petta failed to reappear and O'Neill was forced to throw Stéphane Mahé into the fray in the 36th minute.

The game came to life in controversial circumstances after 40 minutes when Hibernian had shouts for a penalty rejected. Agathe had brought down John O'Neil in the box, but the linesman was flagging for offside on the near side.

In the second half O'Neill continued to be the more animated of the two managers, but McLeish was forced to take off keeper Colgan in the 66th minute through injury and Mike Franks replaced him.

Franks was immediately called into action. Stilian Petrov fired in a fierce free kick from the left flank and Sutton almost got a touch as the ball went through to the stand-in keeper.

Hibs had Laursen yellow-carded late in the game for a foul on Agathe, and after a poor game the referee's whistle could not come quick enough.

The draw helped Celtic keep a seven-point gap at the top of the table, with Hibs in second place. The lead over Rangers had also increased to 13 points. But Rangers still had 2 games in hand as the teams went into December.

8.

CHRISTMAS

Martin O'Neill, Martin O'Neill
Martin O'Neill, Martin O'Neill
Martin O'Neill, Martin O'Neill
Martin O'Neill, Martin O'Neill

AS NEIL LENNON stepped off the plane at Glasgow Airport, he was deep in concentration. John Robertson and Steve Walford, his former coaches at Leicester, had arranged to meet him and he was keeping an eye out for their familiar figures. He had not seen either of them for a few months, not since they had left the Midlands club to join Martin O'Neill at Celtic, and he was looking forward to catching up on their crack. As he approached the domestic arrivals gate he expected them to be waiting for him, their warm smiles beaming at the end of the long airport corridor. Instead, he was met with a scene of frenzied mayhem and it didn't take him long to work out what it meant. Welcome to Celtic Park.

'The scene that greeted me was unbelievable,' he recalls. 'It was like a reception for U2 or Mike Tyson. The place was just mobbed. I have never seen so many press throwing mikes into my face and notepads and the like. It really took me by surprise. I never expected that. I knew there was interest but not on that scale. I knew the passion for the Old Firm but seeing it at first hand was something different altogether.'

A fortnight before those scenes Martin O'Neill was feeling under pressure for the first time in his short Celtic career. He still had much to do to prove to the fans that he had the ability to provide them with the success they craved so badly. Now questions were being asked in some quarters. Was the honeymoon over?

A few days after that humiliating 1–5 defeat by Rangers, he took a party of players to Ireland. Publicly the trip was billed as a short golfing break to help the players relax and to refocus their attentions on the league campaign. The loss at Ibrox followed by two dropped points at Easter Road meant that, for the first time that season, the team's lead at the top of the table was starting to look vulnerable.

Behind the scenes, O'Neill had other plans. As the players perfected their swing on the fairways of a golf club on the outskirts of Dublin, the manager was finalising a spot of business that would prove crucial in landing the club's first Treble for 30 years. At a private meeting with the club's major shareholder, Dermot Desmond, O'Neill spelt out some stark realities. With characteristic frankness, O'Neill told the millionaire businessman that he could no longer manage the club on a comparative shoestring. If Celtic wanted success, they would have to pay for it. Without additional resources he would be sunk.

The Rangers game had exposed the lingering weaknesses within the team that desperately needed to be addressed. O'Neill still hadn't given up hope of landing Neil Lennon, the midfield general he so desperately craved to give his team strength and security in the middle of the park. Since the deal had collapsed in the summer, O'Neill had received a call from his replacement at Leicester, Peter Taylor, who said, tantalisingly, that Lennon might be available – if the price was right. But there were other problems too. The absence of Mjallby at Ibrox had left the side woefully short of an aerial presence in defence. O'Neill likes his central defenders to be aggressive and offensive, but above all, he likes them to be tall so that they can attack high balls as they come into the penalty area. Tom Boyd, for all his other qualities, simply lacked height.

In other areas of the side, too, the season was taking its toll. Sutton hadn't trained for two months because of his toe injury, Petta needed eight stitches in a shin wound sustained in the match against Hibs, Mjallby had needed a cortisone injection to get through that match and Lambert would not be fit again until after the winter break.

Since arriving at Celtic Park O'Neill had spent a little over £13 million on five signings – Sutton, Valgaeren, Thompson, Douglas and Agathe. But the club had raised £6 million through the sale of Viduka so his net spending had been just £7 million. And he had reduced the club's wage bill substantially by lending out Burchill, Riseth and Rafael Scheidt. Compared with his opposite number across the city, Dick Advocaat, who was able to shell out £13 million for one player, O'Neill was a model of fiscal prudence. His message was blunt. He needed more cash and he needed it now.

Desmond listened with interest. He respected O'Neill and he knew he wouldn't have come to Dublin if his situation had not been serious. Desmond was the manager's champion in the boardroom. He had stuck with the Irishman it had been reported when other directors favoured Hiddink for the Celtic job. By the end of the meeting they had an agreement. O'Neill smiled but his pleasure was mixed with trepidation. Leicester had foiled one previous attempt to land Lennon and he knew they weren't beyond doing it again.

The day before leaving for the Dublin trip, Celtic had entertained Dunfermline at Celtic Park. Seldom the most understanding of people, Celtic supporters recognised that the result of this game was always going to be more important than the performance. And so a pedestrian display was greeted with some relief, not least because it ended a troubled week for Celtic in which they had given five desperately won points back to Rangers and Hibs.

2 DECEMBER: CELTIC 3 DUNFERMLINE 1
(Report by authors)

With only two minutes gone it looked as though they were set to drop more points when Dunfermline went ahead. Defender Jason Dair won a 50–50 challenge with Agathe and cut inside on to his right foot.

He sent in a low, whipped shot and, with the aid of a deflection off Mjallby, the ball found its way into the net beyond the reach of Rab Douglas.

However Celtic quickly regained their composure and drew level in the seventh minute when Petrov sprinted to the line to retrieve Johnson's pass. Moravcik met his cutback first time, using his left foot to slam it past Marco Ruitenbeek from eight yards.

Once again Celtic were indebted to Larsson who broke the deadlock and the silence that had pervaded Celtic Park after 21 minutes. Relieving Justin Skinner in the box, he drove the ball through the legs of Ruitenbeek for the cheekiest of nutmegs.

The Swede's moment of controlled poise effectively killed the game and, with Tommy Johnson providing assistance, he could have netted another two before the break.

Pars manager Jimmy Calderwood changed his team for the second half, bringing Nicholson into the midfield and sending Lee Bullen back to mark Petta who had been causing his side all kinds of problems in the first half.

Dunfermline sensed they could pull themselves back into the game and

Nicholson came close with a 25-yard shot followed, in 74 minutes, with a cross to the back post which was hooked over the bar from close range by the unmarked Crawford.

Bullen was doing well to pacify the threat of Petta, but on the one occasion when the winger did slip his marker he won a penalty. Larsson took the kick but he was denied by an athletic save by Ruitenbeek. Despite it being his second penalty miss of the season, the fans and his team-mates permitted him the momentary lapse. However, from the resultant corner, Johnson headed home Celtic's third and the goal which effectively finished the game.

As expected, transfer negotiations for Lennon were anything but straightforward. After publicly denying that Lennon was up for sale, Leicester then agreed on a £5 million sale. Then, just when it looked like the clubs finally had an agreement, Peter Taylor insisted the deal was off because Celtic had missed an arbitrary five p.m. deadline which he himself had set. Lennon was already going through a Celtic medical when Taylor began to quibble over who would pay the £700,000 Leicester had promised Crewe, Lennon's former club, in the event that they sold him on. In frustration O'Neill decided to bypass Taylor completely and he went straight to Leicester chairman John Elsom to sort out the deal.

Eventually, by 7 December, Leicester were resigned to losing Lennon, and even the eventual signing fee of £5.7 million would have been little comfort for them. O'Neill had landed his man, the player he believed would make his team tick. For Lennon it was a lifetime ambition attained. Not only had he been reunited with his former boss and mentor, he had signed for the club he had idolised as a boy. His father Gerry and the rest of his family were devoted to the club. He was initiated at a young age, making regular visits to Parkhead from his home in County Armagh. One of the great highlights of his childhood was meeting his heroes Roy Aitken and Paul McStay and he longed one day to play in the green-and-white hoops. Now his dream had come true with a four-year deal worth £28,000 a week.

'I had been to Parkhead as a kid and had a tour around the ground. I stood in the Jungle – it's something that has remained in my memory ever since,' he said. 'I never saw them play at Parkhead because we didn't have the money or the means to get across to Scotland but, as a family, we always followed them. It's just part of the community.'

After his arrival at Glasgow Airport from Leicester, Robertson and

Walford took Lennon directly to Celtic Park where he met O'Neill. It was an emotional reunion. There were the signing formalities – the paperwork, followed by a four-hour medical, before he could be unveiled to the press and the supporters. From there he was taken to the Marriot Hotel in Glasgow's city centre, which would be his home for the next four months, with nothing but the hold-all he was carrying. In the space of just a few hours he had committed himself to an entirely new existence. He would not return to Leicester. It had been a difficult, emotionally draining period for the player whose move to the club he loved was tempered by the divided loyalties he obviously felt to his old team-mates and the supporters.

'For a while I was very, very unhappy,' he said. 'It's hard leaving a club where you are happy. I wouldn't have left for many other teams. It was unfortunate for them that Celtic wanted me. Those three months were very, very difficult for me. Very unsettling. I didn't think I would get another chance at Celtic. I thought my chance had gone. And then it came around again and I was ecstatic.'

The fact that Lennon was able to fit into the Celtic team so seamlessly was testament to his professionalism and determination to be successful at his new club. He was immediately impressed by the steely will to win that he detected among his team-mates. 'The Leicester dressing-room was quite boisterous, with a lot of characters,' he said. 'The Celtic dressing-room seemed to be a lot more focused. I was made very welcome, especially by the English lads like Tommy Johnson who was brilliant. We hit it off really well.

'There are no cliques. They wouldn't be allowed. As a team you go through too much together and, although there are a lot of strong characters in the dressing-room, it's the family spirit that's important.'

Lennon is now happily assimilated into his new life, dividing his time between the East End, where he works, and the West End, where he lives and socialises. 'I love the West End, it's just brilliant,' he says. 'The people are really friendly. I never get any bother. I hope to put some roots down and stay here for a few years. When I go away I really miss being around the place.' His signing brought to an end one of the most protracted transfer sagas in the history of Scottish football.

'O'Neill and Peter Taylor fell out very badly over the whole Lennon thing,' said Jonathan Northcroft of the *Sunday Times* Scotland. 'There was ridiculous jousting going on. Lennon obviously wanted to come and Taylor was playing silly buggers, saying you need to fax us by five o'clock with an offer, and then moving the goalposts.'

'Taylor was really out of his depth. He tried to play O'Neill to get more money out of him and all he ended up with was an unhappy player and he was then forced to climb down. For O'Neill however the effort was worth it. He knew that Lennon, more than any player, knew instincctively the way he liked the game to be played.'

Iain Campbell added: 'Lennon is not the flashiest of players but his effect on the team is impossible to overstate. He's like having another captain without giving him the armband. He thinks nothing of bossing Paul Lambert and Tom Boyd about. Lennon gets to the point of trouble before the team even realises it's there. He nips so many opposition attacks in the bud. He makes it difficult for the opposition midfielders to play and makes it all look deceptively easy.'

'Martin doesn't like people to make mistakes,' said Billy McNeill, Celtic's most successful captain. 'He feels that if he is secure at the back and in midfield, then something will always happen. There's a caution about the way in which he sets his team out, which means that the one or two goals that you get become very important because they turn a defeat or a draw into a victory.

'Lennon plays that game entirely right for him because he allows people to progress. If the wing-backs are going forward, Lennon sits in the middle and he seems to know exactly the pattern of play. He slows the game down and doesn't give the ball away.'

Lennon would make his debut in Celtic's next league game, a Sunday evening kick-off against Dundee at Dens Park. From first appearances it was not apparent to everyone that this was the final element in a carefully crafted sporting ensemble. 'He looked like a wee barrel,' said Joe O'Rourke, vice-president of the Celtic Supporters Association. 'I remember him running down the tunnel and thinking, look at the haughs on him. He had thighs like giant hams. But in the first 15 minutes he made four outstanding tackles. He played right from the start. There is no doubt that Lennon was one of the telling factors of the season.'

Celtic travelled to Dundee the day after Rangers had defeated Motherwell 2–0 at Ibrox, aware that defeat would peg back their lead at the top of the league table to just four points, compared with the 13-point advantage they had enjoyed just a fortnight before.

The significance of a football match, like the passage of history, is rarely apparent from the present perspective. This most prosaic of games threw up an unlikely moment of history in the making. A scrappy goal at the end of a dour match on a foul night in Dundee hardly possessed the measure of drama on which crucial sporting turning-points are measured. And yet it was the clearest signal to date of a change in the power balance within Scottish football. By the end of the season it would be widely recognised as the goal that won the league.

As the game spilled into injury time there was little to suggest that this game would be the marker of such a paradigm shift. It looked as though Celtic had earned a battling 1–1 draw. On the positive side, they hadn't lost and Lennon had more than shown how valuable he would be. In these circumstances any normal team would have settled for a draw. But this was no normal team. This was a Martin O'Neill team.

10 DECEMBER: DUNDEE 1 CELTIC 2

(Report by authors)

In the closing seconds a Petrov corner was flicked on twice by Mjallby who found Agathe loitering at the back post and the Frenchman glanced in the winner. The goal gifted Celtic the win but, more importantly, it preserved their seven-point lead at the top of the table.

In fairness the result was a travesty for Dundee who, led by the example of Claudio Caniggia, had tested Celtic more thoroughly than any other side that season. If not for the combative qualitities of Lennon, Celtic might even have lost.

The Irishman stamped his authority on the game after Thompson had gifted the ball to Juan Sara. The Dundee striker passed to Caniggia on the edge of the box but his progress was halted abruptly by a biting tackle from Lennon.

A minute later Celtic stormed into the lead following some neat interplay between Agathe, Larsson and Petta. The Dutchman passed down the left flank to Moravcik who hit the byeline and looked up to see Petrov timing a late burst into the box. Moravcik picked him out with the perfect cutback and the Bulgar thrashed his shot into the roof of the net.

Dundee were forced to replace defender Marco de Marchi, who limped, with Chris Coyne. Celtic took advantage before the new formation had time to bed down. Moravcik held the ball up as Petrov ghosted in behind the defence but the midfielder failed to connect with the cross.

But it didn't take long for Dundee to play their way back into the game. Beto Carranza connected with a volley from Javier Artero's cross but he missed the target by inches. Moments later Caniggia provided an angled pass for Carranza, which he switched back towards Sara. The disguised pass caught Valgaeren off balance, but with Sara waiting to end the move, Petrov appeared with a vital intervention.

After 30 minutes Canniggia was released into space by Marrocco. The Argentinian rounded Douglas's dive with graceful simplicity and, with the goal exposed, he shot from a tight angle. His effort was destined for the net until Valgaeren arrived in the nick of time to head clear.

Johnson replaced Moravcik at half-time in an effort to provide a more penetrative threat to Dundee. However, it was Dundee who continued to pose the more potent threat and it took them just ten minutes after the restart to draw level, with a little help from Tom Boyd.

Carranza released man-of-the-match Caniggia who drove forward with a burst of pace that both defied his advancing years and tore Celtic apart. He delivered a cross that was destined for Sara but Celtic captain Boyd tried to intervene and succeeded only in steering a diving header past Douglas.

The nature of the Celtic performance left few fans in any doubt that this was a battling performance worthy of champions.

'The fans were ecstatic that night because it was a game in which we should have been beaten,' said CSA president Gerry Madden. 'They were a far better team and we won. Normally when we are second best, we get trounced.'

'I can remember coming out of the Dundee game and saying to my brother that I thought we had won the league,' said Eddie Toner. 'You just got the feeling that it was a team who were going to fight tooth and nail. We were getting the breaks.'

For Celtic legend Charlie Nicholas, commentating for Sky, the game marked a turning point. 'They got stretched as much that night from Caniggia in particular than they did at any other time of the season,' he said. 'I really did think he pestered the living daylights out of Valgaeren. O'Neill played a clever card again by telling them that they were wonderful and magnificent. They went down the road together, they were in buoyant mood and I think that was the night they said to themselves, "It's definitely going our way." Neil Lennon performed that night as well as any player all season. He just came in and filled the role. He looked as though he had been playing for the team all season. I remember going back to Glasgow that night thinking it's there for the taking if they want it. That's the game that really stands out in my mind because they were really tested as much as at any time in the season.'

O'Neill's performance at Celtic was already attracting international attention when he was ranked tenth in a survey of the world's top managers. However, he was more acutely aware than anyone that he had won nothing. To do so he would have to further strengthen his team and his next foray into the transfer market was to provide unlikely results. But few questioned the manager's judgement.

Part-time fashion model Ramon Vega was tall, athletic and powerfully built – everything O'Neill was looking for in a central defender. The problem was he had earned more acclaim for his fancy footwork on the catwalk than on the football field. He was famously pictured in a powder-blue Vivienne Westwood vest and pants ensemble at a Paris fashion show – a photograph that was to return to haunt him when it fell into the hands of his new team-mates and was hung with pride of place in the Celtic dressing-room.

Booed by his own fans at Spurs, he was desperate to leave White Hart Lane after being sidelined in favour of first-team regulars Sol Campbell, Luke Young and Chris Perry. Few managers were prepared to touch him – until O'Neill came knocking. Vega scored two goals in his debut against Aberdeen and remained in the first team for the rest of the season, rarely putting a foot wrong.

Handsome, charming and erudite, it wasn't long before he became a firm favourite with the fans, who dubbed him the David Ginola of Scottish football. The Spanish-born Swiss international – who speaks five languages – soon became an established fixture in Glasgow's café society along with his stunning fiancée Lucia.

'You almost felt O'Neill was getting to the point where he wanted to prove he could do anything, because Vega was so ridiculed at Tottenham,' said Northcroft. 'It's part of the O'Neill psychology that he likes a challenge, he likes trying to do things that people don't think are possible and there might have been an element of that in the signing of Vega.'

16 DECEMBER: CELTIC 6 ABERDEEN 0
(Report by authors)

Ramon Vega may have grabbed two in his début but anything he could do Henrik could do better – he notched a hat trick. This was a game that showed that Celtic were well and truly over their recent dip and back to their swashbuckling best. Aberdeen, so long the whipping boys for the Glasgow side, were again the hapless victims.

However, the biggest cheer of the day was reserved for Morten Wieghorst who returned to Celtic Park for the first time following his brain illness. Morten visited his team-mates in the Celtic dressing-room before taking his seat in the stand to the deafening cheers of 60,017 fans.

And it didn't take long for his friends to start entertaining him as they scored the first of their six goals after just four minutes. Thompson sent Petta on a run down the left with an inch-perfect pass and, when the winger reached the by-line, he cut the ball inside for Larsson to poke the ball past keeper Ryan Esson.

Weak defending was responsible for Celtic's second, this time scored by debutant Vega. The Pittodrie backline were caught static as Mjallby powered a long-range free kick into the box. The ball bypassed every red shirt but landed comfortably for Vega at the back post to volley it into the net.

Aberdeen were at sixes and sevens and Johnson – standing in for suspended Sutton – should have killed the game when he was played into space inside the box by Larsson. He unleashed a drive before defender Solberg could recover but frustratedly watched his effort shave the bar. Vega's positive contribution and willingness to press forward almost earned him a second goal in the 36th minute but his backward header flew wide.

The visitors managed to create only one significant opening in the first half when Robbie Winters provided a cross from the right which Cato Guntveit brought down and played McAllister into the box. However, the youngster's effort was high and did little to trouble keeper Douglas.

Celtic almost scored again four minutes into the restart when Petta found Johnson in acres of space, but the Geordie couldn't make his header count. Petta was replaced by McNamara and Aberdeen put striker Alex di Rocco on for McAllister. But, as ever, it was Larsson who was to provide the telling contribution of the afternoon with a deadly double strike.

The first came after 76 minutes when Agathe released Thompson. He played in Larsson with a precision pass, and with only the keeper to beat he rolled a cool finish into the net. Two minutes later he notched his third. Thompson linked with McNamara before sweeping the ball to the back post where Larsson was waiting to unleash a powerful half-volley into the top corner. Not to be outdone, Vega grabbed his second, heading home a poorly defended Thompson cross.

Sensing humiliation, Aberdeen replaced Winters with Rachid Belabed in an effort to limit the damage but their misery was completed in the 81st minute when Celtic youngster Jamie Smith, who had replaced Agathe, scored their sixth from a tight angle after a quick free kick by Lennon.

Encouraged by their last two results, O'Neill was now confident that his

RIGHT: Chris Sutton goes wild after his first-minute goal opened the floodgates in Celtic's 6–2 demolition of Rangers back in August

BELOW: Henrik Larsson chips his sensational first goal in the same game

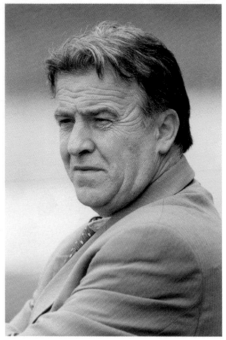

ABOVE: Martin O'Neill
and John Robertson
conduct matters from
the dug-out during the
6–2 win over Rangers

RIGHT: Celtic's assistant
manager John
Robertson

TOP: Alan Thompson blasts past Stefan Klos to give Celtic a 1–0 win over Rangers in February, Celtic's second Old Firm victory in five days

ABOVE: Celtic fans in full voice during the match

ABOVE: The Celtic team celebrate winning the CIS League Cup after beating Kilmarnock 3–0 at Hampden in March

RIGHT: Henrik Larsson lifts the the CIS League Cup after scoring a hat trick to win the match

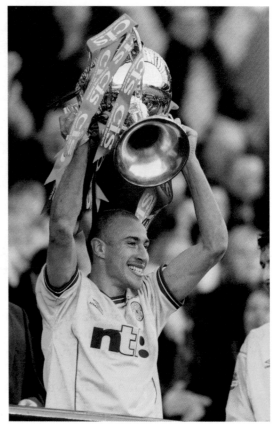

TOP: Larsson chips Stefan Klos as Bert Konterman looks on helplessly in the 3–1 CIS Cup semi-final victory at Hampden

ABOVE: Henrik Larsson rounds Stefan Klos and lines up his 50th goal of the season during Celtic's 3–0 mauling of Rangers at Ibrox on 29 April

ABOVE: Martin O'Neill celebrates Neil Lennon's first goal for Celtic in the 3–0 win over Dunfermline at East End Park

RIGHT: Captain Tommy Boyd lifts the SPL trophy after Celtic beat Hearts 1–0 in April. The title had been clinched 2 weeks earlier after a 1–0 win over St Mirren at Celtic Park

ABOVE: Tommy Boyd and Paul Lambert seal the treble with a kiss as they lift the Scottish Cup after beating Hibs 3–0 at Hampden on 26 May

RIGHT: Super Swede Johan Mjallby lifts the SPL trophy

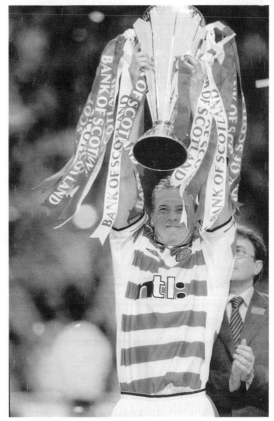

Slovak Lubo Moravcik lifts the SPL trophy

Scotland's Player of the Year for a second time, Henrik Larsson, notched up an incredible 53 goals for the Hoops during the treble-winning campaign

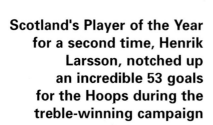

team had negotiated their sticky patch and were back to winning ways. The winter shut-down provided a tangible target and he set his players the challenge of securing maximum points in their remaining three fixtures.

Across the city Advocaat was setting his players a similar target. At an Ibrox shareholders' meeting – which coincided with chairman David Murray's 12-year anniversary – the management team prepared for angry questions over the team's performance: 12 points behind league leaders and bitter rivals Celtic, and again knocked out of Europe twice before Christmas.

At Celtic Park there was relief for the second time in as many months that a player had overcome a major illness. News came through that Alan Stubbs had again beaten cancer. It had been a deeply troubling time for the popular centre-half who was given the all-clear by experts after undergoing an intensive course of chemotherapy. He was told that he would have to undergo one more course of the drug treatment at the Beatson Oncology Unit at Glasgow's Western Infirmary, but that would rid him of the disease for good. He was finally out of the woods and he could, at last, look forward to resuming his life and his playing career.

The players celebrated at their traditional Christmas party by dressing up as their favourite cartoon characters. Tom Boyd turned up as Peter Pan's Captain Hook in a long curly wig, giant black moustache and buckled shoes, Jonathan Gould came as Barney Rubble and defender Jackie McNamara was Postman Pat. It was bit of light relief from the serious business of trying to win the league, enjoyed by the players who knew they had to take advantage of their relaxing breaks when they could.

Paul Lambert, meanwhile, was giving a revealing insight into the motivational methods used by the seemingly mild-mannered O'Neill. He claimed the manager had transformed Celtic into runaway SPL leaders by scaring his players stiff. 'If you don't play well you don't stay in the team,' he told the *Daily Record*. 'He doesn't suffer fools and that's the way it has to be. You have to have the respect of the players and if you ask anybody in that dressing-room they'll tell you they respect him. You go out there with a fear in you because you know if you're not playing well all the time somebody else will come in. He doesn't mess about and everyone knows that. He is a passionate guy and there is also the fear of knowing you're likely to get a going over from him if you let him down. Thankfully, though, apart from one game, everything has gone really well and he's been great with us.'

St Mirren beckoned next. After this match Martin O'Neill was asked for his usual prediction about the destination of the league title. He told reporters he might be tempted to offer a response with one game to go. This result was further confirmation that his side had recovered from the psychological damage inflicted by the Rangers result and it was back to business as usual.

His brawny team required little effort to neutralise the threat of St Mirren and with Valgaeren, Vega and Mjallby it was evident O'Neill finally had the defence he wanted – tall, powerful, good in the air.

If this game revealed anything it was that Celtic weren't giving the ball away or conceding needless goals the way they did under Barnes and, before him, under Dr Jozef Venglos. O'Neill's side was visibly more solid at the back and it worked harder as a team. When a ball went over one defender's head there was someone behind him to retrieve it. Elsewhere Petta, whose fragile confidence had withered to nothing under Barnes, again showed the metamorphosis he had experienced under O'Neill.

23 DECEMBER: ST MIRREN 0 CELTIC 2
(Report by authors)

As they had done against Celtic earlier in the season St Mirren battled manfully, but they couldn't help but expose the shortcomings that had plunged them to the foot of the SPL. Their midfield duo of Hugh Murray and Ricky Gillies competed fiercely with Lennon, Thompson and Petrov but in attack they had nothing with which to trouble their visitors.

St Mirren started energetically enough, but soon they were running out of breath and ideas and it was Celtic's turn to take over. The gulf in standard between the sides was exposed after only 14 minutes when Agathe broke free of his marker. Assisted by a clever decoy run by Sutton which drew defenders from his path, Agathe was unchallenged as he charged forward into the St Mirren penalty box. He rounded the exposed McCaldon and even had time to check back on to his favoured right foot before delivering a decisive shot on target.

The second half followed the same pattern with St Mirren creating bluster rather than substance. After 15 minutes of frenetic activity, again they fell behind to a sucker punch. Again Sutton, only coming back to full fitness after playing through a toe injury, released Petrov who made for the by-line. The Bulgar's cutback left Henrik Larsson with a simple tap-in for his 27th goal of the season. Larsson, who had a comparatively quiet game, returned the favour moments later with a cute back-pass that allowed Petrov to crack home a drive which was blocked by McCaldon.

St Mirren eventually carved out a meaningful chance close to the end but Jose Quitongo hesitated too long in front of goal and the chance was gone.

Celtic headed north for the final game of 2000 on a high. At the start of the season few could have predicted their astonishing rebirth following the débâcle of the previous season. Larsson had played his best month yet. With barely half the season gone he had already scored an astonishing 28 goals in all competitions. No Celtic player in the past generation had such a phenomenal scoring record. If Larsson continued to score as freely as he had been doing, he was on course to smash Charlie Nicholas's post-war scoring record in the 1981–82 season when he notched 48 goals. But Larsson's prolific performances were not the only factor keeping Celtic in the hunt for the title. Sutton was back to fitness after playing through a niggling injury and the new signings were also proving their worth.

'There was a feeling that if we could keep the gap going into the break then we had a great chance,' said Eddie Toner. 'Rangers were dropping points. If you were to ask any Celtic supporter at the beginning of the season what their aspirations were, pushing Rangers all the way would have been the realistic priority. There was a general acceptance that we would have to give Martin O'Neill two or three seasons to turn it round. Yet here we were riding high at the top of the league and still in both cup competitions. No one wanted to admit it quite yet but there was a growing feeling that we could do something really special this season.'

Nine days earlier bottom-of-the-table Dundee United had held Rangers to a draw. Celtic's performance in this game would provide another important measurement of the gap between themselves and their main rivals.

26 DECEMBER: DUNDEE UNITED 0 CELTIC 4
(Report by authors)

If anyone at Ibrox was hoping for the Taysiders to do them a favour, that notion was dispelled in a devastating 18-minute first-half spell when Celtic stormed into a three-goal lead. Celtic's ruthlessness in front of goal cruelly exposed the weaknesses of a side at their seasonal nadir.

The visitors were assisted by a less-than-convincing penalty award that brought the opening goal. Even Henrik Larsson, innocuously challenged by Hasney Aljofree, seemed surprised when Hugh Dallas pointed to the spot. But the Swede was clearly not going to argue and he stepped up to slot the ball beyond the reach of Alan Combe.

A further two-goal burst provided enough of a cushion for Celtic to rest without the need to move out of third gear for the remainder of the match. Their second goal came after 34 minutes when Petta surged down the right wing before ending in a cross which found Sutton unmarked and in space and the Englishman was able to nonchalantly tap the ball over the line. Sutton's second and Celtic's third was an even simpler affair, coming five minutes before the break.

This time the ball came in from a Lennon free kick on the left and Sutton was able to rise unchallenged to head the ball into the net. Jim Hamilton, who had tracked back into the penalty box as a reinforcement to counter Sutton's aerial threat, was left isolated, rooted to the spot.

United posed no real threat to Celtic and seemed devoid of conviction. Even when Celtic's industry perceptibly dipped in the latter stages it seemed the home side could not summon the resources to mount a serious challenge.

The Glasgow side's dominance was confirmed in the 73rd minute when Agathe attempted a shot on goal. The ball flew into the penalty box and Petrov extended his foot, deflected the ball away from Combe and into the net. Victory secured, O'Neill rested Larsson, Petrov and Petta, replacing them with Moravcik, Smith and Johnson.

United manager Smith also rang the changes, replacing Jamie McQuillan and Danny Griffin with Hugh Davidson and David McCracken but by then it was too late. United were chasing shadows and Celtic were already looking forward to a well-earned winter break.

Celtic would end the year perched loftily at the top of the league, gazing down at their rivals beneath them. It was a giddying experience for the supporters who had had precious little notion of such a position over the past decade. December had proved a crucial month in consolidating that position, not only on the park but also in the transfer market, where O'Neill had to be at his shrewdest.

The month was an important step in the chase for the title but it was also one in which the manager's stature was transformed from mere club employee to legend-in-the-making. In the stands of Tannadice on a briskly cold Boxing Day afternoon there would emerge a refrain that was to be repeated ad infinitum by the Celtic support for the duration of the season. It was, and remains, one of the most lyrically challenged anthems to grace the hallowed crucible of football in Glasgow's East End and yet, in its laconic simplicity, it perfectly articulated the prevailing mood.

The music was, as with many celebrated art forms, highly derivative. In fact it was a straightforward theft of a melody formerly adapted to that other Hoops classic of 1998 vintage 'Cheerio to ten-in-a-row'. That was a lexical epic compared with the 2000 version which contained just two words – and what else could they have been but 'Martin O'Neill'?

The work, in its full unexpurgated version, is as follows:

Martin O'Neill, Martin O'Neill
Martin O'Neill, Martin O'Neill
Martin O'Neill, Martin O'Neill
Martin O'Neill, Martin O'Neill
(Repeat and fade)

Supporter Jason Henderson recalls the poignant moment when he first heard the opening strains of the haunting chorus.

'The singing started close to the corner flag in the Celtic end and slowly spread like the winter thaw,' he said. 'All the way round the Celtic end, then into the stand above the dug-outs occupied by the Celtic support. It was like a scene from the movie *Gladiator* as "Martin O'Neill" echoed around the stadium. It was truly one of those moments where the hairs stood up on the back of your neck. For ten whole minutes there was not a let-up in the singing.

'During this period O'Neill must have realised what was going on and you could see him stop watching the play and pause to listen to the support. Being the cautious guy that he is he was probably checking it was his name. When he was sure that it was he raised his hands and applauded the support.

'And that was not the end of it. After the final whistle the crowd had hardly budged and still his name was being chanted. He made his way to the Celtic end and again saluted us. It was as if he was the matador and, had he stayed any longer, then I've no doubt red roses would have been thrown on to the park as well. Though on this performance it won't be long until he does get roses.'

9.

WINTER SUN

Ramon, Ramon,
Ramon, Ramon,
Ramon, Ramon,
Ramon . . .
(To the tune of: 'Come on Come on')

IT IS HARD to dislike Ramon Vega. For a start he laughs a lot. And he calls you 'man'. 'See you later, man, thanks a lot, man'. A sort of Huggie Bear, '70s thing. He also says 'you know' at the end of every sentence which can be charming when it's one of the few signs you are speaking to a foreigner. In all he's pretty sophisticated for a footballer. When we talk in the summer of 2001 he is right slap-bang in the middle of a bit of mud-slinging with Martin O'Neill. Yet during the whole conversation he describes Celtic, Glasgow and the club's supporters with warmth and affection.

He arrived on a cold Friday in December and after signing was pitched straight on to the team bus to meet his new colleagues. 'It was very strange,' he recalls. 'A new guy is coming in. Everybody really stares at you in a way. I never trained with these guys. I don't know them. It was a very, very weird feeling, in a way quite tense, you know. The tension was there because I needed to perform straight away.

'I went on the bus that was going to take us on to the hotel. It was the first time I had seen the other players. So Gouldy was the first to introduce himself to me and then Tom Boyd came up and introduced me to everybody straightaway. Really that first introduction gave me strength and confidence. The warmth . . . it was quite like a family. It was the same at the dinner after, very close.

'I came from Spurs and it was nothing to do with family. It was just very arrogant, very individualist and a very bad spirit. That is London. A big city where they think they are the best in the world. That's why I loved it in Glasgow. They are very nice people.

'I was four years at Spurs. You had all this nervous thing with all the players. Then suddenly I'm off up to Glasgow. Celtic, new players, you know. It was quite like the first day in the school, you know, after the holidays. That kind of feeling. It was a nice feeling because they made me straight away welcome.'

Ramon, pronounced 'Raymon' by the commentators to give it a Glasgow feel, was under such pressure to prove himself after his miserable time at Spurs that he had hyped himself up massively for his first game against Aberdeen and scored two goals – not bad for a defender. However, he quickly learned the Martin O'Neill style of straightforward management. 'He puts some points to you during the game. "You see this, Ramon. You should have done it better." That sort of thing. You know. He's just going straight to the point. Not talking around it. He would say, "Ramon, you should have put the ball that way or you should have defended this way." That's a good thing about him, he is not going around and around.

'John Robertson and Steve Walford, those guys, they try to make the spirit in the team. In the dressing-room, all that kind of thing. I think it is one of the most important things in management. The manager is important. A top figure. Respectable and everything, a man who says during the game what he thinks of the game. But I think when it comes to the work on the football pitch Robertson and Walford are the main figures. They were the guys you dealt with, for the five-a-sides, with the yellow jersey for worst player, all that stuff. They joked about too. It was good. It worked.

'There was a great team spirit. There was also jokers in the dressing-room. Chris Sutton mainly. He had a dark, very, very dark English humour. Always doing things like putting toothpaste in your jeans pockets. Most of the jokes they played on me because I was obviously new. The first thing was the Vivienne Westwood outfit. They cut the pictures out. It was a nice welcome in the first couple of days, that. Of course I had shampoo in the jeans pocket too. You always knew it was only Chris Sutton that would do that.'

O'Neill jokes with the team too but in a different way. He subtly keeps his distance. One player remembers: 'He would meet you in the corridor and joke about with you and have a great time. Like real friends. The next day you might see him again and he would just say "Hi" and hurry by. It is a great tactic because it keeps you warm but also keeps you on your toes. There is that little bit of distance as though you don't really know the man. It's important for respect too.'

Tom Boyd was the club's social covener as well as captain, organising nights out and golf tournaments and such like. But Lennon, Johnson and Sutton were also great fun-time organisers. Vega joined in on team nights out but said the pressure to succeed on the park was so intense he tried to minimise nights out. 'I was so busy it was quite an intense time for myself. I wanted to concentrate so much on the football because it was quite an important time for my career. I had a flat in London. I was up and down. I was out there a couple of times with the lads. It was very good. Rangers fans were, of course, very upset. Sometimes they said things. Sometimes they were very positive. Rangers fans are very positive people. They said "You deserved to win" or "You deserved the league", or "You guys played well".

'I would have loved to stay up there. I really enjoyed Glasgow and the West End. It was beautiful . . . and the team with Champions League football and everything next year. It would have been great. I had to move on for the security. Once you are finished with football it is finished. I couldn't risk it. I was only offered a one-year contract at Celtic. If I got injured at my age who knows what would have happened to me?'

January was winter shutdown month and the team were going to Florida for a welcome break – but before they left there was one league game to get out of the way. The first of January was traditionally the day the Ne'er Day Old Firm clash took place. Because of the tensions in previous years the schedule had been rearranged and now Celtic would play Kilmarnock on the second of January at home. Kilmarnock had been, at times, a difficult fixture for Celtic to deal with. The Ayrshire club were tough and they could play when they wanted to. But it was Larsson's day as he took his goal tally for Celtic to over 100. It was an extraordinary feat for any player but when they came from a player whose career had appeared to be all but over the season before, it was stunning.

2 JANUARY: CELTIC 6 KILMARNOCK 0
(Report by Ken Gallacher: *The Herald*)
The near 60,000 crowd at Parkhead rose to acclaim Henrik Larsson as he left the field at the end of a magnificent performance yesterday. When he completed his hat trick in the 72nd minute his total for the club reached

the magical 100 mark and he added to that before the end of the game.
It was a virtuoso display from the man who was sitting on the sidelines at
the end of last year worrying over his football future. Thirty-two goals
already this season have answered any lingering doubts surrounding the
striker.

The manner in which he took his goals yesterday emphasised his
world-class talents as a finisher. And with Chris Sutton adding two more,
poor Kilmarnock were simply swept aside.

Celtic simply powered their way into the Premier League's winter
break with this stunning victory, which emphasised the gulf between the
league leaders and the team sitting in fourth place. It also underlined that
O'Neill has kept his players focused on football as the seemingly
inevitable boardroom troubles have surfaced at the club yet again. These
arguments most assuredly did not spill over on to the field of play.

Now the Parkhead team can head off to a sunshine break in Florida
knowing that their massive lead over both Hibs and Rangers remains
intact. The two closest challengers have been left struggling in Celtic's
wake as the Glasgow side move closer and closer to the title that they and
their supporters want so desperately.

Yesterday, Kilmarnock offered resistance for 38 minutes and until then,
when Sutton scored their opening goal, the team from Ayrshire had
looked competent enough as Celtic attempted to break down what looked
to be a well-organised defence.

In the second half things changed dramatically. Larsson stepped in
with his four goals and Sutton added his own second, leaving Kilmarnock
looking both disorganised and dispirited. They were just unable to cope
with the surging attacks which Celtic put together after half-time.

Even when O'Neill changed his team around – Alan Thompson
replaced Bobby Petta and then Lubomir Moravcik and Jamie Smith took
over from Stilian Petrov and Jackie McNamara – they did not just simply
relax. Instead, they looked for more goals and still Killie, who made
changes of their own, could not find a way to match them.

Ten minutes from the end Ally McCoist came on to take over from Craig
Dargo to some good-natured barracking from the Parkhead fans in the
59,380 crowd. At the same time, Chris Innes and Mark Reilly appeared as
Freddy Dindeleux and Paul Wright went off.

However, no amount of changes by Kilmarnock's Bobby Williamson
could stem the tide of attacks which moved relentlessly towards his
team's goal. For the early part of the game they looked as if they could
cope and then Gary Hay allowed Sutton to come in behind him and slide

a low shot into goal and Killie were behind; when Larsson took over in that second half, Kilmarnock were doomed.

In 53 minutes, Petrov went down in the penalty box and the Celtic support appealed for a penalty. Referee David Sommers waved play on and Larsson took advantage of the match official's decision to follow up and ram a shot into goal.

In 62 minutes Sutton struck again when he moved on to a long ball out of the Celtic half and into the Killie penalty box. The striker reached it and turned an angled shot beyond Marshall into the net.

In 70 minutes a cross from Petrov on the right found Larsson who scored again then, in 72 minutes, it was Larsson from Alan Thompson to complete his hat trick.

Finally, in 86 minutes, the Swede forced his way through two tackles in the penalty box, took the ball past Marshall and tapped it into the empty net.

Poor Kilmarnock could look back on a header from Jamie McGowne from an Andy McLaren corner which landed on the roof of the net before the main demolition began in the second half.

But, again, few teams would be able to live with Celtic when they are so gloriously on song.

Afterwards Larsson admitted: 'I did know before the game that I was just three goals away from getting 100 for the club but I did not think about this too much. But it was great to get the hat trick and realise I had reached that mark. It is very important to me. But, also, it is even more important that the team are winning and playing as well as we did in the second half today.

'Before then it was a difficult game for us but Chris Sutton scored and that gave us the breakthrough we needed. It is maybe a pity that we now have to go into a winter break but what we must do is make sure that when we return we pick up where we have left off.'

O'Neill insisted: 'You can get players who did not cost a lot of money who can come through as Henrik has done. He was terrific today.

'There is better to come from him and I can hardly wait to see it. You know, I did not expect to see the game going that way. We needed that opening goal just to alleviate any nerves which were hanging around.'

Kilmarnock's manager Bobby Williamson admitted: 'That was really embarrassing for me. It was the worst experience I have known in football from the time I started in the game. I think some of the lads in the dressing-room will tell you the same.'

January was also a time for reflection and talk of how Celtic were on their way to a league trophy. It was a prediction that the *Daily Record*'s Jim Traynor could honestly claim he was among the first to make. Traynor, a physical, no-nonsense player in his youth, is similarly uncompromising in his journalism. So when he announced on Radio Clyde's Saturday afternoon football show that he was changing his prediction only weeks into the season he had to be tough to take the incoming flak.

'It would be October, around about October,' he remembers. 'There was Hugh Keevins, Davie Provan and Derek Johnstone and myself. They all stuck with Rangers and asked, Davie in particular, how anyone could change their view this early in the season. You can't just be stubborn and say I chose one team at the start and I'm going to stick with them. Martin O'Neill just seemed to be some sort of magical catalyst.

'I had said at the start of the season that Rangers would win the title. But after only a handful of matches I thought it was clear Celtic were a better side. They had found something under O'Neill. They were much more confident and you could see that players who the season before you felt were not very good were actually looking as though they were real players.

'There was a fluency, a confidence and – the most obvious thing – there was a determination about them, a steeliness. Rangers didn't start too badly. Remember their Champions League stuff. They beat Sturm Graz and won in Monaco. Although I thought they were lucky to win there. You thought, "They're looking okay." But in the league there was always something fragile about them and it all fell apart very quickly from then to the turn of the year.'

In Scotland, and in Glasgow in particular, outing sports commentators is almost the second national sport. Pundits' words are pored over in minute detail by fans on both sides of the Old Firm divide to detect some hint of bias, something that will unmask them as supporters of the 'other' side. It's partly paranoia and partly a genuine puzzlement that people who spend their lives with football, make a living from it, have not been seduced by one team or another. In a city as charged with football emotion as Glasgow, many fans are also looking for that slip which will reveal a commentator has secretly and subtly being putting the knife into their side.

When Jim Traynor switched predictions he got a backlash. 'Oh aye, I got all of that. They'll come up and they'll say, "We just knew you were a Tim, changing your mind. You were just waiting for them to show a wee sign then you would show your true colours and you have done that." It's the same the other way as well. You get daft Celtic supporters shouting: "Ah, you see, see, you are one of us after all." I did get a bit of stick from Rangers supporters but then I don't think I'm unique in that. I thought it was stupid to stay on one team when I clearly felt they were going to win the title.'

Traynor has no doubt that O'Neill was the deciding factor in Celtic's initial turn-around. 'Martin O'Neill seemed to instil great confidence in them, bearing in mind they never really got a challenge although Rangers cuffed them at Ibrox. It was largely the same players. Of course Sutton and Larsson turned out to be a great partnership. Even Larsson on his own when Sutton was injured at the end of the season scored great goals.'

Although he was impressed by Henrik Larsson, Jim Traynor reserves particular praise for Lubo Moravcik. Moravcik, a little Slovak wizard, as one journalist called him, had been brought to Celtic Park from France by Dr Jo Venglos. He was written off as an over-the-hill dud by the tabloid press before he had even kicked a ball. Then he played up front in the 5–1 Old Firm game at Parkhead and proceeded to demolish Rangers in a fashion that had not been seen around London Road for years. Closer inspection of his track record quickly followed and, lo and behold, it turned out he had had an impeccable career including 70 caps for his national side.

Tabloid headlines are often clever and amusing. Scotland's defeat by Egypt some years ago had prompted a *Sun* headline 'Scotland humped by the Camel Corps', and the *Sun* had called it right with their 'Supercaley' headline the day after John Barnes' team met their downfall. But it wasn't all glory when it came to Celtic. Wim Jansen had arrived from managing a team in Japan with the headline 'Worst Thing To Hit Hiroshima Since The Bomb' hanging around his neck. In his case too there had been some rapid readjustment as he went on to win the league and stop Rangers beating Celtic's nine-in-a-row record.

But that was all in the past and Lubo had been unquestionably a brilliant performer since his arrival. Now, at 35, he had matured like a vintage wine. Already in Martin O'Neill's season he had scored a stunning goal against Bordeaux and scored an even better one against St Johnstone with a left-foot curler straight from a corner three days later. There was more to come.

'For me he is the complete player,' added Traynor. 'I know Larsson is the most valuable player on Celtic's books, but Moravcik has got everything. He does drift out of games, certainly. But lots of quality players do. If you look at Rivaldo you see him playing a lot and you think he's not making a contribution. But when he plays, he plays. Just look at his contribution when he scored a hat trick in Barcelona's final league game of the season. It won them a Champions League place. I think Moravcik has got vision, he's got skill, he's got touch. He has got everything. I think he is a genius of a football player. He is one of the best players we've ever seen here. It's just a pity he has come late in his career. He is marvellous to watch.'

But individual talent aside, it all comes back to Martin O'Neill. Traynor concedes: 'I think he is a very cunning man, not just with his players and supporters, but also with the media. I think sometimes he can be a bit patronising. He will say in press conferences, "That's a very good question." You know when he says that he's not going to answer it.

'As a manager I think he has that great ability that he can go in and convince an ordinary player that he is good, a good player that he is great and a great player that he is a genius. He is one of these managers that people want to play for. The stark contrast is Dick Advocaat because there were players there who were not happy with Dick Advocaat. I know that when you're not winning and you're not in the team, you tend to dislike your manager. But I think Martin O'Neill is probably one of these guys who can just keep most people quite happy. Berkovic would suggest otherwise but I think Berkovic is a waste of space anyway. I think O'Neill just reads people better than most managers. All the great managers will tell you anyway that probably 70 per cent of their job is man management. You get that right and you're not far wrong. People will want to play for you. The contrast in mood between that place and the season before with John Barnes and Kenny Dalglish on his own is just, it's just stunning. It is night and day. People do just want to do things for Martin O'Neill.'

'How far will he go?' Traynor muses. 'As far as Old Trafford, probably,' he laughs, raising the one issue which has been a bone of contention between the Celtic manager and the press all season. 'For all his indignation Martin O'Neill has never answered that question properly. He says, "I'm so happy here, Celtic are wonderful," all that stuff. All he has to say is: "I'm not interested in going to Old Trafford." He has never said that. Of course, who is going to turn down Manchester United? Then again he might, because you don't want to follow Alex Ferguson. You can't emulate him. You want to go one after him. But if they come and say:

"Here's your budget. Alex Ferguson is not going to be part of this," it would be very difficult to refuse because Manchester United is the biggest club in the world. I think Martin O'Neill, though, is an honourable man. He was always getting offered jobs down south and he always honoured his contract. Of course, if he honoured his contract at Celtic that would give him two more years and that would be perfect timing because it would give somebody a year to fail after Alex Ferguson.

'Of course,' Traynor laughs, 'if by chance the Old Firm end up in the Premiership, and they have one of the largest supports in Britain, then Martin O'Neill won't be going anywhere.'

The *Record* journalist, like almost every other Scots commentator on the game, comes back to the bond between the players.

'I only know that the camaraderie that was at Ibrox the year before is now down at Celtic Park. When a team is winning everybody is happy and everybody is pals. I don't think they would fight with Martin O'Neill anyway. The Rangers nine-in-a-row mob, McCoist, Gough, Durrant, McCall and so on, all did go out quite a lot. All this sort of bonding. That was a lot of crap. They were just out getting bevvied like guys in ordinary jobs do. There was nothing wrong with that. The guys were fit enough to play and they were winning everything. You can gain from that because if you're in a game and you're losing and it's wet and it's muddy and you're cold and things are not going for you that's when that camaraderie kicks in. In that nine-in-a-row season Rangers won a couple of titles that you thought "They don't really deserve it." Plus the manager Walter Smith was part of it. They were all big mates. Martin O'Neill's got a bit of that, though he's not really as close to his players as Smith was.

'It's hard to do that sort of thing now. That nine-in-a-row mob were there too long. They were tired. That's why they didn't get ten. They were clapped out. It doesn't happen now in football because the turnover is rapid. I think O'Neill can be very hard and quite cold about it all when he needs to be. I don't think he is a ranter and a raver but he has got this ability to connect with people.'

Traynor's encounters with irate Rangers fans are proof, if proof were needed, of the passion for football in Glasgow. A quick glance at how Old Firm fans coped without their daily fix during the shutdown should dispel all arguments of the hunger for the Old Firm. On 18 January a charity match between Old Firm greats took place at Ibrox. The Auld Old Firm game attracted an attendance of more than 50,000, the second biggest gate of the weekend in Britain. Rangers won but the circumstances didn't prevent arguments raging for days over their squad being about 20 years younger than Celtic's.

The young Old Firm had cleared off for some peace. Celtic and Rangers took advantage of the winter break to head for Florida and the sun. While there Celtic trained at Disney's Wide World of Sports complex, a beautifully manicured sports city fitted out with a full-size baseball stadium and immaculate football pitches.

Celtic were to play two fairly meaningless friendlies. The first was against the University of South Florida. The American students went down 5–1 in what was just a stroll in the sun. But the game was significant because it marked the comeback of Paul Lambert who had been out for two months with an ankle injury. The next match was with Tampa Bay Mutiny. It gave O'Neill the chance to roll a seemingly never-ending succession of substitutes on and off the pitch in another training game which ended in a 2–2 draw. Not that anyone would have known the relative unimportance of the match. More than 3,000 supporters travelled from all across the United States to watch the fixture and take part in a fans' evening at Orlando's TGI Friday and an association evening at the new Marriot Hotel in downtown Orlando.

The high turnout impressed O'Neill yet again. And he was reminded of the depth of feeling Celtic supporters have for the club wherever they are. Henrik Larsson was prompted to tell the *Daily Record*: 'It really is a special kind of feeling when you're thousands of miles from home but surrounded by your own fans. It gives you a funny feeling inside and makes you really proud to be wearing the green hoops.'

The Marriot was the scene for two memorable incidents involving Martin O'Neill. They shine a little more light on his magpie mind with its thirst for all sorts of otherwise unusual information. It's well known that O'Neill is fascinated by crime, that he has queued to get into the public gallery at murder trials, but it's less well known that he is fascinated by ghosts and American football too.

Both incidents took place at a dinner organised by John Howley, the president of Orlando Celtic Supporters Clubs. It was attended by members of North America's 66 Celtic supporters' associations. They are to be found together every year in Las Vegas (unusually the most recent convention was in Bramalea in Canada) attended by members of the Lisbon Lions and players from the first team. The stories that filter back across the Atlantic, via the internet, usually leave those not fortunate enough to attend green with envy. Members still talk about the $65,000 bar bill that was run up during a convention a couple of years ago.

During the dinner John Paton, secretary of the South Florida Celtic Supporters Club, was sitting at Martin O'Neill's table. He remembers: 'The conversation took a funny turn. Somebody asked why Celtic weren't playing their match with the Tampa Bay Rowdies in the Tampa Stadium. He was told that it was because the Superbowl was being held there the next week. Then someone asked Martin O'Neill if he liked American football and, of course, he's a big fan. The next thing we were all talking about betting for the Superbowl and the conversation moved on to players. Martin was asked what team he liked in the States and he said the Buffalo Bills. Then Jacky Meehan of the St Catherine's CSC, which is up there, asked who his favourite player was and Martin said Steve Christie (the team's place-kicker).

'Jackie turned towards him and said, "You're not going to believe this, but I know Steve Christie and he's a Celtic supporter and a member of our association. He comes to watch a lot of games with us and he even trains wearing a Celtic shirt." Martin couldn't believe it. Jackie then told him, "Steve Christie has been to Parkhead to see Celtic play on a number of occasions." I tell you, Martin was amazed. He insisted that Jackie tell Steve Christie to go and see him the next time he was in Glasgow.'

Christie, who was born and brought up in North America, is an American football legend, having played in two Superbowls. He has Irish roots and played football in the States as a youngster before moving into a professional career with the oval ball.

He and O'Neill did meet in Glasgow, at the second Old Firm game of the season at Celtic Park. The manager invited him into his office to share a pot of tea. 'For years, I'd seen him kicking for the Buffalo Bills and never thought for a second that he would even have heard of Celtic,' O'Neill recalls. 'And yet here he was, telling me that this was something like his tenth visit to Celtic Park and presenting me with a signed shirt!

'I told Steve that, even before I met him, one of my ambitions had always been to watch Buffalo play in the middle of their winter at about minus 15 degrees. However, although he made it clear that I'd be more than welcome to visit him, I might have to put that one on hold considering that it would be taking place at a time when I would probably get the sack if I left Glasgow!'

Christie said an Old Firm match was very similar to the Superbowl: 'Both times I played in the Superbowl, I found it all hard to take in – after all, you're being watched by something like one billion viewers. The Old

Firm match is similar in that it is the match that the whole season revolves around. But here you have the situation where you have to go to work with fans of the opposing side the day after and that gives it an edge. There's a lot more on the line with the Old Firm and that shows in the atmosphere in the stadium.

'In the NFL, there's nothing like it – the only thing which could hope to ever compare is the New York Giants v the New York Jets . . . but they're not even in the same division. At Buffalo, our main rivals are the Miami Dolphins, and they're in Florida, for goodness sake.'

The second story relates to the same evening. The Florida Celtic Supporters had invited thriller writer Campbell Armstrong over to the States from Ireland to give a talk to the players and delegates. Armstrong, who is originally Scottish, has made his name with a succession of gritty plots but his first big break came when he was asked to write the books for two of the Indiana Jones movies. After he had given his speech he and O'Neill had a long conversation and it emerged that the Celtic manager is also a keen fan of ghost stories and ghosts. Armstrong lives in a haunted castle in Ireland and one evesdropper recalls O'Neill virtually inviting himself over to see it because he was so interested in the author's tales of his spooks.

On the team's return to Britain there was more good news. Morten Wieghorst, now on the way to a full recovery after his brush with death, resumed training. He told the *Daily Record* that nothing was sacrosanct where football players were concerned – even the slight limp he sustained as a result of his illness.

'I have missed the simple day-to-day involvement of being with Celtic. You miss the banter and even the mickey-taking. The day the players slagged me off about the way I was walking was below the belt but at least I knew I was back.

'I've been told in no uncertain terms to get back playing and the jokes are flying. It's much nicer than the environment I was in when I felt chained to a hospital bed. I'm part of the squad again and even at training I could lie down on the grass and do my keepie-uppie tricks.'

Through hellish weather 2,000 Celtic fans headed south for the Scottish Cup tie with Stranraer at Stair Park. Piece of cake? Well, there was the small matter of Inverness Caledonian Thistle lurking in the background. Never one to turn away from the scent of blood Sky television had spent £100,000 getting their cameras and crews into the tiny ground just in case there was an upset.

28 JANUARY: STRANRAER 1 CELTIC 4

(Report by Iain Campbell: *Daily Mirror*)

Martin O'Neill should have known that nothing would go seriously wrong when he was so close to home.

The Celtic manager was closer to his Northern Ireland home than he was to Glasgow as he watched his side cruise into the fourth round of the Scottish Cup at Stranraer last night.

O'Neill may have been tempted to board a ferry home along with hundreds of travelling Celtic fans after a result which never came close to providing him with his worst nightmare.

The Irishman spoke before the match of the possibility of seeing his side slide out of two cup tournaments in the space of ten days, but his paranoia never came close to being realised on a chilly night at Stair Park.

Goals from Joos Valgaeren, Jackie McNamara and the unfortunate Stranraer defender Keith Knox ensured that the tournament favourites retained the Treble hopes that O'Neill is so keen to play down.

The tiny Division Two ground was full to bursting point with the locals hoping for, though not expecting, another Caley Thistle-style upset.

But although Billy McLaren's side bravely took the game to Celtic as often as they could, the result was never in doubt – particularly after Belgian Valgaeren had given his side the lead after 25 minutes.

A soft and uneven pitch – and Stranraer's determination to stick to their task – ensured that the Celts had to earn their fourth-round place, but it wasn't the toughest test they could have faced after their winter break soaking up the sun in Florida.

Those not lucky enough to get hold of one of the 6,000 tickets were still able to watch Henrik Larsson come close to giving his side the lead in just 90 seconds.

Ramon Vega, who featured strongly in the opening stages, swung over a telling cross and the Swede's first-time shot was smartly saved by keeper Mark McGeown.

Vega almost completed the job from the resulting corner but his snap shot looked like a defender's effort, clearing the bar by several feet.

The difficult pitch ensured that Celtic weren't able to totally dominate from the start and there were a couple of scares for them before they fully took control.

Keeper Robert Douglas was slack with a clearance and hit the ball off the in-rushing Paul Walker, though the little striker wasn't quite able to capitalise on the error.

Celtic had what appeared to be a decent penalty claim when Sandy Hodge brought Bobby Petta crashing down after seven minutes.

And hope began to rise among the home fans when Billy MacDonald sent Walker racing towards goal, but with Joos Valgaeren and Vega racing back to reduce his options, his shot only required a straightforward save from Douglas.

That was really Stranraer's only chance of causing an upset because the defenders combined to put Celtic ahead around midway through the first half.

Neil Lennon's free kick found Vega who headed the ball back across goal for Valgaeren to head in, somewhat painfully, at the far post.

A collision with a despairing home defender left the Belgian with a sore head, but another goal to his growing collection.

The goal had the immediate affect of depressing the home side and virtually assuring the visitors of victory with the result that the game was in danger of dying on its feet as half-time came and went.

But before millions of Sky viewers succumbed to the temptation of switching off, Jackie McNamara came to the rescue with the goal of the match six minutes into the second half.

Chris Sutton and Larsson combined in typical fashion to set up a chance for the wing-back on the edge of the area.

The Scotland international looked up and hit a clinical drive past the helpless McGeown into the net.

That goal, scored while the unfortunate Knox was off the park receiving treatment for a nasty head knock, really finished off the contest.

There was worse for Knox, who had returned with a heavily bandaged head, when he played the ball past his own keeper five minutes later following a cross from Bobby Petta.

It was by then a case of Celtic playing out time, but an uncharacteristic error by midfielder Alan Thompson allowed the home side to cheer their fans by grabbing a consolation goal.

Thompson lost possession to Paul Blair who switched the ball into striker Ian Harty who finished with some style from a tight angle with Douglas unable to save.

That upset the Celts, Douglas in particular, and they stepped up a gear to re-establish their three-goal advantage.

McGeown should have stopped Lubo Moravcik's less-than-ferocious drive, but he allowed the ball to squirm under his body and over the line – he will have cursed the cameras for being there.

The announcer credited the goal to Moravcik much to the delight of the

Celtic fans in the main stand who proceeded to chant his mispronounced name from then to the end of the match.

In the end, though, everyone was happy.

Banana skins aside, league football was beckoning and Celtic should have been cruising with their dozen-point gap over Rangers.

Chris Sutton was trying to keep a lid on things: 'Whatever happens now we have done better than last season so in that respect we are improving but we know it's a tough situation we are in. We are not nervous but no one wants to blow it from this position. We have a good lead but we can't be complacent. If Rangers go and win the last 14 games or Hibs go on a roll then it will be very, very tough for us to win it. We have two vital away games against St Johnstone and Hearts as soon as we go back, followed by massive games against Rangers and Hibs at home. Winning all four would be a dream but the players are disappointed the break came when it did as we were on a roll.

'There's a good spirit in the camp but we have to stay focused. We feel at times that some of the Celtic fans think it is all over when it certainly isn't.'

How right he was. Within a few days the gap between the two sides would have been cut dramatically.

10.

DOUBLE GLORY

We shall not, we shall not be moved,
We shall not, we shall not be moved.
Not by the Hearts, the Hibs or the Rangers,
We shall not be moved.

BILLY MCNEILL has staffing problems. One of his barmaids is off sick and there's no one to cover the evening shift. It's already midday and he's due to knock-off at five p.m., so the race is on. He phones one of his part-time barmen in a mood of hope rather than expectation but he can't make it – he's got a date that night.

'Does your mother know you're winching?' McNeill asks.

The situation demands a joke but he's going through the motions. As the phone goes down he sighs with an expression that implies running a pub is not as simple as it looks. Today he is drafting the staff rota for his bar, McNeill's, a shrine to Celtic Football Club which sits nestled in a side street in Glasgow's residential south side. There was a time when he had less mundane staffing issues to address as he set about marshalling some of the most gifted football players on the planet.

Back in 1969 McNeill was captaining the team to their second Treble in three years. For many football observers, the side which swept the domestic board and reached the European Cup semi-final in that year were even better than the Lisbon Lions. They produced more unbeatable performances and played with greater zest and vigour. They had a more mature professionalism than the all-conquering team of 1967. Just as dominant, they had flair and speed, and were able to dictate the pace and direction of every game.

But for a split second of lost concentration against AC Milan at Celtic

Park, they would, arguably, also have lifted the European Cup that season. The Italians, whom Celtic had matched and at times outplayed over their two-leg tie, went on to win the trophy, thumping Dutch side Feyenoord in the final.

'The attitude of the AC Milan manager that season was that the winners of the European Cup would be either his team or Celtic,' said McNeill. 'That was before the tie against us and obviously he was right because they went on to win it. That was a measure of the respect we had in Europe at the time.'

As the present Celtic players returned from their winter break speculation among the supporters had become more ambitious. There was a general agreement that this was a side who could win the league. The question now on everyone's lips was could they go further? Could they lift the Treble? Comparisons inevitably surfaced with the last Celtic side to achieve that momentous feat. The team of 1969. The European dimension aside, there are similarities between then and now in how both teams developed and matured. Crucially, there were also parallels in the way the seasons had developed.

In September 1968 Celtic suffered an early setback to Rangers, losing 4–2 in the first Old Firm match of the season. It was the Ibrox side's first win at Celtic Park in four years and it was to herald a false dawn in the south side of the city – a belief that Rangers were again the dominant force in Scottish football. Like the 5–1 game last season, Rangers had dominated the midfield, taking advantage of the absence of Bobby Murdoch who was out through injury. Rangers scored first through their Swedish striker Persson who gave Tommy Gemmell a torrid afternoon. Willie Johnston scored a hat trick, including a goal in the final minute, while Celtic replied twice through Wallace to give the final scoreline a more respectable feel. However the tabloids were in no doubt that this was to be Rangers' season. Such premature hyperbole was exposed for what it was before the month had ended after the side dropped points against Kilmarnock and Hearts.

Then, as now, Celtic relied heavily on an inspirational midfielder who, while not possessed of lightning pace, orchestrated the team with the precise rhythm of a metronome. Where Martin O'Neill has Neil Lennon, Jock Stein had George Connelly, a tall, powerful yet desperately shy Fifer who it was said 'could play as a sweeper while sitting in an armchair'. Like O'Neill, Stein was able to slowly evolve his teams without affecting results. Connelly and Charlie Gallagher had seamlessly replaced Bobby

Murdoch and Bertie Auld, who were the engine room that drove the Lisbon Lions.

Similarly, both teams also relied on an inspirational forward to unlock defences. Instead of Larsson, the Celtic side of 1968–69 had Jimmy Johnstone, one of the most naturally gifted ball-players of all time. His worth to the team was never more forcefully demonstrated than in an early European Cup tie against St Etienne in September 1968. Trailing 0–2 from the first leg, Celtic trounced the French 4–0 in Glasgow following an outrageously flamboyant display by the little winger who was dubbed 'the flying flea' by the French press.

Like O'Neill, Stein was not afraid to offload players he felt were not part of his long-term plans. Although Joe McBride had been an integral member of the Celtic squad over a number of years, scoring an important goal against Nantes in the 1967 European campaign, Stein knew he was past his best and could not be guaranteed a starting place in the Celtic team. Though it was an emotional wrench for both parties, Stein sold McBride to Hibernian midway through the season.

Both managers also won trebles by shrewd rather than extravagant dealings in the transfer market. A measure of O'Neill's budgetary caution was the purchase of pacey midfielder Didier Agathe from Hibs for just £35,000 – with the exception of Henrik Larsson and Lubo Moravcik, the most astutely successful purchase made by a Celtic manager in recent times. The price-tag was just the same as Stein paid Dunfermline for the versatile Tommy Callaghan at the back end of 1968. Like Agathe, Callaghan was a midfielder who could play well up front. He was also equally at home on the right and left side of the field. Curiously both players also bore a striking resemblance to Hen Broon.

Like last season, the Celtic side of 1968–69 stumbled across the finishing line rather than bursting through the tape with an ostentatious flourish. Where the 2001 side struggled to a nervy 1–0 win over St Mirren, Stein's side eventually won the league title when Rangers were defeated 2–3 at Dens Park.

The League Cup was won courtesy of a 6–2 hammering of Hibs. However, the highlight of the season was the side's memorable 4–0 win over their Old Firm rivals in the Scottish Cup final. The match would attain historic significance for another reason. It was Alex Ferguson's last match for Rangers. It was not a happy afternoon for the Manchester United manager whose slack marking left Billy McNeill unguarded to score Celtic's first goal after just two minutes. Connelly, the youngest player on the pitch, put Lennox through for Celtic's second before scoring the third after dispossessing John Greig as the Rangers captain tried to dribble the ball out of his own penalty area. It was 3–0 at half-time and Celtic dominated the second half, Stevie Chalmers adding a fourth goal with 15 minutes left.

Ironically Stein's side, like their modern counterparts, were also to lose their final league match of the season once all the hard work had been done. While O'Neill's team lost 0–1 at home to Kilmarnock, the 1969 side went down 2–4 to Morton, with an unknown player called Bartram scoring the fastest hat trick ever seen at Celtic Park. The manager, like his modern successor O'Neill, did not tolerate carelessness. Irate at the result, Stein berated his players publicly in the next issue of the *Celtic View*.

McNeill's nickname in those days was Caesar, not because of the patrician grandeur which he still possesses, but because he drove the same car as Caesar Romero, the Hollywood actor who played the Joker in the *Batman* TV series. McNeill looks like the kind of man who's got better things to do than to be drawn into frivolous parlour games but, after being prompted, he reluctantly agrees. Who, out of the current squad of players, would be good enough to play in the team of 1968–69?

'It's easy to say a player like Larsson could have played in that side but would he have had the same communion with the rest of the players? Would he have made the same impact and who would be left out? If you look at Stevie Chalmers and Bobby Lennox and Willie Wallace, they more than did the business, not just against Scottish opposition but in Europe as well. Larsson is a supreme player but it will be interesting to see if he can now go on to produce it on the big European stage. That is a challenge facing the whole team.'

It's an unfair question based on a spurious premise, not least because there's an implicit criticism of those who are left out and, after Celtic's most complete season in a generation, even inadvertent criticism is unworthy. Stein's teams were a product of their time. The game is different today in every respect, commercially, physically, socially. The team of 1969 was built on relationships between players established over a number of years. Relationships that persist to this day. The Lisbon Lions are like a travelling social club with the most exclusive membership list in Scotland. They appear at the top table of dinners together; they go to charity fundraisers together; they travel to supporters' functions halfway across the world together. Barely a week goes by when some of their number don't come together as a group.

The nature of the modern game means players move on more frequently and those relationships no longer exist. Or at least not to the same extent. Yet, for McNeill, what unites both teams is more important than what sets them apart – like the spirit and determination exemplified by the attitude of Neil Lennon, a player 'bursting out of his skin to be a success at Celtic Park'.

'The attitude to football has changed,' McNeill insists. 'Comparisons like that add unfair pressure on to Martin O'Neill. He will set his own standards and his own record. Big Jock was a manager of his time. At his time he was the best. It would be lovely to think that Martin could emulate the type of success that Jock established.

'In a sense Martin's job is easier because he enjoys a greater independence than Jock ever had. Jock was working to establish himself. He would earn well but he would never have earned the kind of money that would have made him totally independent. The job was always important to him. The present-day Celtic, because of the manner in which you are able to sell season tickets, are able to compete in a market that big Jock was never able to do. I am hoping the board are aware of the demands of modern-day football and are prepared to back the manager. I don't think Jock ever got the backing that he wanted or would have needed.'

Celtic returned from the winter shutdown with more than a little trepidation. Unlike rivals Rangers, who used the break as an opportunity to regroup and to nurse their injury-hit squad back to fitness, it had come at a bad time for Celtic. They had been in electrifying form at the start of January and there was a fear that, having fallen into that enforced gap in the schedule, they might not be able to recapture their form.

Their first test was against Hearts who, under Craig Levein, had become better organised and possessed of a mental toughness that O'Neill knew would be difficult to break. A good start was important but the two games that followed – a double-header against Rangers in the semi-final of the CIS Insurance Cup and then in the league – were the key to their season.

Rangers, who played the day before the Hearts game, piled pressure on Celtic by leapfrogging Hibernian into second place. They reduced Celtic's lead at the top of the SPL to 6 points following a 2–0 win against Dunfermline at Ibrox. The first Scottish match to be broadcast on pay-per-view television included a Kerimoglu Tugay volley which gave Rangers the lead. Michael Mols slotted the second in the 89th minute.

Celtic knew dropped points against Hearts followed by defeat against Rangers would all but eliminate their lead. This was a time when the season's most important questions would be asked and answered. As their team coach traversed the M8, the elements seemed to be conspiring against them. It was a dark, bitterly cold Sunday which, as night descended, would become shrouded in a fierce blizzard. As the players ran out on to the Tynecastle pitch they knew this, more than any before, was the moment of truth. Had their consistently solid, sometimes inspirational, form over the past six months been a flash in the pan or was it something more sustained? The next 90 minutes would tell.

4 FEBRUARY: HEARTS 0 CELTIC 3
(Report by authors)

Celtic made a perfect start when they took the lead after just four minutes. Alan Thompson fired in a dangerous free kick from the left wing and Larsson got ahead of Grant Murray to emphatically head into the bottom corner.

But the visitors were dealt a cruel blow in the sixth minute when Joos Valgaeren was carried off after appearing to fall awkwardly when going up for a header with Hearts striker Gordon Durie.

The inspirational Belgian was rushed to hospital with a suspected broken ankle which would be the only title worry from an otherwise faultless match.

Celtic were rampant in the opening exchanges and almost created another great chance for Larsson in the eighth minute when Ramon Vega crossed from the right only for Steven pressley to make a vital interception.

Chris Sutton was booked moments later after clashing with Gordan Petric off the ball – but that failed to knock Celtic out of their stride.

Hearts goalkeeper Antti Niemi was their hero in the 12th minute after Didier Agathe had left pressley and Colin Cameron in his wake with a burst down the right.

The Frenchman got to the by-line and cut the ball back but the former Rangers keeper made a telling save as Larsson set himself up to shoot.

Hearts were clearly rattled and Niemi again had to keep his side in the match as Sutton got to Thompson's free kick, but the goalkeeper did well to get down low to his right to deny him.

Celtic were far from fazed by the loss of Valgaeren and they were unfortunate not to double their lead in the 24th minute following a flowing move which ripped the Hearts defence wide open again.

Larsson rounded Niemi, after a great interchange of passes from Lambert and Sutton, and the Swede tried to return the ball to his fellow striker but the ball was too high for him to capitalise.

Former Rangers star Durie was booked in the 27th minute for a late challenge on Tommy Boyd before his strike partner Andy Kirk was presented with Hearts' first chance to draw level two minutes later.

Robert Tomaschek made a determined run to the by-line before picking out the youngster at the near post but Kirk blasted just wide on the volley.

Sutton was inches away from adding a second Celtic goal in the 38th minute when Larsson burst through on the right and squared the ball across the face of goal but the former Chelsea player was unable to reach it.

But Hearts were still in with a shout and in the 41st minute they mustered their first shot on target when Tomaschek rose to head Cameron's free kick but Robert Douglas comfortably saved.

The visitors, however, survived a last-minute scare when Cameron's corner fell to Scott Severin on the edge of the box and he hit a fierce goalbound strike which Boyd, on the line, did well to head over.

Celtic continued to press Hearts back after the interval and on the hour mark Sutton was again presented with a glorious chance.

Jackie McNamara found the striker on the edge of the box and after jinking past pressley only a crucial block from Murray denied him a shot on target.

Hearts went close in the 67th minute when Cameron's free kick came off the head of Boyd and past the far post – but Celtic killed the game off just a minute later in superb fashion.

Thompson broke down the left wing before crossing for Larsson, who flicked the ball with the outside of his right foot and into the bottom corner.

Larsson was not yet finished and in the 84th minute he was celebrating a brilliant hat trick.

The Swede played the ball through to Agathe down the right flank and his return cross was fired home past Niemi by the Swede, who wheeled away in delight. Agathe could have made it four but his shot was well saved.

The only Celtic fan who was not celebrating that night was Nick Woods, president of the Edinburgh University and Heriot-Watt Celtic

Supporters Club. Before the game he had foolishly proposed that, if Larsson scored a hat trick, then he would run naked through the International Bar in Tollcross. So it was that, on one of the coldest nights of the year, the regulars of that venerable hostelry were given their own sneak preview of a Celtic Treble. Fortunately the performance attracted some charitable donations.

The result of the Hearts match did two things. It consolidated Celtic's league position but, perhaps more importantly, it sent a chilling message to Rangers that this was a side significantly improved since the last Old Firm encounter in November. Larsson's hat trick was the majestic highlight of a dominant performance, three of the most expertly executed striker's goals seen in any league all season. They brought his domestic tally to 29, rapidly closing on Brian McClair's Scottish league record of 35 in the 1986–87 season.

However the jubilation was tempered with the loss of Valgaeren. Some newspaper reports predicted that his season was over after breaking his ankle. Their diagnoses were premature as X-rays confirmed that he had suffered only a sprain, but it was still inevitable that he would now miss both of the Old Firm encounters.

As Celtic approached the first of their two matches against Rangers, the players could hardly have been in a more positive frame of mind. 'What I remember going into that double-header was a feeling among neutrals that, for the first time, Celtic were actually a better team than Rangers and that Celtic would win,' said Jonathan Northcroft. 'I certainly thought they would win the double-header, which was an unusual feeling after 12 years of watching Rangers being the best team. Rangers did have dreadful injury problems, particularly for the CIS game, but there was a feeling that if Celtic couldn't do it now then they never would.'

7 FEBRUARY: CELTIC 3 RANGERS 1
(Report by authors)

Celtic controlled most of this CIS Cup semi-final, but there was stilll plenty of controversy with two penalties, one for each side, a plethora of bookings and three red cards.

The result was never in much doubt after Sutton fired Celtic into the lead after only six minutes, followed by a second by Larsson midway through the first half. From then on Rangers looked distinctly second rate.

Even when Rangers pulled one back through a highly questionable penalty, converted by Jorg Albertz, Celtic never surrendered their grip on the game. In the second half Rangers flattered to deceive but when

Larsson converted a penalty he himself had won after being brought down by Scott Wilson, there was only ever going to be one winner.

That did not stop the game igniting into life when Reyna directed a lunging tackle at Petta and, having been booked earlier, was sent from the field of play. In the ensuing argument over the merits of the dismissal Michael Mols clashed with Lubo Moravcik and the pair were also dismissed by referee Willie Young.

Rangers started with an unpredictable line-up, 20-year-old Robert Malcolm replacing Fernando Ricksen. Also demoted to the bench was Michael Mols, who sat alongside Kenny Miller. Celtic started with a full-strength side with the exception of Douglas and Agathe, who were both serving suspensions.

They looked the more assured side from the start and it was no surprise when they took the lead. Konterman fouled Larsson and, from the resultant Thompson free kick, Vega headed against the bar. Sutton was first to react, knocking it goalward.

Celtic went two up after 17 minutes when a speculative punt upfield by Mjallby bounced awkwardly in front of Malcolm. The youngster appeared to stumble and his mistake was cruelly exploited by Larsson, who was in like a whippet. He composed himself before hoisting the ball over Stefan Klos and then touching it over the line.

On the half-hour mark Rangers were showing signs of life. Barry Ferguson played in Reyna who had Celtic retreating and Jonathan Gould was forced into an agile save from a shot which Vega then helped to clear. Rangers' persistence paid off in the 37th minute. Albertz sent a cross into the Celtic area and, when Sutton and Wilson brushed against one another, Young spotted an infringement and pointed to the spot.

Reyna joined Jackie McNamara in Young's notebook after a foul on Lambert, a move which excited the passions of Tugay, who continued to argue with the referee as the teams left the field for the break.

The Turk never emerged for the second period. Advocaat signalled his desire to chase the game further when he put Mols on for the ineffectual McCann after 58 minutes.

However nine minutes later the game was over as a contest when Celtic earned a penalty, despatched by Larsson. From then on the game settled down and the Celtic crowd rose to applaud the Swede as he was replaced by Moravcik with 15 minutes to go.

Of the two Rangers games, the CIS tie was the least important because, for both sides, the league was the priority. However, both sides also knew that whoever won the first game would have the advantage for the second leg.

'I thought the first Rangers game was crucial,' said Bob Crampsey. 'It showed it was not a one-off and that Celtic were likely to win the great bulk of games they played against Rangers. I think it created uncertainty in the minds of the Rangers players. If Rangers had at least held their own then they could have gone into the second game in the series and the season thinking they could turn things around.'

Celtic, having overcome their toughest rivals in the cup competition, knew that a win on Sunday would be the making of their season. No one in the dressing-room was prepared to openly articulate the 'T' word but everyone knew a clean sweep of domestic trophies was now a credible possibility. And it wasn't just sporting ambition that was driving the players on – there was also a financial incentive. In the post-biscuit tin era, each player had been promised a reported bonus of £70,000 to wrest the SPL title from Rangers – and double that amount if they scooped the Treble.

'At that stage the Celtic players would undoubtedly have been thinking about the possibility of the Treble,' said Billy McNeill 'The most important thing is to keep your mind focused on the game ahead. But it's amazing when you are in that type of run. People talk about the burden of having to play so many games in a season. I think that is the best thing that can happen to you because they just come upon each other, one after the other, and all your thoughts are on the next game. That's exactly what Celtic did. You only had to look at the attitude and the appetite in individual players. Nobody was prepared to dwell on an injury.'

O'Neill knew better than to underestimate his Ibrox counterpart Dick Advocaat. He would have to plan meticulously, not least because he would not have the luxury of a full-strength side. Stilian Petrov was serving a two-match SPL suspension and, as expected, Valgaeren would also be absent.

However, not for the last time in the season, his preparations would be disrupted by unnecessary distractions. Even before winning a single item of silverware, he was already a victim of his own success. Alex Ferguson had signalled that the 2001–02 season would be his last at Old Trafford and, with nothing more meaningful to write about, the Fleet Street sports writers began to speculate on his successor. O'Neill had all the right credentials and so the press began what was to become a protracted campaign linking him with the job. The speculation, much of it ill-informed, would become more fevered as the season progressed, particularly after a public fall-out between Ferguson and the Manchester United chief executive Peter Kenyon towards the end of the season. But it was doing little to foster a spirit of settled continuity at Celtic Park. It seemed to the supporters that, just as their love affair with O'Neill was beginning, he was being snatched from their grasp by a richer, more successful rival.

Ahead of the league game against Rangers, Ramon Vega was doing his best to calm tempers by pledging that there would be no vendettas carried over from the midweek encounter. It was a genuine attempt to defuse tensions but sadly others outwith football were doing otherwise. Celtic-supporting superstar Rod Stewart turned up the heat for the crunch game by taunting rival Rangers supporters. 'To all you blue-nosed bastards out there, Celtic Football Club will win the Scottish league this year,' he told *GQ* magazine.

11 FEBRUARY: CELTIC 1 RANGERS 0
(Report by authors)

Martin O'Neill refused to accept that the league was in the bag even after his side scored the victory that hoisted them 12 points clear of Rangers.

Absent were the histrionics of Wednesday night, although there was a sending off – now almost a mandatory element of an Old Firm encounter. Fernando Ricksen received his marching orders for a second bookable offence before the break.

Ricksen, who was pulled off by Advocaat after being mesmerised by Petta's skilful wing play during the 6–2 game, again lost his rag. Though even before his dismissal Rangers had looked vulnerable at the back.

Referee Hugh Dallas produced his first card of the game after only 11 minutes when Ricksen brought down Alan Thompson.

Six minutes later the Celtic support was in delirium when Thompson put them ahead. Sutton played the ball through to Larsson who squared it to Thompson and he fired it home from close range. The visitors regrouped with furious Advocaat orchestrating the manoeuvres from the sidelines. Celtic came close when Lennon crossed for Sutton to head on target – but Klos made a desperate save with Vega scavenging in the background.

Celtic had two clear chances before the break but Robert Malcolm blocked Sutton's shot in the 31st minute and eight minutes later Thompson pounced on a momentary lapse by Konterman. Sutton collected but Klos made a timely block. Lambert collected the rebound and the German had to race back to keep Rangers in the game.

Ricksen's red card came in the last minute of the half following a late tackle on Boyd. Playing a man short for the second 45, Rangers showed some resilience and Albertz could have scored after Malcolm had found him in space but he blasted the ball over the bar.

Celtic grabbed the game by the scruff of the neck and imposed themselves on Rangers' goal. With Ricksen gone Petta was free to exploit extra space on the wing and a threatening, dangerous, in-swinging cross in 48 minutes had to be cut out by Albertz.

Moments later he outfoxed Tugay on the touchline and raced down the left wing before curling another cross into the box which Sutton connected with but Konterman intercepted and put it out for a corner.

Rangers' only meaningful move came four minutes after the break when Neil McCann passed to Tore Andre Flo who played in Albertz but the German blasted the ball directly at the keeper.

Dallas rejected Rangers' claim for a penalty nine minutes from time when Sutton tussled with Flo just as the Norwegian was teeing up a shot. As Dallas blew the final whistle the home supporters began to sing 'We're going to win the league!'

Celtic, unable to cope with superiority against their Old Firm rivals so often in the past, made sure they didn't throw away their hard-won advantage. They did well to maintain their concentration during a humdrum performance punctuated only by the sending-off of Ricksen. Much of the post-match autopsy would centre on the player's inability to contain the skilful flair of Bobby Petta on the wing.

After the midweek game, Advocaat had accused Petta of 'showboating' and warned him not to try it at Ibrox in front of the baying Rangers hordes. O'Neill, who had studiously avoided being drawn into media slanging matches, felt obliged to respond to the besmirching of his player's talents. He simply pointed out that Petta rolled his foot over the ball in a similar fashion every day in training and none of his players ever felt compelled to kick him up in the air.

The league game revealed that the players had finally shed their inability, most evident under the stewardship of Tommy Burns, to translate superiority against Rangers into tangible results. It also showed that, with the additions made to the team since November, Celtic now possessed an assuredness in midfield that could match and outplay Rangers in every respect.

'What the two Rangers games showed conclusively was that the

Lennon–Lambert partnership could work,' said Charlie Nicholas. 'When Lennon initially came a lot of people thought they might be too similar. When it came to those Rangers games, Lennon just sat on the left side of Lambert and upset the Rangers midfield. Mentally he just knew he was winning it. I remember thinking, "That's it, Celtic have the knowledge now." Lennon and Lambert were just too much for Rangers. Barry Ferguson at times had to play on his own and it was too much. You are talking about two guys with positional knowledge, temperamental knowledge, and they just sat and basically frustrated the living daylights out of Rangers and I think that was the time when you thought, "That's it, it just doesn't get any better than this."'

Celtic Park had become something of a mecca for the rich and famous during the season, something Martin O'Neill quite rightly did nothing to discourage. Among the many celebrities who had shared a pot of tea with the manager was Billy Connolly. Connolly could quite rightly claim to be no flash-in-the-pan supporter as he had been coming to games quietly for years. He had already met Martin O'Neill earlier in the season but the two were about to have a more unusual encounter.

It came as Connolly was being shown around the stadium in the company of John Robertson and a friend. It was long after the players had departed with their families and friends for homes and pubs or wherever players go to celebrate. The stadium was quiet as Robertson led Connolly into the hallowed first-team dressing-room. As they stood at the door a figure emerged from the steaming shower with just a towel wrapped around his waist. It was Martin O'Neill freshening up before he went home. He stopped for a second and then with a glint in his eye and a flourish he pretended he was going to whip the towel back. A stunned Connolly quickly got the joke and the men all roared with laughter. It was O'Neill's way of taking the mickey out of the comic who, only weeks before, had done his own strip for charity in London.

Behind the scenes everything may have been a laugh but in the outside world trouble was brewing. The Celtic fans, jealous guardians of the club's history and traditions, were unhappy with the new shirt design. For the first time in almost 100 years the world-famous barrel hoops had disappeared. A white band running vertically beneath the arms meant the hoops were broken. It was a sacreligious affront. Among those most concerned was the club's mascot, who was now faced with changing his name to the unacceptably non-alliterative 'Stripey the Huddle Hound'. A boycott was organised, with three of the club's official supporters' associations urging fans not to buy the new Umbro jersey. They demanded the club scrap the strip and order the sportswear firm to design another one. But the club and the company stood firm and eventually the fans agreed to back down.

The catalyst for peace was O'Neill, who agreed to meet a delegation from the Celtic Supporters Association. He sympathised with their plight but pointed out that, with success on the pitch now within touching distance, it was not sensible to rock the boat. The culture of confrontation which had characterised relations between supporters and club so often in the past had gone and, crucially, O'Neill was at the very heart of the new spirit of rapprochement. 'He expressed some concerns from a superstitious point of view,' said Eddie Toner, secretary of the CSA. 'He didn't want to change the strip because they were doing well in the old one. He certainly understood where we were coming from. He's the kind of guy who, if he thought we were in there for something really trivial, I am sure would have told us in no uncertain terms.'

The decision to launch the new strip had been taken when Dalglish was still in charge of team affairs. O'Neill would ensure that any future strip designs would not be given the go-ahead without his say-so. 'O'Neill is involved in most of the decisions along there,' said Toner. 'He is very much an old-fashioned manager – he's not just the head coach. He takes an interest in everything that goes on.'

Celtic's next challenge on the park was a Scottish Cup tie against Dunfermline. The shocked expression which O'Neill displayed at the final whistle was testament to the Pars' tenacious determination. Rarely had a side challenged Celtic so closely all season.

17 FEBRUARY: DUNFERMLINE 2 CELTIC 2
(Report by authors)

Even Henrik Larsson's double failed to subdue the home side who fought for every scrap. The fact that he managed to break free from Andrius Skerla, who handles him better than any other defender in the SPL, at all was one of the biggest surprises of the afternoon.

In a drab opening spell Celtic's best chance fell to Petta, who always looked unlikely to add to his single strike of the season as he weakly attempted to place the ball past Marco Ruitenbeek in goal with his right foot.

With Skerla capably shackling Larsson and Andy Tod keeping close tabs on Sutton, Celtic's chances were few and far between. The greatest threat to the Dunfermline goal came from their own players. Ruitenbeek failed to deal with a routine clearance and, as Sutton sought to take advantage, the keeper appeared to hold on to his shirt. Fortunately for the home side, referee Willie Young saw nothing amiss in the challenge and waved play on.

Dunfermline turned to route one in an effort to breach the solid Celtic defence, by punting a series of high balls into the area. A Tod header ended up on the roof of the net after a Nicholson corner. Then Scott Thomson sent in a low, awkward strike which Douglas, blinded by the sunlight, only just managed to scramble away with his left hand.

The game failed to spark into life until the second period. In the 66th minute Larsson eventually managed to escape the iron grip of the Lithuanian to glance home from an Alan Thompson free kick.

Clearly disgruntled, Skerla more than made up for his lapse when he fired home from close range after Dair and Skinner had combined neatly to send the ball into his path. Soon afterward Dunfermline should have gone ahead when Scott Thomson hooked a shot just wide with his left foot.

However, they missed the opportunity and it wasn't long before Celtic again asserted their superiority with another inspiring Larsson strike. Lennon played a low ball in from the left and Larsson edged away from Sutton to gently lob the ball over Marco Ruitenbeek in goal.

Instead of buckling under, Dunfermline pushed forward and a penetrating run from Chris McGroarty allowed Lee Bullen to play in Nicholson, who scored with a drive from 22 yards.

Celtic were not the only side having an off-day. Barry Ferguson spared Rangers' blushes with a 62nd-minute winner against lowly Ross County. Rangers had looked to be coasting after a double strike in the opening 15 minutes from Tore Andre Flo but County hit back with a double from Alex Bone in the 19th and 53rd minutes. A major Cup upset seemed possible as the Victoria Park outfit more than matched Rangers for most of the game, until they were hit by Ferguson's late sucker punch.

The result seemed to bring O'Neill down to earth following the euphoria of recent days. The ever-cautious manager attempted to inject a bit of realism into his players when he pointed out that they had yet to prove themselves at a higher level. O'Neill said it was just as well Celtic were out of Europe because it would have added an impossible distraction to the players. And he insisted they were not ready to mix it with the big boys of Europe like Barcelona and Liverpool.

As he prepared for the midweek visit of Motherwell, he said: 'In the future we would need a decent-sized squad if we're contemplating European football on a serious note. If we had been in European football this side of Christmas it would have been very difficult with the squad we have at present.'

Not for the first time Celtic relied on the mercurial talents of their midfield orchestrator Lubo Moravcik who, like a good French wine, becomes more pleasing to the senses with age. Like everything possessed of great quality, the diminutive Slovakian is best used sparingly and O'Neill seemed to have perfected the skill of deploying him in moments when his talents were utterly decisive.

21 FEBRUARY: CELTIC 1 MOTHERWELL 0
(Report by authors)

For 83 minutes Celtic huffed and puffed, unable to breach a resolute Motherwell defence. As the muted Celtic support shuffled nervously, wondering if this was the moment when their title ambitions would finally become unstuck, up stepped Moravcik with a bending free kick from 25 yards which almost punctured the net. It was a strike of such noble quality that even Andy Goram, stranded on the Motherwell goal-line, didn't know whether to cry or applaud.

Celtic began the game brimming with confidence. O'Neill was able to field virtually a full side, with only Jackie McNamara missing through injury.

However, it took the home side 12 minutes to open up the Motherwell defence following a rapid interchange between Larsson and Thompson. The Englishman raced to the byline and he whipped in a ball across the face of goal but Chris Sutton was fractionally slow and failed to connect.

Scott Leitch was booked for impeding Larsson and, from the free kick, Thompson drilled a shot from 20 yards which Goram only just managed to punch clear. Celtic were denied a penalty claim in the 19th minute when Larsson clashed with Kemble inside the box and it was to be another 20 minutes before Goram was significantly troubled again when he threw himself to his left to prevent a long-range effort by Lambert breaching his goal.

O'Neill was forced to replace Petta with Petrov before the break after the Dutchman injured himself charging down a McMillan shot. Vega should have put Celtic in front moments later when he charged on to a

182

Sutton lay-off two yards from goal. But the giant Swiss international missed the ball completely.

Within minutes of the restart Motherwell should have been ahead when Spencer trapped a high ball and fed it into the path of Lee McCulloch whose dipping first-time shot would have gone in had it been inches either side of Rab Douglas. Celtic injected more urgency into their play and, in a furious five-minute spell, Petrov came close twice and Lennon also narrowly missed from 25 yards.

Celtic thought the breakthrough had come after 70 minutes when Larsson sent Thompson on a darting run to the by-line. The Geordie swung over a deep cross which hung in the air above Goram's back post, which Sutton reached but his header rebounded agonisingly off the left-hand post.

Sensing a stalemate O'Neill sent on Tom Boyd for Joos Valgaeren and Moravcik for Lambert in a move that was to ultimately change the course of the game. Thompson hit woodwork in the 87th minute and Larsson headed the rebound over but by then Celtic had secured the points.

Moravcik was a £300,000 bargain buy by Dr Jozef Venglos from the German side MSV Duisburg in October 1998. A sporting legend in his native Slovakia, the player was a virtual unknown in this country before his move to Celtic.

Technically the most gifted player in Scotland, his worth could not be overestimated. It was remarked repeatedly that if he was a younger player he would be gracing the Spanish or Italian leagues. However, at the unlikely age of 35 he was approaching his footballing dotage and Celtic were fortunate to be blessed with such a rare talent. No one was more aware of his worth than O'Neill, who began a campaign to convince the player to extend his contract for another year.

At this relatively early stage in the season even O'Neill could not have known what an astute piece of business that was to be, for in the later stages Moravcik was to take his genius to greater heights, providing the Celtic faithful with an afternoon of delirium almost unsurpassed in recent years.

Neil Lennon was in no doubt that Moravcik could provide a special dimension to the Celtic side. 'If he was ten years younger he would be at Real Madrid or Barcelona with the ability he has got,' he said. 'We're trying to build a squad here and there is talent like Lubo's oozing through it. It's good to be part of it.'

'Any championship-winning side needs at least one outstanding player,' said Bob Crampsey. 'Celtic were lucky because they had two – Larsson and Moravcik. These are the players who can do things nobody else can. Then there was a whole raft of very good players like Mjallby, Valgaeren and Lennon. But Celtic won the league because they had Larsson and Moravcik.'

The squad were given a further boost before their final league match of the month when popular club captain Tom Boyd was given a year-long extension to his contract. The inspirational skipper was the longest-serving member of the squad and the gesture was important in maintaining morale. Celtic has never been the most assiduous of clubs in rewarding faithful servants but again, under O'Neill, that was all changing. The manager joked that he had only offered Boyd a new deal because he made a decent cup of tea but he knew that the player's presence in the dressing-room was important for squad harmony. Before the end of the season Boyd would also be rewarded with a high-earning testimonial tie against the superstars of Manchester United.

February had been the most crucial month in the season so far. The players had emerged from their winter break and devastated their opponents, establishing for themselves a place on the cusp of sporting greatness. The reward was in their grasp – all they had to do was to hold their nerve for a place in history, the first Celtic side in 32 years to win the Treble.

As they contemplated equalling the achievements of Celtic legends like Billy McNeill, Bobby Murdoch and Jimmy Johnstone, the players enjoyed a rare moment of relaxation. Henrik Larsson proved that blondes have more fun by glamming it up as singer Benny from pop group Abba at a fancy dress birthday party for Jackie McNamara's wife Samantha. 'Everyone was gobsmacked when Henrik teetered in on huge shoes wearing this tight, sequinned outfit,' said one party-goer. 'He always comes across as quite a shy guy but he seemed to be having a ball.'

25 FEBRUARY: CELTIC 1 HIBERNIAN 1
(Report by authors)

Mjallby's first-half strike looked like giving Celtic the points but substitute Libbra equalised to keep Hibs' slim championship hopes alive.

The breakthrough for Celtic came after 23 minutes when Larsson rose to head Thompson's corner towards the goal. John O'Neil blocked the effort but Mjallby was on hand to slot the rebound straight in from close range.

Celtic should have gone further ahead in the 34th minute when

Larsson put Petrov through with an incisive pass, but with only Colgan to beat he hooked his effort round the post. Slowly Hibs imposed themselves on the game and they almost caught Celtic dozing after 37 minutes. O'Neil played Ulrik Laursen in and Robert Douglas was forced to make a last-ditch save. Hibs came close again three minutes before half-time when Zitelli put through Laursen, but Mjallby made a telling tackle to deny him a shot on target. Vega then tried to chip the keeper after a determined run through the middle and the keeper had to look sharp to save under his post.

Hibs pressed forward in the second period and Franck Sauzee attempted a shot in the 50th minute, but Lennon took the sting out of it and Douglas gathered his retake with ease. But as they pushed up, holes emerged in the visitors' defence and they were lucky not to go further behind in the 63rd minute when Petrov's cross flew across the face of goal, but Vega was unable to reach it and Larsson could only put it into the crowd. Two minutes later the Hibs defence were torn apart again when Petrov played in Lambert, but the midfielder's cross missed everybody.

The Edinburgh side needed a spark of inspiration and it arrived in the shape of new signing Mark Libbra who was brought on for the industrious but ineffective Lehmann. With just five minutes to go he capitalised on a loss of concentration in the Celtic defence to slot the ball below Douglas from close range and give his side a share of the points.

Earlier Larsson had almost secured the win for Celtic when he hit Lennon's pass on the volley but Colgan got down well to deny him. The Swede had another opportunity in the 76th minute when Sutton put him through, but Lovell made a vital interception. Sutton then headed Petrov's corner over the crossbar from close range.

March and the League Cup final was now on the horizon. A date with history. But before that Neil Lennon was to discover the price of playing on one side of the Old Firm divide. The dark underbelly of Scottish football was about to be exposed. He had his own date with bigotry.

11.

ALMOST THERE

Oh Hampden in the sun,
Celtic 7 Rangers 1,
That was the score when it came time up,
The Hoops had won the cup.
I see Tully running down the line,
He slips the ball past Valentine,
It's nodded down by 'Teazy Weazy',
And Sammy Wilson makes it look so easy.

MOLISE IS POSSIBLY the poorest and most forgotten region of Italy. It has no magnificent architecture, few memorable ruins and no significant cities. It tumbles down to the Adriatic coast from the spine of the country through a series of beautiful valleys, ugly concrete factories and tiny feudal, mountaintop villages. Collemacchia is one of these villages. It's not on any map of any significance but if you wanted to find it you could do worse than locate Naples then lay a ruler straight across the country. It's somewhere about halfway across – somewhere around the highest bit, in the national park where bears and wolves are said to roam and rich Neapolitans enjoy the most southerly skiing in Italy. Not that there's any skiing in Collemacchia. Like the dozens of tiny hamlets scattered around, it's known only for the overwhelming desire its inhabitants once had to get away from it and the terrible poverty caused by too many people and not enough land. And, of course, briefly during the war the great armies of Germany, Britain and America, along with Poles, French and the brutal Moroccans, took it in turns to pass bloodily by on their way to the terrible carnage at nearby Monte Cassino. Now the village seems to be permanently sleeping. The 20 or 30 simple but attractive houses lie still for much of the year until the children and grandchildren of those emigrants roll up for their summer holidays.

Still – but for the voice of a Scotsman which has sounded around it for more than 40 years. Willie Hughes is 79 now. His red, red hair has turned white and his face is leathered with the sun but his accent is still pure Glasgow. His house is perched halfway up the village's only real road. It looks much like it must have done since the night 60 years ago when Kesselring slept under the hand-painted murals in the main bedroom. The German General and his troops had just arrived and he wanted the most comfortable bed in the district. The bed is still there, with its feather mattress so soft that it bares the imprint of the last person that slept in it for days afterwards.

In the evenings Willie and Lisa sit on either side of the big wood fire in their simply furnished dining room. The room is like many others in the village except that to the left of the door as you come in is a shrine to the famous Glasgow Celtic. Pennants, pictures and signed photographs jostle for space, all brought by Scots as gifts for the biggest Celtic fan they know.

Willie left Glasgow in 1961 to be with Lisa, the Italian woman he met as she helped out in the café near his own workplace of Weir Pumps in Cathcart, Glasgow. His life then was his work, his brothers and Celtic. Circumstances have meant he has rarely been back. Yet throughout those years he has always kept the faith for his team burning brightly.

There was no surfaced road in the village when he arrived, no cars or phones nor televisions. Electricity arrived via a set of bare wires in the piazza and they blew out a couple of times a week. Willie worked the land for Lisa's father, making wine in October, picking olives in January and toiling in the sun for the rest of the year. It was Willie and his friend Bene Coia who dug the ditch up the main street many, many years later to put power into the houses. But the village was busy then. Families and their animals were crammed into the small houses living on top of each other. It was a blessing, not just for the company, but also for the match reports.

'At first I used to knock people's doors and see who had a shortwave radio, because I certainly didn't have one,' says Willie. 'It was the only way I could tune into the World Service and get the scores.' Then television came and then much later satellites and for a while Willie could watch games at Parkhead live. I sat in his house to watch the first game of the season the year Henrik Larsson arrived. Larsson was terrible and Chic Charnley, a Celtic supporter, scored a cracker for Hibs. Shortly after that decoder cards arrived and Willie's live football coverage was over. Instead he tunes into Teletext reports umpteen times a day to get the latest on Parkhead's comings and goings. And also, of course, to sit and watch the scores flash up when the games are on.

March in the year 2001 was the month of the League Cup final and League Cup finals are often in Willie's mind. He was one of the 82,293 people who were at Hampden Park in 1957 for the most famous of them all. 'I remember it well,' he says. 'I was there with my brother and it was just wonderful.'

Willie's passion for Celtic began like that of so many others when he was a child. During the war, as he took part in the Allied landings in Italy, it was put on hold. The Celtic he returned to support after being demobbed was a team of under-achievers. He remembers going through the turnstiles throughout the terrible '40s as the team was displaced as Rangers main rivals by Hibs and continually failed miserably to make any impact in either the league or the Scottish Cup. He was there during the infamous 1947–48 season when Celtic plunged down Division 'A', as the Premiership was known. And he kept the faith at Celtic's lowest point when on the last day of that season defeat by Dundee would have meant the shame of relegation. Celtic won 3–2 but they were, he concedes, grim times. The arrival of the electrifying Charlie Tully from Belfast lifted the gloom from the grim '40s and the otherwise dull '50s. 'They say Tully liked his fags and his booze and they say he wasn't much good at the training either,' Willie laughs. 'But I never saw any of that and, boy, could he play. Everybody was talking about him. The city was mad for him. There were Tully jokes. Every phrase had the word Tully added, as in Tullyvision and things like that.' Indeed, Tully had a flavour of green ice cream named after him. And sparked a craze in Tully ties.

But the real Tully was nothing like his public image. In sharp contrast to the way today's superstars must live cloistered private lives away from the monster that the sport has become, Charlie Tully could wander around Glasgow in a manner that would be unimaginable now.

Willie Hughes used to meet him regularly and listen to the legend's tales. 'On a Sunday when myself and four of five of my pals would go for a walk Charlie Tully would often join us. In those days the pubs weren't open on a Sunday evening like they are today and people would go out walking. We always used to go for a walk up Clarkston Road. Sometimes Charlie Tully would join us, sometimes he wouldn't. We would go up through the south side to Stamperland where he lived. He always brought his wee boy, who was about seven or eight then. You couldn't meet a nicer, more down-to-earth bloke than Charlie. I never saw him with a cigarette once, though none of us smoked and maybe that discouraged him. He just wore ordinary clothes the same as the rest of us. And we always talked about the game.

'He also used to come to our supporters' dances at the Couper Institute. I used to run the lemonade bar and it was my job to see Charlie home in a taxi. I never ever saw him drink and I dropped him off right at the gate of his house.'

Tully was to play in the '57 League Cup final, dazzling Rangers with his twists and turns and feints. 'He was brilliant. I was down the front of the Rangers end with my brother,' Willie added. 'I always stood there if it was Hampden. It was closer to my house. It was just goal after goal. I'll tell you, Charlie Tully ran circles around them all.'

Willie's decision to stand in amongst the opposition supporters nearly cost him his liberty, he remembers. 'I almost got arrested at that game. The Rangers supporters weren't happy and they were setting fire to their scarves and throwing them, burning, onto the pitch. There was this big policeman near me and he was getting mad at what they were doing. He was obviously going to wade in and start arresting people and he was eyeing me up. I had just stood throughout the game and said nothing. Of course, they all thought I was one of them. But I certainly didn't want to be arrested for a Rangers protest. In the end I just managed to slip away before any trouble started.'

Of course the League Cup of 2001 wasn't won yet and Celtic had a full fixture card of matches in the league and the Scottish Cup to take care of before meeting Kilmarnock at Hampden on 18 March.

But first Neil Lennon was on international duty for Northern Ireland, heading for Windsor Park and a match with Norway. It would have been an otherwise straightforward fixture were it not for the fact that he had now joined one side of the Old Firm and given those who preached intolerance an opportunity. He knew what was coming. He had been visiting his family in his home town of Lurgan in County Armagh when he heard about the 'Neil Lennon RIP' graffiti that had been daubed on a wall in the town. He'd received hate mail and, reportedly, a death threat and there were rumours that tickets for the Norway game were being purchased by Glasgow-based Rangers fans.

Lennon hadn't left the dressing-room when he received the first signs of a difficult evening: a few scattered hisses greeting the announcement of his name over the public address system. By then the crowd was still streaming into Windsor Park and the bully-boys were only clearing their throats. As kick-off approached they had massed on the Spion Kop, a 200-strong mob determined to exact retribution on a player who had committed, in their eyes, the cardinal sin of signing for Celtic.

Midway through the singing of the national anthem the old loyalist chant, 'No surrender to the IRA', began to reverberate around the ground. It was to be the start of 90 minutes of endless barracking and abuse for Lennon. It was a low point in the history of the international team. During the previous year the absence of sectarian singing at Windsor Park, reflecting the improving situation in Northern Ireland, had been clear to everyone. Now it was back and bent on making itself heard.

Lennon could have pulled out of the game but bravely insisted on facing the bigots. 'Neil felt he had to go,' said a friend at the time. 'He felt it was something he had to tackle head on. What else was he going to do? Stay away from every game at Windsor?'

Not everything had slipped back to the bad old days. The Ulster-based *Belfast Telegraph* defended Lennon in a manner that would have been unthinkable at the height of the troubles.

It said: 'It's little consolation that so many of the genuine home fans tried manfully, but unsuccessfully, to drown out the boring, predictable and unoriginal chants, and it's true that the currency of a supposedly new 21st-century Northern Ireland took a severe battering. But change will happen, because most of us want to move on and cease these relentless tribal hostilities. They bring no credit to any of us in this land who want to be able to live peaceful lives.'

When Lennon returned to Glasgow he looked to O'Neill for support. Martin O'Neill understood Northern Ireland as well as anyone. He may have been born and brought up in a small, end-of-terrace, three-bedroom house in the peaceful town of Kilrea at the edge of County Derry, but he and his family later moved much closer to the Troubles. O'Neill's father Leo was the local barber and he served both sides of the community with an ability to bridge the divide that Martin would later show. When Leo took the family to Belfast in the late '60s they lived near the same Antrim Road that was later to become notorious as one of the hot-spots of violence. Meanwhile the young Martin had begun his footballing career with Rosario Youth Club based on the Ormeau Road, another area later linked with extreme tensions during the marching season. At the same time young O'Neill studied for the law degree that he would eventually give up for the game. He began to make a name for himself with another club, Distillery's. It was located on Grosvenor Road, yet another dividing line between Catholics and Protestants where the flags and banners that hung from windows left no doubt as to the occupants' religious persuasion. Yet the Distillery club contained players from both sides who fought together for footballing honours without letting the terrible hatreds surrounding them intrude.

It wasn't until the '70s, as the violence escalated and turned the Antrim Road and New Lodge area into one of the most murderous places to live, that Leo and his wife Greta took their family across the water to Nottingham where Martin was already playing for Forest.

Martin O'Neill never turned his back on Northern Ireland and played for his country 64 times in a career that spanned two World Cup campaigns and included a lengthy spell as captain.

O'Neill would also have reminded Lennon as they talked at Parkhead that his international career was played out during the height of the Troubles when the squad was regularly forced to switch hotels at the last minute because of the incessant bomb threats. But like the squad that Lennon played with there was no sectarianism within the dressing-room. Fellow player Jimmy Nicholl recalls: 'The players never bickered about religion and I honestly don't remember our fans having a go at any of our Catholic players.'

O'Neill did play in one of the most controversial, politically charged Irish matches of all time when he turned out for a united Ireland side in 1973 – at precisely the moment when the violence in Northern Ireland was at a frenzy. More than 34,000 people turned out to watch them lose by just one goal against a Brazil side that included legends Jairzinho and Rivelino

Despite his manager's support, Lennon had clearly been shaken by the incident at Windsor Park. All eyes were on him as he turned out for Celtic against Dunfermline at East End Park.

4 MARCH: DUNFERMLINE 0 CELTIC 3
(Report by Michael Ballie: *Daily Mirror*)

Neil Lennon ended his week of torment in spectacular fashion as he helped Celtic continue their relentless march to the title.

The Celtic midfielder was jeered by his countrymen every time he touched the ball last Wednesday in Northern Ireland's friendly against Norway.

But this time, his every touch was greeted with huge cheers by the Celtic faithful, as they constantly sang his name throughout.

He ran the show at East End Park and inspired Celtic to a 3–0 win, which maintains their 13 point lead over Rangers.

And he topped off the sensational display with his first goal for the club, when he netted Celtic's third with 13 minutes remaining.

Celtic controlled the game from start to finish and raced into a two-goal lead.

Stilian Petrov got the opener and Henrik Larsson, as usual, got his name on the scoresheet, when he scored a spectacular free kick.

The Swede has amazingly notched 40 goals this season, 32 in the league, as Celtic steamrolled towards the championship.

Celtic welcomed back Joos Valgaeren at the expense of the evergreen Tom Boyd.

Dunfermline's form has seen them strive for a place in the top six. But those hopes were further damaged after just 11 minutes when Celtic took the lead.

Petrov slipped the ball to Larsson, who played a cushioned pass into the path of the Bulgarian.

The home side defence were posted missing leaving Marco Ruitenbeek exposed and Petrov kept his composure to slip the ball over the advancing keeper.

Two minutes later O'Neill was forced to make an alteration when Chris Sutton, who had already been off for treatment after falling awkwardly when jumping with Andrius Skerla, hobbled out of the action and was replaced by Tommy Johnson.

Larsson came within an inch of increasing Celtic's lead when his volley, from a Johnson cross, flashed across the face of goal.

After 21 minutes, Mjallby clipped the top of the bar with a lobbed volley, then Skerla was alert to nick the ball off the Swede's toe as he tried to get on the end of a Ramon Vega knock-down.

It was only a matter of time before Celtic increased their lead and they did so in spectacular fashion.

Alan Thompson was hauled back by Ian Ferguson as he weaved his way through three Pars defenders and referee Hugh Dallas blew for a free kick.

Ruitenbeek took time setting his wall but he need not have bothered as Larsson struck the ball over the wall with pace and bend, sending it right into the top corner before the keeper had a chance to move.

Dunfermline started the second period in a determined mood but, for all their possession, they failed to get in behind the Celtic defence to trouble Robert Douglas. Eventually, Celtic tied up the three points.

Thompson's cross was kept in by Johnson, then Larsson knocked the ball into the path of Lennon.

From the edge of the box he drilled a low shot through a packed area into the bottom corner.

The joy was clear to see on his face as he spun away in delight and sprinted to the Celtic dug-out to hug assistant boss John Robertson, before being surrounded by his ecstatic team-mates.

With Celtic in three competitions the fixtures were crowding in on one another, throwing up unusual mixtures. It must have been with a collective sigh that the squad greeted the realisation that they were playing Dunfermline again at Celtic Park three days later in the Scottish Cup fourth-round replay. It was the third time they had met in the space of about three weeks and Celtic were definitely getting better, as the results showed.

Once again Celtic Park had been blessed with celebrities. This time it was the comic duo who were the team's undoubted favourites, Greg Hemphill and Ford Kiernan. Their *Chewin' the Fat* show was a nationwide phenomenon but nowhere did it go down better than in the first-team dressing-room at Celtic Park. Their videos were played on the bus before every game, home and away, and the players regularly regaled each other with the show's catchphrases. Hemphill and Kiernan both drank in the West End pub that Lennon liked to drop into occasionally. Through a mutual journalist friend, Thomas Jordan, a visit was arranged at Parkhead. Thomas remembers: 'The players just loved them. I took them into the players' lounge and the reaction was fantastic. It was quite humbling to see a genuine superstar like Henrik Larsson asking if he could be introduced to the two lads.'

Although it wasn't planned, the comedians were also to meet Martin O'Neill on the same visit. 'We were going out of the stadium past the manager's office,' Thomas adds, 'and John Robertson saw us passing. He called us all in and was clearly delighted to meet them. After a few seconds he said he would go and get Martin O'Neill and the next minute he was there too. It was quite funny because the guys had been doing imitations of people from the world of football and Martin O'Neill immediately started teasing them about it. He said to the lads: "I saw your imitation of me the other day and it was crap." The boys immediately started laughing and said: "You must be some man because it was on the radio." Then they just started taking the mick out of each other. It was a really good atmosphere.'

If O'Neill had only known it, the *Chewin' the Fat* stars weren't the only ones who liked to mimic him. His trademark sign of encouragement on the training field was to bring his hands up to his chest and clap quickly while voicing some words of encouragement to the players running by. They had noticed.

In the dressing-room in March, however, when the joking was over it was Treble talk that was starting to become one of the main topics of conversation. With every match the confidence grew and Dunfermline was to be no different.

7 MARCH: CELTIC 4 DUNFERMLINE 1
(Report by Michael Baillie: *Daily Mirror*)

A double apiece from Ramon Vega and Henrik Larsson made sure Celtic booked their place in the last eight of the Scottish Cup and kept the club well on course for a domestic Treble.

But the scoreline slightly flattered the home side as Jimmy Calderwood's side made sure they knew they were in a Cup tie.

Two crucial penalty decisions turned the game in Celtic's favour, although referee Willie Young was spot-on with both his calls.

The game was nicely poised at 2–1 but once Larsson slotted both penalties away Dunfermline's chance of an upset had gone.

Vega had given Celtic a deserved lead after 24 minutes but Scott Thomson's equaliser three minutes later put the tie on a knife edge.

Celtic's desire told after the interval as Vega once again headed them into the lead before Larsson tied up the game.

With so many crucial games on the horizon, O'Neill had taken the opportunity to rest key players Paul Lambert and Stilian Petrov, with Lubo Moravcik and Jackie McNamara slotting in instead.

Celtic, clearly wanting to kill off Dunfermline's challenge early doors, set out their attacking intentions from the first whistle.

Red-hot Swedish strike ace Larsson was first to threaten after seven minutes – glancing a header from a Moravcik cross just wide.

Then three minutes later the little Slovakian midfielder forced a fine save from Marco Ruitenbeek with a low shot from the edge of the box.

It was all one-way traffic and whenever the Pars did manage to clear their lines it would only give them brief respite before another wave of Celtic attacks.

And in 24 minutes Celtic's pressure paid off when they took the lead with a simple goal.

Alan Thompson curled in a corner and the towering figure of Vega rose unchallenged to nod the ball past Ruitenbeek.

The Pars roared up the park to nick a shock equaliser. O'Neill was clearly unhappy with his side's first-half performance and the way they seemed to ease up after taking the lead.

But the Celtic boss's half-time team talk did the trick and the reinvigorated home side burst out of the starting blocks after the interval.

A minute after the restart Moravcik unleashed a shot that skimmed the top of Ruitenbeek's bar.

And just two minutes later Celtic reclaimed the lead and once again it was Swiss defender Vega who did the damage.

The loss of a goal again galvanised Dunfermline and they came back at Celtic. Agathe did well to clear a Thompson header off the line with Douglas stranded.

And right on the hour mark the Celtic keeper could only beat out a low shot from Thompson, and with Stevie Crawford ready to pounce for a tap in, Joos Valgaeren stepped in to clear off the striker's toe.

Then Larsson, who has made a habit of grabbing crucial goals for Celtic, raced up the other end to nab the vital third on 61 minutes.

He cleverly ran across Andrius Skerla's path as he burst into the box and the Lithuanian pulled him down.

Larsson picked himself up and made no mistake from the spot. And 12 minutes later Larsson repeated the trick – this time after being barged in the back by Ferguson inside the box.

Everybody could now see that the Celtic team was settling into a solid, regular line-up. Give or take injuries, it was one they would finish the season with. Astonishingly all seven of O'Neill's new signings were playing regular first-team football. And O'Neill was showing the trademark of the great manager: the ability to elevate the performance of all his players into something special.

It was a trait Jock Stein had and one that Britain's most successful manager, Alex Ferguson, also has. Glenn Gibbons has noticed the similarities. 'You can compare O'Neill and Stein as managers, if not personalities,' he says. 'Although it's certainly harder now to be a manager than it was in Big Jock's day. You can't get the players you want for a start. Martin has had to do it from that poor position. More than anything his ability to put into players what Alex Ferguson can do and what Big Jock did is significant. I said to Alex once "How do you do that?" and he told me, "You just keep chipping away at it. Just keep the drip going. There are some players that don't need it, of course. They are the godsends. They are the rocks you build it on. They help you."

'O'Neill himself has said the most important thing for him at Celtic was the guys who were already there and the improvement in them. He was talking about Mjallby, Petta, Petrov and even wee Jackie MacNamara.

'That was vital at the beginning. But in the team that ended the season there were hardly any guys remaining from the early games because all Martin's new players were in the team. That is just incredible. I think that is where you look for the key to what he does in a sense. The recruitment thing has been very astutely done. Look at who he signed. Look at the guys in his team who have gone from misery into this golden dawn: Chris Sutton, Allan Thompson, big Vega. It's no coincidence that all three of these guys were in dark places.'

Gibbons believes that talented players who are rescued from misery are often incredibly loyal to their new manager. It is a technique Martin O'Neill must have seen Brian Clough and his managerial partner Peter Taylor utilise with great effect at Nottingham Forest. Virtually the whole Forest squad were in that category, such was the team's lacklustre perfomances before Clough and Taylor arrived. John Robertson certainly remembers the transformation. The talented winger told Clough's biographer Tony Francis: 'Brian and Pete saved my career. I was wasting away at Forest. The life was nice and easy until Pete took me apart. After that, Brian helped me an awful lot by watching every part of my play and pulling me up on little things . . . It helped that I was in awe of him, we all were.'

But Clough and Taylor also specialised, like O'Neill does now, in bringing in players who appeared to have hit a dead-end elsewhere. They brought in England centre-half Larry Lloyd who had been transferred to Coventry from Liverpool for just under a quarter of a million. Lloyd, in his own words, was swinging the lead at the smaller club and his attitude had made him extremely unpopular wih his own team-mates.

He was trouble but he was also talented. Peter Taylor bought Lloyd because he thought he and Clough were strong enough to switch him back on again. 'I was only good where there was a strong manager,' Lloyd later told Francis. 'Not many could handle a big, proud, arrogant bugger like me, but Clough did.'

O'Neill has the strength to handle such players and to motivate those who need the carrot more than the stick. His ability to give players back their self-belief cannot be underestimated.

Glenn Gibbons recalls being told by former England and Rangers player Ray Wilkins what it meant to have someone put faith in him again.

'Ray told me once that when Graeme Souness came for him at Paris St Germain he was in a dungeon,' Gibbons says. 'Wilkins said he would always be grateful because Souness brought him into the light. I think big Sutton has got that same feeling. Watch the way he talks and looks, the way he carries himself and you'll think "He loves it here." Allan Thompson too. He had a complete nightmare at Villa. It happens to players. They just make a wrong move. Of the seven signings three have that in common. I reckon O'Neill thought, "I know they're better than that. And they will be better when I bring them into the light." It also makes them available and affordable.'

After the Dunfermline game there was no doubt that Celtic's squad were on fire on the pitch. They met Hearts on a Sunday when the rain came down in stair rods and few in the crowd doubted that the march to glory was taking place. Fate was to lend a hand too, as a faltering Rangers lined up against Dundee United in the quarter-finals.

11 MARCH: CELTIC 1 HEARTS 0
(Report by Ian Paul: *The Herald*)

Celtic did no more than was required to dispose of Hearts and continue their impressive journey towards prize-giving day. Hearts did give them some nervy times in the final minutes, but overall the Edinburgh team rarely looked capable of preventing the Parkhead side from moving into the Tennent's Scottish Cup semi-final.

Henrik Larsson, the scourge of so many teams this season, has given Hearts a hard time, too. Inevitably, it was he who scored the winning goal and, at the same time, chalked up his seventh strike against the Tynecastle team this season.

Even so, Stilian Petrov would get my vote as Celtic's top man. The Bulgarian, whose uncertain form last term raised questions about his future, has become a seriously good midfield player under manager Martin O'Neill this season.

He was the main playmaker yesterday, but also a genuine goal-seeking supporting act to the frontline. With Alan Thompson providing excellent service on the left and the dazzling speed of Didier Agathe on the right, Celtic had Hearts clinging on grimly during the first half before Larsson struck with a well-placed, authoritative header four minutes before half-time.

Hearts were much better, more assured in the second half and did cause some flutters in the Parkhead penalty area, but it would hardly have been justice if they had snatched a replay.

Larsson, who has hit 43 goals to date this term, is now within reach of

Jimmy McGrory's all-time scoring record of 50 goals in season 1936–37, and Charlie Nicholas's post-war milestone of 48 in season 1982–83.

O'Neill said: 'I thought Henrik's goal was fantastic, an absolutely brilliant goal. No matter how great the ball is in you still have to put it in the back of the net so that was fantastic – he is a truly top-class player.'

Hearts' manager Craig Levein also was magnanimous enough to praise the Swede. 'I'm thinking about buying him. It would be the only way to stop him scoring against us. We may agree on the noughts with Celtic, but the place where the decimal point goes could be the problem.'

Neil Lennon waxed lyrical about Thompson. 'He has been a revelation to me, although I always thought he was a good player with Villa. England are short of left-sided players and they could find it hard to do better than him. He has pace, delivers a great ball, is strong and aggressive. I believe he has what it takes to play at international level.'

The barrier was broken four minutes before the break. A Thompson cross, measured to perfection, reached Larsson, who had evaded his markers, and the striker took deliberate aim before sending a powerful header high into the net.

We didn't know it at that point, but that was effectively game, set and match.

The road ahead suddenly looked very clear as the news came back that Rangers had gone out of the tournament to Dundee United at Tannadice. The fans could taste the Treble in the air. But it wasn't going to be that easy. Attaining the greatest domestic triumph has always been like following a path strewn with landmines.

Glenn Gibbons has seen a few: 'Trebles are very difficult. Big Walter Smith always used to say nobody has any idea how hard a Treble is. Look at the stats. During Rangers' nine championships in a row they only won one Treble. It's incredible. Celtic only won two in their spell. Celtic's was a crazy one because they kept losing the League Cup final. It should have been the easiest one of the lot. They played in 14 successive League Cup finals only winning five in a row and one later. So they lost eight of the 14 against teams you would have thought shouldn't have been on the same pitch as them. It just kept happening. They kept doing the hard bit, like winning the league and the Scottish Cup, and then failing the League Cup hurdle. It's a very strange thing but Walter Smith was right – it's very hard to win a Treble.

'The funny thing is you can lose it when you think it's almost won.

Take the Scottish Cup final which Rangers lost to Dundee United in '94 for a Scottish Treble.'

Despite history's grim warnings of last-minute slip-ups, Gibbons believes Celtic were shaping up for greatness early on. 'I thought Celtic were probably going to make it in March. I felt they had established such dominion. I thought if they are not going to make it, it will have to be before the Scottish Cup final. They wouldn't be stopped in the final. They were just so far ahead of everybody else. The overwhelming impression was their strength, both spiritual and physical. They just looked too strong for everybody and their self-belief just grew throughout the year.'

There was lots more drama on the cards for the team before anything would be sewn up. Next up was a game that will remain etched on the memory of every Celtic supporter who was there because of the curious mixture of sadness and happiness that came at the same time.

It was St Johnstone at McDiarmid Park. Rangers were playing Dundee at Ibrox. It started so well. As the fans queued outside St Johnstone's ground the news flashed back that Rangers, who had kicked off 15 minutes earlier, had lost a goal already. Amid the backslapping and grinning faces the Celtic support settled down for an epic night which could, if only Rangers lost, put them 16 points clear at the top of the table. Johnson scored first for Celtic, then St Johnstone equalised. It was tense, tense stuff. Thompson sent in another screaming low cross. Bang. Larsson smacked a header straight past Alan Main. The game was all but won. All ears were straining to pick up the latest news from Ibrox. It arrived. Rangers had lost.

Supporter Austin Barrett takes up the tale. 'Up until then the fans had been going wild. We were just waiting for that Rangers result. When it came we were too sick to cheer. I can see it now. Stilian Petrov was lying on the ground with his leg broken. They were all fussing around him. You knew from the atmosphere and the reaction of the playing staff that it was bad. It was just sickening.'

The horror of the scene was obvious by the shocked look on the faces of Martin O'Neill and John Robertson as they turned away to hide their expressions from Petrov.

14 MARCH: ST JOHNSTONE 1 CELTIC 2
(Report by Steven Sullivan: *Celtic View*)

An uncharacteristically tired performance from Celtic nevertheless yielded another three points as the Hoops continued their inexorable march towards the SPL title.

Tommy Johnson opened the scoring in the 28th minute when he

headed home an Alan Thompson corner-kick, but the teams went into the break on level terms as Stewart McCluskey pegged a goal back for the visitors after some sloppy Celtic defending.

Celtic dominated the majority of the second period, but it took until the 60th minute before the visitors regained their earlier cushion when Henrik Larsson headed home his 44th goal of the season.

It ought to have been another happy evening for the Swede but after watching Petrov sustain a painful injury, the game perhaps evoked memories of his own misfortune in Lyon last season.

Indeed, Europe's top scorer was the first at Petrov's side to offer words of encouragement and was quick off the pitch at the final whistle, giving the travelling support a brief acknowledgement before making his way to the dressing-room.

O'Neill reintroduced Tommy Johnson as Henrik Larsson's partner in front of goal, perhaps with one eye on Sunday's CIS Insurance Cup final.

The importance of the St Johnstone result was not lost amid the shock of Petrov's injury. It was to be remembered as the night Celtic really won the league. Lifelong supporter Jim Smith was on his way back home after the match when he pulled into Perth's Tesco for something to eat. 'I couldn't believe it,' he remembers. 'The place was full of Celtic supporters queuing up beside the mums and dads with their shopping. There were scores of them and they were all buying bottles of wine to celebrate. It was the same out in the car park where these guys were wandering round with bottles of Chardonnay, obviously there was no Buckfast, trying to work out how to open them. It was a real party feeling.'

Cup final day came and the hordes in green and white swarmed all over Mount Florida. Police lined the roads, traffic wardens cleared the cars and there was a taste of Celtic victory in the air. Celtic went into the match at Hampden as the holders. No great achievement, many will say, because the League Cup is the Cinderella competition overshadowed by the other two major honours. But it takes on a magical significance when the Treble is still possible.

Celtic had won the League Cup last year. Then it had been a hollow victory because it also signalled the end of the season as far as trophies were concerned.

The League Cup will, of course, always hold a place in the heart of Celtic supporters because of the 7–1 game. The result has resonated down the years even amongst those who didn't follow either side.

'I remember it,' says Gibbons. 'I was walking into Cambridge Street in Glasgow and somebody said it was 1–0, then it was 2–0. I think it was 4–1 at half-time. I listened to the rest of it on the radio. It became a formality and Willie Fernie scored. At the age of 12 the impact isn't the same as it is in adults, but I still thought it was something. I wasn't aware of the barrenness of the period Celtic were undergoing then. In actual fact it hadn't seemed that barren because although Celtic had won the Double in '54 and nothing since they had been in three successive Scottish Cup finals in' 54, '55, '56. Rangers weren't dominating either so you didn't notice so much.

'You've got to remember how different it was then. Hibs were the first team invited into the European Cup. They were the first British team to play in it and not because they were Scottish champions. It was by invitation only and Hibs were seen as the best team in Scotland.

'The '50s were like that, well spread. Nobody would realise that for Celtic there would be the 11 years between '54 and '65, interrupted only by that League Cup final. The 11 barren years as they called it then.'

Celtic had had their barren years in recent times too. But even the bleakest periods were broken by the occasional League Cup win. The victories were always celebrated magnificently even if the champagne quickly went as flat as the rest of the season. The 2001 final would never be among that category. At first, though, it was simply memorable because of the magnificent hat trick notched up by Henrik Larsson in the second half of the game. No goal was more beautiful than his last. As he picked up the ball in his own half with just ten minutes left on the clock, and the match clearly won, Larsson proved his hunger for goals was insatiable. Spinning into the Kilmarnock half with defenders trailing him like dogs chasing a passing car, he came face to face with goalie Gordon Marshall who spread himself wide with his legs and arms flailing. Henrik coolly rolled the ball to the side and ghosted past the downed keeper before stroking the ball into an empty net.

The more perceptive also sensed a growing feeling that Martin O'Neill was increasing in stature as every extra inch was gained in the battle for the Treble. Now he had the League Cup under his belt and the Martin O'Neill story had really begun.

18 MARCH: CELTIC 3 KILMARNOCK 0
(Report by Graham Spiers: *The Herald*)
This CIS Cup final will be regarded as the beginning of the rest of Martin O'Neill's career. The Celtic manager has tasted Worthington Cup success

in England, but it is in Glasgow guiding Scotland's champions-elect that the mould for his future experiences will be cast. Yesterday, as Celtic anticipated their first Treble for 32 years, O'Neill secured the first in a series of achievements that might delight and unnerve the Celtic support.

A noisy battalion bellowed in celebration at Hampden, and if this match is an indication of how O'Neill's Celtic react at the critical hour, the club's future will be decorated indeed. The more O'Neill hauls silverware towards Parkhead, however, the more the prying eyes from bigger footballing environments will commence their siren call. Meantime, Celtic and O'Neill are a love affair that seems destined for great days.

With his lithe frame and relentless motion, Henrik Larsson in this match resembled a greyhound that could not be caught. Already awash with goals this season, Larsson's second-half hat trick inflicted not just damage but misery on Kilmarnock, whose wariness turned to depression over a player who is simply unstoppable.

Those who wonder why Larsson is so reluctant to go to England should have been at this match. For Larsson, life with Celtic is improbably charmed.

His ludicrous goals statistic for the 2000–01 season stands at 47, which, if it partly damns the quality of defenders he has faced, is also a testimony to his insatiable poaching. Yet one of the many remarkable aspects of Larsson's game which was evident yesterday was the time he finds amid bulging nets for chasing and harrying opponents. At least one of them, Frederick Dindeleux, was on a yellow card through being harassed by the Swede, and was surely heading for another from Hugh Dallas before being mercifully substituted by Bobby Williamson.

Larsson's havoc was such that Celtic could endure a series of setbacks. Bobby Petta limped away after 11 minutes, the result of two heavy tackles which caused fresh injury to his groin. Celtic's greatest handicap, though, and the most fiery moment of the afternoon, should have been the red card shown to Chris Sutton by Dallas after 59 minutes.

This affair was yet another instalment of the Englishman's misery in Glasgow. After two red cards and a flurry of bookings this season, if Sutton isn't careful he'll develop a persecution complex in Scotland. Dallas spent the afternoon repeatedly chiding the striker over his inability to challenge cleanly for the ball, and when Sutton and Gary Holt competed for a loose ball, his frustrations boiled over.

His tackle on Holt was ghastly. Arriving knee-high with his studs showing, it was the sort of stamping motion that, in the past, has ended careers. Dallas flourished his red card while Holt sprawled on the grass.

Deep in his own half and by the left touchline, this antic from Sutton seemed not just crude but a mite stupid.

Amid all of this, Kilmarnock failed to make an impact. A morose feature of their day was that, following Sutton's dismissal, they could not make a single threatening gesture around Jonathan Gould's goal. Williamson resisted throwing the ageing menace of Ally McCoist into the fray, instead replacing Dindeleux with Peter Canero, while leaving Kilmarnock sparse at the back. If anything, as this game got older, it was Celtic who assumed control.

Perhaps Williamson rued the manner in which injuries took their toll. Christophe Cocard had to be replaced after 48 minutes, but Kilmarnock's true misfortune was the loss of Ian Durrant ten minutes earlier. Back after four months out with knee trouble, Durrant's craft had been not just a delight but significant, in a period in which his team excelled. Along with Alan Mahood and Holt, the 34-year-old had embroidered Kilmarnock's play. Durrant hobbled away at the point when the match swung towards Celtic, but the news that his career may be over was of far greater concern.

Without Stilian Petrov, Didier Agathe, Alan Thompson, and ultimately Sutton, Celtic might have toiled, should Larsson not make such notions absurd. He struck thrice between 47 and 80 minutes, and it was his third which embodied his extraordinary powers. Grabbing possession 15 yards inside Kilmarnock's half, Larsson's head went down as his pace increased, boring through on Gordon Marshall's goal.

Garry Hay made helpless pursuit which didn't affect the striker, and when Marshall advanced, Larsson dribbled around him before prodding the ball into the net. It was an exquisite completion which few other strikers could so perfect from start to finish.

Larsson's opening goal boasted no such architecture – it was simple plundering in the penalty box. Colin Healy worked a short corner with Lubo Moravcik, whose out-swinging cross was met by a galaxy of heads. Above the six-yard line the ball looped up and Larsson arched and swung his right boot to hook the ball past Marshall. Kilmarnock, now lacking Durrant, must have sensed their nauseous fate.

Strictly speaking, at the decree of killjoys, perhaps Larsson's wasn't a hat trick at all. His second, in 73 minutes, took a wicked deflection off Chris Innes, forcing the shot up and spinning into a mesmerising trajectory as the ball wafted over Marshall and just under his crossbar. After so much pillaging, though, this Swede doesn't appear fussy about the manner in which he strikes. His goals here had the quality of almost predestined bedlam which scarcely any Celtic striker in history has enjoyed.

Lifelong Celtic supporter and *Herald* journalist Keith Sinclair took part in the partying that rolled on that evening. 'It wasn't over the top,' he says. 'There was just a feeling of anticipation in the pit of your stomach like when you know something is going to happen and it's going to be very good. It was a very special time for Celtic fans. We could sense the club was on the beginning of a new era.'

Frank Murphy of the *Four Four Two* football magazine had the same sensation. 'It was all unfolding right in front of everybody's eyes. The players, the groundstaff, the fans could sense that something big was happening right in front of their eyes. History in the making, all that sort of stuff. I never doubted from then on in. Neither did anyone else. The whole thing had a sensation of being preordained.'

It was a case of one down, two to go.

12.

CHAMPIONES

Championes, Championes,
Away, away, away
Championes, Championes,
Away, away, away.

IT'S MIDWAY THROUGH the first half of Celtic v St Mirren and O'Brien's is packed with more than 100 fans watching the match live on TV. The atmosphere is tense and a nervous silence has descended. Supporters adorned in Celtic T-shirts and replica strips lean anxiously on the edge of their seats. Pints of beer and Guinness line the tables, largely untouched. The bar is filled with the familiar, comforting aroma of warm Scotch pies. A fresh delivery has arrived from Jim McGill, who hails from Carnwadric. But Jim's a Rangers fan so, understandably, he's not in the bar today. Margaret, from the Garngad, asks if anyone wants a pie or one of her special rolls and sausage. She prepared the sausage meat herself, with spices she bought from the Gallowgate. But nobody's hungry. The punters are too nervous to eat.

With more than half an hour played the score is still 0–0. Celtic have had plenty of possession but they have not managed to convert their advantage into goals. Normally that would not be a cause for concern but this is no normal game. Celtic need all three points to secure the league championship – and the second leg of the Treble – so that the partying can begin in earnest.

Suddenly a few of the regulars sit forward excitedly, sensing that something is happening. Henrik Larsson has found a chink of space on the left. He plays in Tommy Johnson, who's been left unmarked inside the box. Some fans stand up in nervous expectation. The Geordie attempts to control the pass with his left foot but it spins free from under his studs and it looks like the chance is gone. The bar breathes a collective sigh of frustration as some fans begin to sit back down. But Johnson is not finished. He steadies himself before connecting with his right boot. The ball is fired straight at the keeper but somehow it wriggles under his outstretched form and beyond him. The ball is in the back of the net.

The bar erupts in a cacophony of unrestrained jubilation. The noise is unchained and formless and it seems to go on forever. Tables are edged on to their sides and glasses upended, the contents spilling over legs and on to the carpet. But no one cares. Celtic are ahead. Gradually the noise becomes less anarchic and begins to take shape into a recognisable chant: 'For it's a grand old team to play for . . .'

The same ritual is being repeated in a thousand pubs across Scotland but O'Brien's is different – it's 6,000 miles away in downtown Santa Monica, California. At half-time Joe Cook steps outside to catch his breath, free from the smoky, oppressive atmosphere inside. He squints in the blinding sunlight and looks at his watch – it's barely 8 a.m.

The punters inside are all members of the Los Angeles Celtic Supporters Club, one of dozens of such organisations in North America. If Celtic's very existence is about perpetuating the legacy of the Irish community in Scotland then this is the foreign legion – a far-flung colony keeping the same traditions alive in some of the world's unlikeliest spots.

Joe, the club's co-secretary, is a self-employed insulation engineer from Pollok who brought his family to live in LA 12 years ago. His accent may still be unmistakably Glaswegian but Joe is perfectly assimilated into his new Californian lifestyle. He's one of the beautiful people. There's little he misses about Scotland but he does miss his beloved Celtic. Back home he was a founder member of the now defunct West End Celtic Supporters Club, along with Alan Storer, Ronnie Mahér and Paolo Mazzoncini. He didn't have to look far in his adopted country to find a home from home. LA has had a thriving Celtic supporters club for 35 years.

Thanks to the wonders of satellite communication, Joe and his fellow club members get to see more live action than most fans back home. Every game, home and away, is beamed direct to their little piece of Parkhead in the heart of the golden state. 'It's important for the Scots and Irish people who live here to remember who they are and what they are about,' says Joe. 'Following Celtic helps them to do that.'

It takes a dedicated follower to keep up with their team in a time zone that is no respecter of Scottish kick-off times. For most matches Joe has to be up by six a.m. to be at the bar in time for kick-off. 'The 6–2 game was a one p.m. kick-off in Glasgow which meant it was five a.m. over here but the pub was still jumping,' says Joe. 'This season has been unbelievable, not just because of what's happened with the team. We have had dozens of people turn up for every single game. The support has been amazing. People are just so happy that we are winning again. It hasn't always been easy in the past, keeping the club going through the bad spells. Last year we only had a handful of devoted souls who turned up for the Inverness Caley game.'

When the LA club was started in 1966 it had just 14 members. Back in the early days, before live satellite games, members would sit round a shortwave radio hoping for snatched items of news about anything to do with Celtic. With the advent of video they had tapes sent over from family back home and they would watch the matches a few weeks after they had been played. Now the club is the focal point of an entire community which can meet and talk about all things Celtic. The club has four dances a year, which raise funds for the club, and an annual convention in Las Vegas where they invite players and ex-players. This year's special guest was Chris Sutton.

Andy Rock, who is the club's vice-president, has lived in California since 1961 when he was four years old. His father Billy, who grew up in Anderston, is now a well-known face among the LA Celtic community. 'I came here to find work. Found work but there was a huge void in my life called Celtic,' he recalls.

People like Joe, Larry, Andy and Billy have kept the faith for the past decade and a half or so when being a Celtic supporter was often a burden they were forced to drag behind them like a leg iron. Remaining true and bold was all the more difficult when they were doing so from the other side of the world, when the results were going against them, when good players were being sold and when the club was being dragged through the mire by people who thought little about Celtic and cared less.

Now the good times were returning. When Celtic travelled to Pittodrie on 1 April their task was clear. A defeat by Rangers the previous day against Dundee United had simplified all the mathematical permutations. If they beat Aberdeen, followed by victories against Dundee in midweek and St Mirren the following Saturday, then the league crown would be theirs.

The implication of Rangers' defeat had not been lost on Davie Welsh, a 36-year-old police officer from Glasgow. He hadn't planned on travelling north to Aberdeen, for the first of Celtic's crucial trio of games the following day, but suddenly he felt compelled to be there. He didn't want to miss a thing. Despite working complicated shift patterns, Davie had barely missed a game all season, home or away. Through a combination of arm-twisting sympathetic colleagues and nimble footwork around the shift rota at Johnstone CID, he had managed to secure all the necessary time off, even for crucial Sunday and midweek games in farflung destinations like Perth and Dundee.

While Rangers were losing to Dundee United, he was on a stag weekend with 11 mates in Perth. They were due to return to Glasgow at lunchtime on the Sunday but suddenly he hit on an ingenious plan. He would set out from Perth a couple of hours earlier and join up with three other mates back in Glasgow, who had a spare ticket. He would then retrace his tracks back up north, arriving in the Granite City in time for the early evening kick-off.

It was a consummately cunning plan, perfect in every way, except that he had not told his wife about it. His devotion to the Celtic cause, while applauded by his fellow supporters, had done little to foster amicable domestic relations and, as he contentedly sped up the M90, she was busily pacing the length of chez Welsh, her face contorted with rage, using what was left of her rational faculty to devise her own plan – how to quell her husband's Celtic-fuelled wanderlust without getting bloodstains on her good carpet.

'I decided not to tell her I was going to Aberdeen,' the father-of-three admits coyly. 'I just told her that I wouldn't be back from Perth until late in the evening. It would have worked too if she hadn't started phoning round the other wives who told her the rest of the boys had returned in the early afternoon.

'After the Aberdeen game we were on such a high that we went for a couple of pints. It was about 11 p.m. by the time I got home and she was absolutely raging. I can't even tell you her name because she won't think this is funny. It's still a sore point in the house. We were supposed to be saving up for a holiday and she gave me all this grief about how I was neglecting the family to follow Celtic.

'But I don't regret a thing. It's the best season that I can remember. It's like a fairytale – Martin O'Neill's arrival, the 6–2 game, all the games when it looked like we were going to drop points but we pulled it off in the dying moments. It took a while for my wife to calm down but it's all sorted out now because we've got a holiday booked.'

1 APRIL: ABERDEEN 0 CELTIC 1
(Report by authors)

One down, two to go. This was generally regarded as the most testing barrier to the league title and Celtic negotiated it with craft and determination. It was hardly a convincing display, one which had the band of travelling support shuffling nervously in their seats for well over an hour.

But when the breakthrough finally came, after 72 minutes from a goal by Didier Agathe, it perhaps decisively vindicated the belief that this would, indeed, be Celtic's year. His strike sparked rapturous celebrations among the Celtic supporters who remained in the ground long after the final whistle, united in their joy.

The Frenchman, largely anonymous for most of the match, picked up a stray ball on the edge of the Dons defence and, with his back to goal, created space. Losing his marker with a dexterous spin, he fired the ball beyond the reach of the despairing keeper Ryan Esson.

It was the introduction of Moravcik for Johnson after 64 minutes which was to prove tactically decisive. Other than providing the initial penetration which led to the goal, the Slovak introduced a calm assuredness which the midfield had lacked until then.

Celtic dominated completely for the remainder of the match and they could have increased their lead on several occasions. For Aberdeen the only consolation was that they appeared to have broken the jinx which has afflicted them in past seasons where they cannot play Celtic without conceding six goals.

However, for much of the game a Celtic win seemed as unlikely as a balmy spring evening in the North-East.

Celtic were barely able to create an opening in the first half. When they did, it was Lennon who was the creative force. A free kick from the Irishman in 22 minutes found Larsson who, unusually, failed to hit the target when he rose for the header.

Neither the Swede, who had been treated for a head injury after colliding with Whyte, nor Johnson were able to find a chink in a tight Aberdeen defence. Johnson powered a cross along the six-yard line when, with more composure, he might have spotted Larsson in space and later he headed a Thompson cross straight into the arms of Esson. In between times Vega failed to hit the target after being picked out with pin-point accuracy by a Lennon free kick.

Sensing that things were not going his way, O'Neill switched Agathe from the right wing to a midfield role, immediately behind the two strikers, and then to the left wing but his versatility was not having much impact. Rather it was the home side who were looking the more dangerous approaching half-time when Rab Douglas fluffed a Robbie Winters corner, allowing defender Philip McGuire a free shot at goal, but his powerful shot deflected over the bar.

The introduction of Moravcik in 64 minutes was followed closely by the replacement of Jackie McNamara for Colin Healy and things started to move in Celtic's favour. After Agathe's goal, Larsson might have added a second, only denied by the intervention of Whyte, who back-heeled the ball to safety. Moravcik almost finished things off when his drive from the edge of the area struck the far post and was scrambled away in some desperation.

For the first time since arriving at Celtic Park, O'Neill permitted himself a modicum of self-congratulation although, true to form, he didn't allow himself to become too carried away. His team, after all, had not yet won the league. 'It's a bit premature of the fans to celebrate the title, although I can't do anything about that,' he said afterwards. 'However, we are tantalisingly close now – and we will throw absolutely everything at the charge to get it over these two games. We're in a fantastic position – even I can't deny that.'

It was appropriate that the winning goal was scored by Agathe, perhaps O'Neill's most astute purchase in the post-Bosman transfer market. Despite it being only the winger's third goal in 28 appearances, it was yet another timely strike from the Frenchman. He had grabbed the crucial winner in the dying seconds at Dens Park four months previously. Rarely a headline stealer, Agathe had nevertheless more than proved his worth to the side during the league run-in, providing electrifying pace and penetration, hence his nickname, the Road Runner.

The son of an Indian Ocean island merchant banker, his career had looked to be in terminal decline when he was forced to leave Montpellier because of a knee problem. He was picked up by Raith Rovers and forgotten about in his homeland until he was signed by Hibs manager Alex McLeish, who recognised his enormous potential, and then by O'Neill.

His strike meant Celtic remained on course to lift the championship by the weekend. They had overcome the most difficult hurdle at Pittodrie and now all they had to do was hold their nerve at home against Dundee and St Mirren. It sounded straightforward. It was anything but.

4 APRIL: CELTIC 2 DUNDEE 1
(Report by authors)

The champagne was put on ice at the end of a pulsating match which set up a title party the following Saturday. Johan Mjallby's 85th-minute winner ensured Celtic needed only to take full points from their clash with St Mirren to claim their first-ever SPL championship.

Few could have anticipated such a nervy ending to a match which had seemed a formality after five minutes when Johnson fired Celtic into the lead. However, the title party went distinctly flat when the side, wearing their new non-hooped strips for the first time, conceded an equaliser in the 68th minute, stunning the home support. Only the sending-off of Barry Smith with seven minutes remaining offered the Bhoys renewed hope and that was justified with the Swedish defender's strike, only his third of the season.

O'Neill had vowed that his team would seek to wrap up the title as quickly as possible but suddenly the unthinkable was happening. Henrik Larsson was suffering a goal drought. That is to say, he had gone three games without a goal. For most strikers such a statistic would largely go unnoticed but Larsson is far better than most strikers.

The Swede could have put Celtic ahead in the first minute after connecting with a Moravcik pass but keeper Jamie Langfield deflected the striker's effort with his left leg. Ramon Vega started the move which led to the goal, feeding Thompson on the left. He put Larsson further down the line and the striker crossed the ball low into the area where Johnson was able to steal space between Steven Tweed and Chris Coyne to flick the ball past Langfield from eight yards.

Four minutes later Dundee survived another attack when Larsson's shot deflected into the path of Johnson who was unable to dig the ball from under the feet of the prostrate Langfield. The Geordie striker almost made amends in the 37th minute after he was played in by Larsson, but he misfired from in front of goal.

Dundee replaced Caniggia with Fabian Caballero at the break and the visitors came close minutes into the restart when Rab Douglas was forced to beat away a low cross from Javier Artero which was destined for the boot of the substitute. Tweed was booked ten minutes into the second half for a foul on Larsson but Dundee continued to push forward, with Douglas forced into some impromptu acrobatics as he dived to tip a long-range shot by Antonio Garrido around his left-hand post.

McNamara came on for Johnson after 62 minutes to tighten up the midfield but the switch failed to prevent Dundee drawing level six minutes later. Georgie Nemsadze found Juan Sara in the box with an angled cross, and the striker composed himself before guiding the ball past Douglas with the inside of his foot from six yards.

With time running out, Moravcik tried to put Celtic back in front after Larsson flicked on a Lennon free kick but his shot lacked the power to trouble Langfield. However, as the game looked to be approaching stalemate, the home side were given renewed hope when Smith was then sent off for hauling back Mjallby after Larsson had played his team-mate in on goal. Langfield managed a terrific save from Thompson's resultant free kick but two minutes later Dundee failed to clear Thompson's corner and, as the ball dropped into the box, Mjallby powered through to force the ball over the line.

And so the party preparations begun. At last the winning post was in sight and Celtic supporters across the country geared up for a massive celebration. On paper the match was as close to a formality as was possible. Celtic were placed comfortably at the top of the league, St Mirren were ten places behind in bottom position. Celtic had lost only once en route to the title-decider, St Mirren had won only a handful of games and were now destined for relegation. Celtic had a team full of comparative superstars. The entire St Mirren squad cost less than Neil Lennon.

And there were precedents. St Mirren had proved convenient fall-guys in the past when Celtic needed precious points to wrap up the league title. Never more so than in 1986 when, going into the final match, Celtic needed to beat the Buddies by at least three goals at Love Street and hope that Hearts lost at Dundee for them to edge the title on goal difference. Happily for the Bhoys, St Mirren were swept aside by a rampant Celtic side who managed to shoot five past their hosts while Hearts, who had an unbeaten run stretching back to the first month of the season, went down 2–0 to the Taysiders.

Four years previously St Mirren had played their part in a similarly anxious scenario. Again on the final day of the season, Celtic knew that a 1–0 defeat for them and a 5–0 win for Aberdeen against Rangers at Pittodrie would mean the flag going north. Most of the 40,000 supporters crammed into Celtic Park believed that to be a highly unlikely prospect until half-time when the match was still goal-less and Aberdeen were leading 4–0. However a George McCluskey goal after 63 minutes put Celtic on the road to a 3–0 victory which brought the title back to the East End.

As the crunch tie approached, Celtic's cause was further boosted by discontent among the St Mirren players who had been promised a paltry £5,000 a man to avoid the drop zone, less than half the bonus on offer to their nearest challengers, Dundee United.

Behind the scenes, staff at Celtic Park were preparing for the biggest party seen there in more than a decade. Champagne was ordered, security gates were erected at the front of the stadium to protect players from adoring fans and the unlikely named Celtic Tenors were hired as the post-match turn.

'It was a nervous few days,' admitted Tony Hamilton, producer of Celtic TV. 'We normally have a staff meeting on a Tuesday, when all the arrangements for Saturday are made. At that stage we hadn't played Dundee yet, so we didn't know if we would even be in a position to win the league. It could have looked a bit presumptuous if we had laid on a big party for nothing.'

He added: 'I always get lots of people phoning me up and asking for tickets. The interest in that game was phenomenal, even more so than the Cup final. The pressure was really on. We had to win. If we had lost, it would have gone totally flat.'

The Celtic players knew that all they had to do was to maintain their equilibrium, go for one final push and the title would be theirs. But by the time kick-off arrived, the pressure was getting to them. Suddenly nerves started to jangle. Perhaps it was the realisation of what they were on the verge of achieving. Perhaps it was the pressure of Celtic Park packed with 60,400 expectant, success-hungry fans plus a worldwide audience watching live on satellite TV. Perhaps it was that St Mirren were actually a pretty decent side who were prepared to come to Celtic Park and actually attack.

Whatever the reason, no one felt the intense expectation more than Joos Valgaeren. His family were visiting him in Scotland for the first time and were watching him from the main stand. The trip had been organised some time before. It was purely coincidental that it happened to fall on the most crucial weekend in the entire season.

7 APRIL: CELTIC 1 ST MIRREN 0
(Report by authors)

The goal that eventually clinched Celtic's 37th league championship came from the unlikeliest of sources. An early strike from Tommy Johnson, who has played third fiddle to Sutton and the heroics of Larsson all season, ultimately proved decisive on a nervy afternoon.

Although their opponents were anchored at the foot of the table, St Mirren had proved among the pluckiest of Celtic's opponents during the course of the season and they set about their latest task with characteristic determination, playing three up front.

It was a high-risk strategy and one that was to prove their early undoing as Celtic, marshalled by the supremely calm Lambert in midfield, set about exposing their defensive weaknesses with cruel ruthlessness. With Paul Lambert, who was superbly calm and controlled, patrolling deep in midfield and springing forward at every opportunity, Celtic took immediate advantage of St Mirren's cavalier approach and created chance after chance.

Yet for all Celtic's bravado, largely orchestrated by the twisting, pirouetting Moravcik, it took them 38 minutes to breach that defence. Larsson played Johnson through and, as the Geordie attempted to control the pass with his left foot, it spun free from under his studs. As the Celtic support breathed a collective sigh of frustration, he connected with his right boot and the ball was poked under the keeper and into the net.

Encouraged by their opener, Celtic started the second half with a degree of vigour and Alan Thompson could have put them two ahead but his header smashed against the bar and bounced behind. Saints became more adventurous as the game progressed and they frightened Celtic when Stephen McPhee surged into the box after beating Vega, only for Rab Douglas to rescue the situation with a bold tackle.

Celtic continued to create opportunities. Vega headed a Thompson cross wide and a Larsson volley also missed the target when Didier Agathe centred from the same position. A second goal eluded Celtic but in the end it wasn't needed as the final whistle sparked the biggest party seen in the East End of Glasgow for years.

Celtic went indoors still only that goal ahead and although Alan Thompson saw a header skim the top of the bar they had to settle for a narrow win but the margin of victory wasn't important. The fact that St Mirren were always only one goal away from spoiling the fun merely enhanced the pleasure at the end.

The roar which greeted the final whistle blew the dust from the rafters and scattered the pigeons, and long after St Mirren had departed Celtic and their fans were still rejoicing, barely able to believe the title was back in their possession even though that had been a distinct possibility for months.

It was a nervy, unconvincing performance and the score signalled just how tight the match had been. Yet by the time the final whistle sounded all that was irrelevant as frenzied scenes of green-and-white mayhem detonated across the East End of the city. The 60,000 people packed into Celtic Park cheered, sang, danced and embraced. Some cried, others stood, bemused and open-mouthed, slowly coming to terms with the new status quo. Celtic were league champions.

Without any silverware to parade, the Celtic players were restricted to a lap of honour. T-shirts worn by every first-team member were emblazoned with the slogan 'No Excuses', an ironic riposte to Advocaat's perpetual refrain that injury problems had cost his side the league. On the back was the enigmatic 'Smell the Glove' message, which had first appeared after their 1998 league triumph. The players ran and skipped and danced before making a series of headlong Klinsmanesque dives across the surface of the pitch, in front of all four stands.

O'Neill kept a discreet distance from the celebrations, allowing his players their moment in the sun. After a while he emerged to accept the applause of the crowd and to thank them for their support. His post-match comments were modest and magnanimous in victory. Even he could no longer deny the scale of the achievement.

'It's been phenomenal,' he said. 'It is as good a day as I've had in football. To win it so early and to win it here at Parkhead is extremely special. It's everything and more that I ever dreamed of. I don't think we'll ever win 28 out of 33 games again. That is sensational and I can't praise the players highly enough.'

Watching from the press box was Jim Traynor of the *Daily Record*. 'He is a great guy to study,' said Traynor. 'The celebrations seemed to go on forever. Out on the pitch, when the team was celebrating, you would see O'Neill tugging some member of the backroom staff to come into the picture. There he is, this great guy in his moment of triumph saying "It's not about me. It's about these other people." Then he stood back with the smile on his face. He was maybe two or three feet away in the background. And then, as though there was a trapdoor in the middle of the pitch, everyone else disappeared and he was on his own. He couldn't resist it. And why should he? I think he knew exactly what he was doing. And as long as his team wins he can do what he wants.'

Tony Hamilton was one of the few non-players privileged to go into the dressing-room and witness the outpourings of delight that came from the squad. The players were shouting at the tops of their voices and there were waves of delight bouncing off the dressing-room walls. 'They were singing "The Soldiers' Song",' Tony recalls. 'Which was amazing because, with the exception of Colin Healy, none of them were Irish and only a couple were Scottish.

'The players have a real feel for the history and traditions of the club, none more so than Henrik. He is the kind of guy who is able to tell you the majority of things that any lifelong Celtic fan will know. He has really done his homework on the club.'

The raw humour that had been building up in the dressing-room all season was evident as Tony Hamilton presented Ramon Vega with the Man of the Match award on Celtic TV. Paul Lambert, who was passing, stuck his face in front of the camera and shouted, 'Man of the match, my arse.'

All over the city supporters partied into the night. In Bargo, a city-centre bar, one unfortunate bystander was appropriated by a group of fans for no reason other than he bore a passing resemblance to O'Neill. He was carried shoulder-high through the streets of the Merchant City to chants of 'Martin O'Neill, Martin O'Neill, Martin O'Neill, Martin O'Neill . . .' As the mob swung into Candleriggs, their path was blocked by a police car, so they sat down in the middle of the road, refusing to budge, singing 'We Shall Not Be Moved'.

In another city-centre bar the community singing was in full cry by early evening. It was standing-room only and strong drink was flowing. As the singing became noisier and more boisterous, so the landlord became correspondingly more foot-stampingly irate. The volume of singing eventually dimmed following scarlet-faced threats of mass eviction. Then the landlord turned his back and the fans swung back into full pelt. Some of the regulars were perplexed at mein host's uncharacteristically party-pooping attitude. Only later was it revealed that Dick Advocaat had been upstairs in a private room enjoying a meal with his family.

After sewing up the league, Celtic were immediately bounced into another crucial game – a Scottish Cup semi-final against Dundee United which they would need to win to keep alive their hopes of landing the Treble. Former Ranger Charlie Miller acknowledged publicly that he and his colleagues would be carrying the hopes of half the country into the match as they stood between Celtic and a clean sweep.

Any concerns that the Celtic players might be suffering from a league hangover were quickly dispelled as they set about destroying their Tayside opponents with the clinical ruthlessness of an assassin. Henrik Larsson could barely have picked a more appropriate moment to break

Charlie Nicholas' post-war scoring record. His double strike took his season's tally to 49, ending a three-match goal famine!

The Swede was developing a fairy-tale relationship with Hampden Park, where his goals effectively killed off Dundee United before substitute Jackie McNamara applied the finishing touch. The scoreline may have flattered Celtic but Derek Lilley gave boss Alex Smith consolation as he watched his dream of becoming the first manager to win the Cup with three different teams disappear.

APRIL 15: CELTIC 3 DUNDEE UNITED 1
(Report by authors)

Chris Sutton and Larsson caused United problems throughout and were showing great movement up front from the first whistle, but United also showed much promise on the break.

Space opened up for former Rangers midfielder Charlie Miller in the tenth minute, but his right-foot shot from 22 yards flew just over Robert Douglas's crossbar.

Celtic looked nervous at the back and in the 15th minute they breathed a sigh of relief when referee Hugh Dallas waved away United's claims for a penalty.

Stephen Thompson played the ball up to Lilley but the frontman went down in the area under the challenge of Paul Lambert and they escaped.

That stirred the champions and Jim Lauchlan did well to head Alan Thompson's dangerous cross-over with Sutton breathing down his neck.

Moments later and Lambert found Joos Valgaeren in the box but the Belgian fired over the bar from a tight angle.

Sutton continued to cause the United defence all kinds of problems and it was the former Chelsea man who came closest to breaking the deadlock in the 27th minute.

Agathe teed the ball up for Larsson to deliver the perfect cross and Sutton soared highest but watched as his header rocketed back off the upright.

But Celtic took the lead with a wonderful move that was finished off by Larsson to equal Charlie Nicholas' post-war record of 48 goals in all competitions.

Sutton chased Johan Mjallby's ball downfield and swung over a cross for Larsson to bullet a diving header past Paul Gallacher.

As expected United came out with all guns blazing after the break but too often their final ball let them down.

Lilley's over-exuberance cost him a booking in the 49th minute when he caught Lambert with an unnecessary late tackle.

As United pushed more men forward they were in grave danger of being caught on the break and so it almost proved in the 57th minute.

Larsson got on the end of Lubo Moravcik's long-range ball and he teased De Vos just inside the box before going inside and curling a superb left-foot shot just around the post.

O'Neill tried to tighten up in midfield and brought Jackie McNamara on for Moravcik in the 68th minute.

United's dreams were killed off in the 78th minute and it was Larsson again who struck to break Nicholas' milestone.

Griffin tripped the Swede in the area and Dallas had no option but to point to the spot. Larsson stepped up to blast past the diving Gallacher.

The day got even worse for United two minutes later when Celtic increased their lead further as Larsson found McNamara on the right and he drilled the ball into the bottom corner.

United were down but not out as they responded with a deserved consolation in the 86th minute when Lilley nipped in ahead of Vega and Douglas to take Griffin's ball in his path before rolling it into the empty net.

The win meant that all that was standing between Celtic and a historic Treble were Hibs, who had seen off Livingston in the other semi-final. Celtic's pedigree under O'Neill was now self-evident. They had won when they had to win and they had acquired that all-too-elusive quality that is the hallmark of champions – they were very difficult to beat. Even Advocaat was forced to admit that something special was happening on the other side of the city.

'Even though there is a little pain in my heart, it is not a problem for me to say that Martin O'Neill and Celtic have done extremely well this season,' he said. 'O'Neill has done a good job and Celtic deserve to be champions. There is no doubt about that because they have been the better side and have played with consistency.

'I see Martin as a very experienced manager. I always like to talk that way if I feel it is correct to do so and I know it must have been quite difficult for Celtic to accept the situation when we did extremely well in the first two seasons with a totally new squad.

'Everyone likes to forget that. We know we have had a bad season but in football you always get a second chance and there is next season and everybody at Rangers is up for it.' (8 April, *Mail on Sunday*)

Unfortunately the same magnanimity was not in evidence among some members of the Rangers playing staff. In an extraordinary outburst Jorg

Albertz claimed Celtic won the title not because they were particularly good, but only because Rangers were so poor due to their multiple injuries. 'They won this league not because they were so good, but because we were so bad and didn't have the players available to win a championship,' he said. 'That's the main thing. In the last 15 years, how many titles have Rangers won? How many have Celtic won? It's a big occasion for them because they won't get it a lot. Just let them enjoy it and wait for next season.'

He added: 'You find it difficult to cope when there are five or six changes every week. If all the players stay fit it will be hard for anyone to beat us in Scotland and in Europe, especially here at Ibrox. We're going to win it back.' (22 April, *Daily Mirror*)

The outburst angered the Celtic players who felt it was a churlish and unnecessary attack timed to coincide with the presentation of the league championship trophy the same day. For the moment they stayed silent but, as the players took to the field to face Hearts, tempers were flaring.

On the park Hearts keeper Antti Niemi almost spoiled Celtic's title party with a string of superb saves from Henrik Larsson and his colleagues. However, despite a vintage performance, he was unable to prevent super-Slovak Lubo Moravcik breaching his goal-line. Not that Celtic required the victory. The party would have gone ahead anyway but it ensured the 60,000 ecstatic supporters did not have to endure a dreaded anti-climax before wallowing in yet more self-indulgent celebration.

The kick-off was preceded by a minute's silence for Rangers legend Jim Baxter, who had died tragically of cancer the week before, observed with such impeccable grace that the raindrops could be heard pattering down on the metal roofs above the stands.

22 APRIL: CELTIC 1 HEARTS 0
(Report by Iain Campbell: *Daily Mirror*)

Didier Agathe was anxious to get the party started and wasted no time in cutting in sharply from the left to fire an explosive drive against the crossbar.

The capacity crowd, which had been fairly quiet, roared to life in anticipation of yet another win from a side which would seem to have forgotten how to lose.

Despite being without Chris Sutton, the home side were able to pour forward.

Tommy Johnson, playing beside Henrik Larsson up front, was keen to become involved. The Geordie fired in a speculative drive from 40 yards with Niemi scurrying across his goal.

But although Celtic were firmly in control the visitors might have taken the lead in 15 minutes.

Colin Cameron cleverly set up Gary Wales 30 yards out who in turn switched the ball to Steven Boyack who was definitely in scoring range no more than 12 yards out but he was thwarted by a brave Joos Valgaeren block.

As Rangers have often discovered in the past, these title parties can take time to warm up and the opening goal did not arrive as quickly as the massed green-and-white ranks would have liked.

Instead they celebrated the ejection of some rival fans from the stadium after an outbreak of anti-social behaviour.

Larsson brought the stadium to its feet, not for the first time this season, when he ran on to a superb Johnson pass after 25 minutes but was denied his 50th goal of the season by Niemi's foot.

Johnson himself headed Jackie McNamara's corner over the bar before the lively and dangerous Agathe fired in a 20-yarder which the Hearts keeper punched away. Hearts did manage a breakaway when keeper Robert Douglas was forced to spring from his line to stop skipper Cameron grabbing the lead against the run of play.

But Celtic's procession towards Niemi's goal continued and the keeper had to pull off another super save from Alan Thompson after Agathe had switched play to McNamara, whose shot-cum-cross broke kindly for his colleague.

For all the champions' pressure, Gary Wales threatened to grab an equaliser seven minutes from half-time when he ran on to a long Scott Severin pass played out of defence. But under pressure from Valgaeren he blasted well over the bar from the edge of the area.

It was a warning for the home side who once again in the current campaign were finding Hearts a stubborn team to overcome. It was youngster Colin Healy who was next to threaten Niemi's goal, though he was no more successful than his experienced team-mates.

The midfielder sprinted on to a nicely weighted McNamara pass and his snap shot had at least a section of the crowd anticipating a goal, but the ball went wide.

Agathe's running had been Celtic's main strategy in the first half but it was McNamara on the right flank who was proving to be the main threat after the break, continuously hitting the goal-line in an attempt to finally put one over the defiant Niemi.

Thompson had another attempt at breaking the deadlock from 25 yards but Niemi was not in the mood to be beaten and coped with the shot comfortably. Martin O'Neill decided that subtlety was the weapon to use against the Tynecastle side's resistance and he replaced Healy with crowd hero Lubo Moravcik.

His impact was almost immediate with Niemi being forced to dive to his left to pull off another superb save from his 25-yard shot.

He was only denied temporarily, however, and he slotted in the goal after Larsson miskicked a shot into his path.

Larsson's 50th goal looked certain to arrive when the Swede raced through nine minutes from time but he merely succeeded in shooting straight at Niemi.

At 8.07 p.m. Celtic were finally awarded the league championship trophy in an emotional ceremony in front of 59,298 delirious fans – a few short of the capacity 60,000 crowd expected. Among those missing was season book holder Tony Spadi who, suffering a hangover from two weeks of celebration, slept in for the 6.05 p.m. kick-off.

Captain Paul Lambert had been nominated to respond to Albertz's pre-match comments and he did so with a stinging riposte. 'We deserve to be champions,' he said pointedly. 'Anyone else outwith this club who thinks otherwise is kidding themselves on.'

The club were now just nine points adrift of the magical 100-point mark with four matches to play after their 29th win in 34 league matches. They had captured the league title, they had won the CIS Insurance Cup and Larsson had broken the post-war scoring record. There was only one major challenge to overcome – a Scottish Cup victory which would gift them the coveted Treble.

In those circumstances their remaining league matches were almost an irrelevance. Or at least they would have been, had the first game not been against Rangers. With the Ibrox side now secure in second place, there should have been nothing more at stake than pride. But there was something more. In a sense the league victory had not been enough. Months of negative briefing from Ibrox had created an accepted wisdom that Celtic were not worthy of their title. That, had Rangers been at full strength, the championship trophy would, once again, be comfortably ensconced in the Ibrox trophy cabinet. Celtic had to demonstrate, unequivocally, that they were a better side. Albertz's comments had fuelled their determination to go to the home of their bitterest rivals and beat them. Despite winning three out of their previous four encounters, they needed this final victory to confirm their superiority. They needed to show that they could beat Rangers, and beat them convincingly, on the majority of occasions that they met. In short they needed to show that they were now the dominant force in Scottish football.

Their preparations were given a major fillip with the return of their two illness victims. Morten Wieghorst moved a significant step closer to a remarkable comeback when he completed his first full training session since contracting the life-threatening Guillain-Barres syndrome. And Alan Stubbs, who had suffered a relapse of testicular cancer, resumed his playing career in the eerie surroundings of a sparsely occupied Rugby Park in an Under-21 encounter with Kilmarnock. An extended contract for Moravcik, who agreed to stay at the club for at least another season, also helped to create a mood of solidarity and stability in the dressing-room.

However, preparations were again distracted by newspaper speculation that O'Neill would be the next manager of Manchester United. The week before, Alex Ferguson had revealed in a series of media interviews that he would be leaving Old Trafford for good at the end of the following season. It had earlier been envisaged that, when he stood down, he would remain at the club in an ambassadorial role. But following a public spat with chief executive Peter Kenyon over the terms of such a role, Ferguson announced that he would instead be severing all links with the club he had managed for 15 years.

The fall-out led to conjecture that the Manchester United board would start to look for a replacement for Ferguson sooner rather than later and inevitably O'Neill was installed as their presumed favourite for the job. A rash of largely inaccurate stories followed, claiming that O'Neill had a clause in his contract which allowed him to leave Celtic early and that he had already been in talks with the Old Trafford club.

Celtic powerbroker Dermot Desmond was pragmatic enough to recognise that he could not keep O'Neill at the club if he received a better offer elsewhere but he made clear he would do everything possible to keep him. 'It's to Martin's credit that he might be in demand by Manchester United, Barcelona or Inter Milan,' said Desmond. 'He's a great manager but I can't handcuff him. If Martin wanted to join the board, he'd be welcome. I think he has the capabilities to be a PLC director of Celtic.'

On a sunlit afternoon, Celtic arrived at the temple of their greatest adversaries. There was a gladiatorial atmosphere and the crowd demanded sport. There was a rare moment of unanimity when a video of Jim Baxter was applauded by both sets of supporters. A minute's silence was also required because this was Rangers' first home match since the death of their favourite son. For the Celtic fans, however, it was the third time in the space of a fortnight that they were being asked to observe the silence.

For the vast majority of Celtic fans that posed no problem. For them Jim Baxter transcended club rivalries. He was, quite simply, an extraordinary Scottish player and they were proud to pay their respects. All was going well until one ill-advised Celtic fan at the rear of the Broomfield Road broke the silence with a crass and disrespectful chant. That drew a reaction from a handful of Rangers fans and the referee was forced to cut short what should have been a poignant tribute.

'The person who broke the silence was quickly huckled out,' said Celtic supporter Jason Henderson. 'Hopefully he will never see another Celtic game. This was as much for the Celtic support as it was for Jim Baxter. For a few minutes after the silence the atmosphere was very subdued. You could sense the Celtic support felt genuinely let down.'

If Celtic's reputation was momentarily tarnished by the actions of an individual, the team quickly set about restoring it on the park with an imperious display which all but destroyed their opponents. Rarely has one team dominated an Old Firm encounter with such stunning grace and rarely has a single player made the match his own. Lubomir Moravcik's enchanting display made the hair on the back of the neck stand on end. The 35-year-old Slovak twisted, turned and tortured the Rangers defence to the point where it was almost disturbing to watch. Ricksen, in particular, seemed as mesmerised by his quixotic display as anyone in the crowd.

29 APRIL: RANGERS 0 CELTIC 3
(Report by Graham Spiers: *The Herald*)

Rangers had enjoyed the better of the first half but after the break, with Celtic applying confidence to their imagination, the home side began to resemble desperation. In fact, near the end of this dishevelled season, there was a symbolic chaos about Rangers. With the game slipping away, Dick Advocaat hatched a bewildering array of tactics and substitutes, each of which appeared more mystical than the last. In the second period, Rangers failed to force a single save from Rab Douglas.

They trudged from the field looking haunted at the end, their supporters already having deserted Ibrox in their droves. Not since August, 1971, have Rangers lost by such a margin at home to Celtic.

Thus was inflicted one more bloody wound on their Dutch coach. Advocaat enjoys strutting around Ibrox as perky as a bantam cock but it is impossible to believe his confidence and pride are not badly bruised. On the nights when they thrashed Sturm Graz at Ibrox in September and then went to France to defeat Monaco, it was inconceivable to envisage it ending like this for Rangers. They will be in the Champions League again next season but will emerge from a season of rubble. Last night, Advocaat tried hard to preserve his bullish appearance but even he was whimpering slightly. 'We just want this season to end; we are looking to next year,' he said wanly.

The game enjoyed the usual fateful moments – random flicks and botched efforts that might have changed the course of its life. In the 22nd minute, with the match still scoreless, you had to rub your eyes to believe Rod Wallace had actually missed from five yards with a header following Arthur Numan's deliciously curling cross. As Advocaat was keen to assert later, had Wallace scored then, Rangers might have thrived. On the basis of the second half, though, there was a chasm between the spirit and technique of these two teams which did nothing to embarrass Celtic's 21-point lead in the championship.

While Celtic drew from a well called Moravcik, Rangers were hampered in other areas. Barry Ferguson played with brisk authority in the opening half but a yellow card shown to him as early as the sixth minute by Stuart Dougal meant he felt his instincts severely curtailed. Rangers also lost Lorenzo Amoruso on a stretcher after 70 minutes following a challenge by Neil Lennon. The game, though, despite being subjected to the usual pre-match baloney in the press, refused to allow its frenzy to become outrageous.

The afternoon also once more honoured the passing of Jim Baxter. In an awkward situation, Celtic's supporters were thus asked to observe their third silence in two weeks for Baxter; something even Erasmus couldn't have imagined being granted. It was an ironic but proper twist of fate, given that this was Rangers' first home match since Baxter's death. With such frequency, and given that this was Ibrox they were visiting, many feared it might prove a test too far for Celtic's legions. The moment, though, passed in impressive observance, with only a solitary lout desecrating its final seconds at the end.

By the time Moravcik had finished plundering, there was still time for one more. Larsson's haul of 50 goals this season is a spate that has football historians scurrying and beavering through all sorts of dusty pages. Jimmy McGrory, by all fabled accounts, was a prince among scorers for Celtic but even he would have toiled to beat Larsson's finish here. In the 86th minute the Swede dragged the ball wide of the advancing Stefan Klos before prodding the ball back across goal and inside the far post. The angle had seemed impossible, it was an excruciating finish, but still not as good as those which preceded it.

Moravcik played in his usual role, in other words no definable one at all. He popped up here, he popped up there, he ran deep, he took to the flanks . . . in an age of team discipline he is a glorious anachronism. Rangers yesterday witnessed the sorest evidence.

The home side already had doom about them when Moravcik broke the deadlock. In the 61st minute, Neil Lennon's free kick was short and sweet to Larsson, who was on the edge of the Rangers box. Feeling buffeted, Larsson nevertheless shielded the ball before tapping it into the path of the on-rushing Moravcik. The remainder was all about balance and skill. The Slovak burst clear of everyone until he was confronted only by Klos, whom he beat with a low drive.

Twelve minutes later, Moravcik's second was fatal to Rangers. Douglas' long clearance was headed on by Shaun Maloney, the young Celtic substitute, and chased by Moravcik in the Rangers box. With Fernando Ricksen in pursuit, Moravcik applied his trademark change of direction, leaving the defender instantly stranded, before then chipping beyond Klos. It might be a long time in an Old Firm game before any player scores such a sumptuous pair of goals.

With the Celtic team at their swaggering, cavalier best it wasn't long before the supporters were in full song, displaying the characteristic, stiletto-point humour used so effectively in the past to prick the egos of their opponents. Jorg Albertz's comments now looked more inappropriate than ever as he was singled out for sometimes barbarous teasing. One large, hand-painted sign seemed to sum up the Rangers' mood perfectly when it said 'Simply Depressed'.

With their team 1–0 up, the Celtic fans broke into chants of 'easy, easy' and 'Albertz, Albertz, what's the score?' At 2–0 they were singing 'Can we play you every week?' and at 3–0, to the tune of 'Knees-up Mother Brown' they chanted 'No excuses now, no excuses now, no excuses, no excuses, no excuses now'. By the time the third goal had gone in, the football was almost an irrelevance as the fans set about taunting their rivals. When Albertz moved to the corner flag to take a corner-kick a group of around 100 fans sat reading broadsheet Sunday newspapers and smoking fat cigars as they sang, 'Here for the party, we're only here for the party'.

'When the final whistle blew, the players came over and saluted us,' said Jason Henderson. 'Neil Lennon looked like he wanted to dive into the crowd. Probably as well he didn't – he'd have drowned in all the emotion.

Eventually we made our way out onto the streets and into the pub just in time to see the kick-off. We watched it twice more on the big screen.'

Back at the Montrose Bar in the city centre the party was in full swing. Among those celebrating was film-maker Peter Braughan, producer of *Rob Roy*.

'He sang this amazing song about Moravcik,' said Celtic fan Austin Barratt. 'He stood up on the bar and the whole pub was silent. Then everybody joined in on the chorus, "Why, why, why, Moravcik?" to the tune of "My, my, my Delilah". Nobody had heard it before but they all caught on.'

The atmosphere was only slightly soured by spurious claims later made by a group of Rangers fans that the Celtic players had taunted them by spraying champagne on them from a dressing-room window at Ibrox. The claims were untrue and the SFA decided that they did not warrant an investigation. But the episode left a bad taste in the players' mouths.

'There was no champagne in the dressing-room,' said Tom Boyd. 'The players were certainly joyful because it was the first time we had beaten Rangers at Ibrox in seven years. I'm sure there would have been a bit of singing. But it was just blown up out of all proportion. For the season we have had we surely should be allowed to have a bit of celebration.'

Later that night, however, there was no one to spoil the party as Henrik Larsson was named SPFA Player of the Year and Stilian Petrov Young Player of the Year. It was a perfect end to a perfect day and few Celtic supporters thought it could get better. But things were about to get much, much better.

13.

THE TREBLE

Oh the Blue Room is bare,
Because there's no silverware
And there's no Mr Sheen,
Because there's nothing to clean
(To the tune of 'The Bluebells are Blue')

GUY WILMET was born in Mechelen, Belgium, in 1969. He has no
Scottish ancestry, no friends in Scotland and, until recently, he had never
crossed the North Sea. When he was five years old his father, a sports
photographer who travelled all over Europe, showed him a picture of the
famous green-and-white hoops. It was love at first sight and it is an affair
that is still burning passionately 21 years later.

'The moment I saw that shirt it was as if it had a magical effect on me,'
recalls the 32-year-old court official. 'I had never heard of Celtic but I
knew instinctively that they were a special team. My best memories as a
youngster were winning their ninth title in a row, playing the semi-final of
the European Cup against Atletico Madrid in 1974 and winning the title
in the last game against Rangers at Paradise in 1979. Names like Dalglish,
Macari, Deans and Connelly are still fresh in my mind although I never
saw them play.

'Kenny Dalglish made a big impression on me. We had this idea on the
continent that Scottish football was simply "kick and rush" and that
technical skill wasn't that important. But when I saw Kenny play I realised
it was a misconception.'

In 1992 Celtic drew the Belgium side Germinal Ekeren in the UEFA
Cup. Guy had just finished his national service with the Belgian military
and, although he didn't have a ticket for the game, he travelled to

Antwerp just so that he could mix with the fans. It was his induction into life with the Bhoys.

'When I arrived at the station I couldn't believe my eyes,' he said. 'I saw all these fans in the Hoops standing, singing, drinking beer and having a wonderful time. It was like a huge ocean of green and white everywhere in the city. At the start the Belgian people were a little sceptical because of the trouble we had had with English hooligans at Heysel. But after a while they changed their opinion. The game ended 1–1 and when the referee blew the final whistle thousands of Celtic fans cheered and applauded the home team. The Belgian TV commentator was speechless. I still remember him saying, "These fans are the best I've ever seen."'

Earlier this year, on a visit to Scotland, Guy met his hero Billy McNeill for the first time when he visited his pub. 'I can't remember anything about the last Treble because I had only just been born,' he says. 'When I met Billy I felt it must be some kind of sign. I knew that we were going to do it – I knew that we would win the Treble.'

At the start of May, however, the final piece of the jigsaw was still missing. Celtic still had to overcome a difficult test against Hibs in the Scottish Cup final. On 6 May they travelled to Edinburgh for a league tie against the Hibees in what was billed as a dress rehearsal for the main event. It was an emotional occasion as it marked the return to first-team football of Alan Stubbs, who capped a remarkable comeback with a dream goal. The centre-half came on at half-time, rounding off a convincing display with a 68th-minute header. His appearance also meant that he qualified for a league winner's medal.

Despite the emphatic scoreline, the result flattered Celtic who benefited from two first-half strikes. And while it must have caused Alex McLeish considerable concern at the way his team were unable to impose themselves, even after Agathe was dismissed for a second bookable offence after 79 minutes, Celtic had a third-gear look about them. They seemed to be lacking the same drive that had swept them to league victory. O'Neill knew that his side would have to be more convincing if they were to emerge winners at Hampden Park later in the month.

MAY 6: HIBERNIAN 2 CELTIC 5
(Report by Robert Martin: *Daily Mirror*)

It took the champions only four minutes to sweep into the lead, even if it is fair to say that McNamara's strike will not go down as one of the goals of the season.

It came from the first corner of the game, which Moravcik played short to Alan Thompson, who then advanced into the Hibs area.

His shot was deflected goalward by McNamara, then also grazed the head of young defender Ian Murray before spinning over the stranded Nick Colgan.

As Hibs looked to strike back Stuart Lovell spurned a glorious opportunity to level the game after 14 minutes when he headed wide from point-blank range after meeting a cross from O'Neil.

Hibs were left stunned as the Hoops doubled their lead with McNamara's second goal of the game after 18 minutes.

This time it was Agathe who did the damage, collecting a pass from Moravcik and driving fiercely at Colgan from the edge of the area.

The keeper looked to have held the ball but collided with team-mate Lehmann, and as the ball broke loose McNamara was on hand to turn home from three yards.

Lovell again went close to bringing his side back into the game in the 24th minute, volleying inches wide after good work from Mixu Paatelainen and Libbra.

And Libbra then saw a shot well saved by Kharine after neat skill had taken him past several yellow-shirted challenges, the keeper doing well to block the Frenchman's effort at close range.

Stubbs replaced Joos Valgaeren at the interval to a generous reception from both sets of supporters, while Colin Healy was also brought on in place of Neil Lennon.

Agathe was booked for a late challenge on Lehmann a minute later.

And Sauzee drove a free kick narrowly, to try to get back into the game.

Kharine did well to beat away a Paatelainen header in the 50th minute, with Ian Murray sending another header a foot wide of the Russian's right-hand post.

The Hoops keeper then pulled off a fine stop to deny Libbra in the 57th minute and Murray crashed the rebound off the post.

Mathias Jack was booked after catching Larsson a few minutes later.

And the Swede then got revenge the only way he knows how in the 62nd minute when the Players' Player of the year notched goal number 51 of his campaign.

Goalscorer McNamara turned provider, playing the striker through on goal, and although Colgan managed to get a touch on his effort, Larsson made sure it crossed the line.

Stubbs completed his fairy-tale comeback six minutes later, rising unmarked to head home from Alan Thompson's corner.

And while Agathe then saw red after catching O'Neil, the unaffected Hoops saw Moravcik add a fifth ten minutes from time, the Slovak racing all of 40 yards to collect a long ball and then drive low past the helpless Colgan.

Libbra capped a decent personal display with his two late strikes, one a shot and one a header.

Following their Olympian performances throughout the season, Celtic were brought further back down to earth with a humbling defeat at home to Dundee. The result brought to an end a 14-month unbeaten home record in the league. Argentine striker Fabian Caballero gave the visitors a shock victory with first-half goals either side of Zura Khizanishvili's sending off. It was a sobering experience for Celtic. It meant they would have to win their final match of the season at Kilmarnock to become the first Scottish Premier League side to reach 100 points in a season.

13 MAY: CELTIC 0 DUNDEE 2
(Report by Tim Gordon: *Daily Mirror*)

Record-breaking striker Henrik Larsson had another milestone in his sights as he aimed to beat Brian McClair's top-flight scoring feat of 35 in a season but he endured a rare off-day today.

The Swedish striker had a glorious chance in the 27th minute when Walter del Rio's slip allowed him a clear run through on goal, but his effort was easily saved by Jamie Langfield.

The home crowd were stunned on the half-hour when Celtic fell behind to a superb Caballero goal.

Gavin Rae found Beto Carranza on the left flank and he played the ball to Caballero, who turned away from Valgaeren before curling an inch-perfect effort past the left hand of Gould and into the bottom corner.

But Celtic were thrown a lifeline three minutes later when Dundee were reduced to ten men.

Khizanishvili attempted to pull down Larsson but the Swede shrugged him off to shoot just wide of the post.

Referee Tom Brown pulled play back and brandished the red card, although it looked to be a harsh decision.

The blow failed to knock Dundee out of their stride and they doubled their lead two minutes before the break by capitalising on some poor Celtic defending and held on after the break for a well-earned victory

Javier Artero found space on the right wing and played the ball across the face of goal. Caballero was the first to react and shot home from close range with Ramon Vega dithering.

O'Neill replaced Vega and Smith at the break with Tom Boyd and Sean Maloney and they certainly came out fighting.

Maloney was a constant threat and was unfortunate not to reduce the deficit in the 48th minute when he headed Thompson's cross down but Langfield made a stunning save to deny him.

The result was a setback to the side's Cup final preparations and, not for the first time, O'Neill was upset and surprised at the barracking his players took from the supporters who, perfectionists to a man and woman, were unhappy with the defeat. The manager refused to offer any post-mortems on the result which he insisted offered few lessons for Hampden. 'I'm mystified people are even attempting to look into what happened,' he told the *Celtic View*. 'It's simply a case of the competitive edge fading when games are not all that important. All the players are very mindful of the Cup final and that's only natural.'

He added: 'I've no worries whatsoever about their mentality. They're very strong in that sense and their attitude in the dressing-room afterwards told me all I needed to know about how they'll approach the next few weeks.'

Suddenly football seemed irrelevant with the news that Lisbon Lion Bobby Murdoch had died after suffering a massive stroke. He died peacefully in the early hours of 15 May with his wife Kathleen and his three children around his bedside. He was 56. Murdoch, once described by Jock Stein as the best player he ever worked with, had been admitted to Glasgow's Victoria Infirmary the previous weekend after becoming ill following a hernia operation. He fell into a coma from which he never recovered.

The news was a shattering blow to everyone at Celtic Park. O'Neill, who had met Murdoch at the dinner he arranged for the Lisbon Lions earlier in the season, was upset. Club captain Tom Boyd spoke for the entire dressing-room when he said: 'Bobby had an aura about him that comes with playing for the club's most successful team. The 1967 team hold a legendary place in the hearts of Celtic fans. We will miss him.'

A product of Celtic's youth system, Murdoch made his club debut as a 17-year-old in 1961 when one of his team-mates turned up for a match without his boots. His basic wage was £12 a week, with a £3 win bonus. He went on to make 484 appearances for the Hoops, scoring 105 goals in 13 years. He helped the club to win 8 championships, 5 League Cups and

4 Scottish Cups, as well as the European Cup, before moving south and joining Middlesbrough in 1973.

The second youngest of the Lisbon Lions, behind Jimmy Johnstone, it was Murdoch's shot which striker Steve Chalmers deflected for the winning goal against Inter Milan in Lisbon. It was also one of his characteristic drives that knocked Leeds United out of the European Cup in 1970 in the unofficial Battle of Britain.

The night he died, there was a minute's silence at Tommy Boyd's testimonial match against Manchester United. The match ended in a 2–0 win for the visitors but by then few people were thinking about football.

At the weekend Celtic travelled to Kilmarnock for the final league match of the season and, for once, Henrik Larsson was not the centre of attention. Instead it was a rotund, ageing TV pundit playing the final match in a long, distinguished – and at times infuriatingly successful – career.

To the last, the Celtic fans would not allow themselves a momentary lapse into magnanimity or appreciation of Ally McCoist's talents. When, shortly before half-time, he missed a sitter the travelling support joined in a rousing chorus of 'One John Parrot, there's only one John Parrot'. His sclaff was all the sweeter because, had it gone in, it would have guaranteed Killie a UEFA Cup spot. In the end it was left to his team-mate Alan Mahood to grab a late winner.

Celtic used the match as an opportunity to rest most of the stars who would play in the Cup final. The chance was there for Killie to exploit the champs' relative weakness, which they did and in the end Hearts' win over Dundee turned out to be cruelly meaningless for the Edinburgh side, who were also chasing the last UEFA Cup spot.

20 MAY: KILMARNOCK 1 CELTIC 0
(Report by Ian Campbell: *Daily Mirror*)

Killie left it late. Mahood's goal came just 11 minutes from time. Chris Innes sent the impressive di Giacomo racing clear of Stéphane Mahé down the right and the attacker's sweep right across the Celtic goalmouth was an invitation the in-rushing midfielder was unwilling to pass up.

Dejected Hearts are bound to ask questions about Celtic's team selection but Martin O'Neill's side passed up chances of their own to win the game.

The young strike force of Jamie Smith and Shaun Maloney both had clear-cut chances to put their side ahead in the first half but pulled their efforts wide, misses which ultimately cost them the match.

Nevertheless, Killie's Spanish midfielder Jesus San Juan was desperately unlucky to see his well-weighted sidefoot shot cannon back off a post after a superbly constructed move by key men Mahood and di Giacomo.

In the end most of the ground was happy, with the departing McCoist and Wright taking their final bows and an emotional Gus MacPherson wondering whether he too will be leaving after recently refusing a contract offer.

And even though his side lost, O'Neill walked over to the Celtic fans still celebrating their champions status to applaud them.

But Celtic's shadow squad is bound to be a major bone of contention at Tynecastle, who did everything they could to win a UEFA place.

Celts were without the injured Henrik Larsson but also left out key men like Paul Lambert, Neil Lennon, Alan Thompson, Joos Valgaeren, Johan Mjallby and Lubo Moravcik.

O'Neill will argue that he was giving players an opportunity to prove they should be playing at Hampden.

Returning defender Alan Stubbs, who appears to be winning his battle with cancer, was one player who may have done enough to book a place. His first task was to make a superb tackle on di Giacomo who had burst through on to an Antonio Calderon pass after 11 minutes.

O'Neill felt his side might have equalised during a goalmouth mêlée seven minutes from time but the best chance of the second half fell to Stéphane Mahé, who won't have helped his own chances by shooting wide from a good position.

That chance came 27 minutes before Mahood's winner and Killie were determined not to be caught out after that, effectively keeping Celtic at arm's length.

In the end the Rugby Park side were back in Europe while Hearts lost out despite beating Dundee. But Killie will return to that grand arena without one of the most familiar faces in the game. It truly was the end of an era.

With the league campaign out of the way O'Neill could concentrate on preparing his players for the Cup final. He had taken them away for a break in the Spanish sun, a shrewd move which ensured they were refreshed, sharp and eager to resume training when they returned.

Publicly he played down the importance of the final. After all, the hard work had been done. The league had been won, a place in the Champions

KEEP THE FAITH

League secured. That's what he was employed to deliver. That was the bread and butter. Anything else was jam. But privately he knew differently. No Celtic manager since the great Jock Stein had secured a domestic Treble. No Celtic team in the past 30 years had reached the holy grail, a clean sweep of Scottish honours. There were 90 minutes of the 2000–01 season remaining and O'Neill knew his team were no longer playing for medals or honours or money – they were playing for a place in history.

But he also knew they had a fight on their hands. Despite their comfortable win over Hibs earlier in the month, the Edinburgh side would be no pushovers. They needed to win the Cup to secure a European place the following season. A measure of how importantly they regarded victory was the £32,000 win bonus on offer to every player if they ended the club's 99-year wait for the Scottish Cup.

As the players ran on to the Hampden turf they were met with a panorama of green and white. With both teams obliged to play in their away strips it was left to the fans to parade the club colours at Scotland's showpiece football event. Brilliant sun beamed down on ecstatic supporters of both clubs who provided the deafening soundtrack to a perfect day.

Beyond the stadium, across Scotland and abroad, supporters crammed, shoulder to shoulder, around TV sets to watch the events unfold. In McNeill's bar in the south side, in the Montrose on the Broomielaw, in O'Brien's, Santa Monica, in Antwerp, Perth, Australia, Florida and Ireland, Celtic fans gathered and prepared for the unfolding of history. In Molly Malone's Irish Bar in Singapore's Boat Quay district the Sing Tims were getting ready for a party. Their entourage included Pat McGinlay, Jim Duffy, Owen Coyle and ex-Celt Mark McGhee who, as the song had it, alternately bounced round the ground and was worth a million pound. In Italy, lifelong Celt Willie Hughes settled down to watch the game live, courtesy of the only person in his village who had access to the satellite channel. His friend was, ironically, a true-blue Rangers supporter. But one who appreciated that football transcends even tribal loyalties when there is history in the making.

'There was a strange mood that day,' recalls Tony Hamilton. 'There was a sense of disbelief that we had got as far as we had and, in a way, it didn't really matter if we won or lost. Everyone was going to have a great time whatever the result.'

The Celtic players had other ideas. Throughout the season Hibs had demonstrated that, with limited resources, they could compete with the best in Scotland. They were well led by Alex McLeish, an astute post-Bosman operator. They had a number of highly skilful European footballers but they lacked one important element – Henrik Larsson.

The Swede capped a glorious season with a double strike which articulated more poetically than anything his value to the side. It was yet further persuasion, if any were needed, why Celtic should do all that was necessary to keep him at the club.

Larsson struck just after the break to add to sub Jackie McNamara's first-half goal and by then the champions were coasting. He added a third from the penalty spot late in the game but by then it was simply icing on the cake.

26 MAY: CELTIC 3 HIBERNIAN 0
(Report by Ian Paul: *The Herald*)

Not even the glorious sunshine that enveloped the stadium was able to bring some light into their whingeing souls. The moaners, the Hammers of Hampden, will never concede that the old/new lady is here to stay. They were at it again, before and after the big finale to the season.

There is no atmosphere, the pitch is rotten, the stands are too far away from the park . . . on and on they go.

Look at the San Siro, at the Nou Camp, at the Amsterdam Arena, they say. I have, and all three are wonderful, but for years the San Siro has had problems with the playing surface, the Amsterdam park has to be relaid on a regular basis and anyone who has sat on the high tiers of the Nou Camp will tell you it is like watching from an aeroplane.

The financial mess that accompanied the make-over for the national stadium was rightly highlighted and berated but the place is there now, and it is not a bad place to be on a sunny May afternoon when the Cup final is being played.

In fact, the atmosphere created by the crowd, especially the Hibs fans, even as they saw defeat inevitably looming closer, and by the SFA stage management of the final, was superb.

Of course, any outdoor event blessed with such sunshine would have a hard job flopping but, inside that casserole of a stadium, with the clear blue sky sitting like a dazzling lid above us, it was easy to feel a touch privileged.

The game was not great, not all that exciting, but neither was it all that bad. There were stars on the stage, of that there can be no doubt.

Abune them a' was a Scot . . . and we have not been able to say that very often in recent times. Step forward Paul Lambert, whose performance was as flawless as is possible in an inexact science. Defensively sensible, attackingly shrewd and always intelligent, Lambert would be hailed as something of a football genius anywhere else. When he gives the ball away it is only to a colleague to take a throw-in.

His display made such a nonsense of the theory expounded earlier in the season that he could not play in the same team as Neil Lennon. The real question, which has been well answered, was whether Lennon could play in the same team as Lambert.

They gel easily but that is hardly a surprise when two players of their talents are involved. Lambert never ceases to credit Otmar Hitzfeld for the improvement in his game after he went to Borussia Dortmund, and that must be so, but he has not gone back the way since he returned to Scotland and Celtic.

In fact, he seems to me to be almost the perfect all-round player nowadays. The one missing ingredient is a goal or two. He is well capable of that, too, but maybe opts out of shooting at times when he ought to have a go.

It was Lambert who won the midfield contest for his club and that was no easy task because Hibs, in the first half, made a real impact in that zone.

He was ably assisted by a player who has had an in-and-out time this season, mostly through injury, Jackie McNamara. Irony being an ever-present interloper in football dressing-rooms, it was predictable that the loss of their favourite playmaker, Lubo Moravcik, would result in Celtic replacing him with a player who would prove to be the key to their success.

McNamara scored one goal, laid on another and had perhaps his finest game for the club this season.

There is no fairness about the business, though. Alex McLeish must have imagined that Lubo's departure would have raised the ante in his side's favour but then saw the substitute top anything he had anticipated would come from the Slovak.

If that left the manager shaking his head, how must he have felt watching Didier Agathe, the man Celtic kidnapped from Easter Road for a paltry £50,000, lay on the opening goal for McNamara? It is enough to make a manager slope off to West Ham.

One more Celtic name has to be mentioned. You got it in one. He did virtually nowt for a while, made a hash of a very good chance and then finished off the game with two goals in the second half.

Henrik Larsson thus won the man-of-the-match award which will join the others in the underground car park he has converted for the purpose.

His first goal was a typical Henrik pre-emptive strike when the ball hits the net before anyone realises he has pounced.

The second was another well-placed penalty after Gary Smith held Larsson's shirt and also tripped him.

Hibs had a good first half and, had they managed to score the first goal, there could have been a real contest, but it was not to be. They were well served by the skilful, tricky Marc Libbra who, if Hibs can afford him, will be a real asset next season and Ulrik Laursen, but especially by their captain, Franck Sauzee.

The personable Frenchman did his utmost to inspire his team-mates and for spells they responded. He said all the right things afterwards, too, in excellent English. Naturally, he dismissed suggestions that, if McLeish is head hunted and taken off by West Ham, he would be a likely successor.

Even as he spoke, however, he sounded more and more like a man with the savvy and maturity to go straight into the manager's office.

However, the Hibees who gave their side such wonderful backing on Saturday don't want to see McLeish leave. The side has made tremendous progress under Alex and there could be more to come yet.

Sauzee said he and his mates would be back at Hampden next season . . . 'and we will win'. For the sake of those supporters, I hope he is right.

The final whistle sounded and Celtic had proved conclusively that they were now the benchmark of Scottish football. No excuses. The players fell to their knees in disbelief at what they had achieved – they had claimed the elusive Treble for only the third time in their history.

After changing into the famous hooped shirts they stepped up to receive the Cup from Chancellor of the Exchequer Gordon Brown. As the strains of Lou Reed's 'Perfect Day' echoed around the ground, the players cavorted on the pitch with the trophy. O'Neill was finally persuaded to join in, to the delight of the fans. Afterwards, in the first-team dressing-room, the words of a song the fans had been singing for weeks could be heard being sung with enormous fervour. It referred to the famous Blue Room at Ibrox where Rangers' dazzling array of trophies is held. It went something like this . . . 'Oh the Blue Room is bare/Because there's no silverware/And there's no Mister Sheen/Because there's nothing to clean.' These are all the words. It isn't sectarian. It isn't offensive. It merely reflects the huge relief at having vanquished their toughest rivals. Curiously, it also proves that neither side can really understand victory without measuring themselves up against the other team in the Old Firm divide. It is a sad commentary on the charged atmosphere that surrounds Old Frim football in Scotland that even this tame chant is not really acceptable. It is a fact Martin O'Neill was aware of and one of the reasons he does not want his players singing it again/

After the match plaudits inevitably centred on Larsson, whose goal tally took him to 53 for the season, enough to win the European Golden Shoe award as the continent's top striker. Lou Reed gave way to the strains of 'The Magnificent Seven' and then to 'The Fields of Athenry' – the unofficial Celtic anthem. The haunting lyrics perfectly articulated the mood – the fans had dreams and songs to sing, never more so than now.

It signalled the start of another round of celebrations that threatened to bring the burgeoning Celtic support to the point of exhaustion. Starved of a reason to party for so many years, they were now overdosing on delirium, mainlining unfettered joy. 'Every game we went to there was another reason to celebrate,' said lifelong Hoops fan Damian Rogers. 'It just seemed to go on and on for ages. A league win here, a trophy presentation there, another cup final. I don't think I stopped smiling for about a month. By the time the Cup final came round I think we were just glad it was all over. My liver couldn't have taken much more success.'

Before leading his team to Argentina in 1978, former Scotland manager Ally MacLeod was asked what he planned to do after the World Cup. 'Retain it,' he famously replied. O'Neill's horizons were more modest. Within days of the Cup final his thoughts had already shifted from achievements past to challenges ahead. The challenges of Champions League qualification, of maintaining the high standards he had set, of taking on an inevitably rejuvenated Rangers.

'I'm well aware of the reality of football,' he said. 'So while I always felt that, given enough time, I could achieve something here, I knew that I had to win and win quickly. It doesn't take people long to forget. We've had a great year and expectations are now higher as a result. But next year is a new challenge.'